3 773114 - City 📞 01603 731252 - Easton f /ccninformationstore
↷ ccnlibraryblog.wordpress.com

College

EASTON COLLEGE
LEARNING RESOURCE CENTRE

Sports Talent

Jim Brown

Human Kinetics

Library of Congress Cataloging-in-Publication Data

Brown, Jim, 1940-
    Sports talent / Jim Brown.
        p.   cm.
    Includes bibliographical references and index.
    ISBN 0-7360-3390-4
        1. Athletic ability--Testing.   I. Title.
    GV436 .B755   2001
    796'.07--dc21   00-052990

ISBN: 0-7360-3390-4

Developmental Editor: Leigh LaHood; **Assistant Editor**: Kim Thoren; **Copyeditor**: Patsy Fortney; **Proofreader**: Sarah Wiseman; **Indexer**: Betty Frizzéll; **Graphic Designer**: Fred Starbird; **Graphic Artist**: Sandra Meier; **Photo Manager**: Clark Brooks; **Cover Designer**: Jack W. Davis; **Photographer (cover)**: Tom Roberts; **Photographer (interior)**: Tom Roberts, unless otherwise noted; **Art Manager**: Craig Newsom; **Illustrators**: figures on pages 100, 199, and 235-237 by Tom Roberts; all other illustrations by Martin J. Bee; **Printer**: United Graphics

Human Kinetics books are available at special discounts for bulk purchase. Special editions or book excerpts can also be created to specification. For details, contact the Special Sales Manager at Human Kinetics.

Printed in the United States of America

10   9   8   7   6   5   4   3   2   1

Human Kinetics
Web site: www.humankinetics.com

United States: Human Kinetics
P.O. Box 5076, Champaign, IL 61825-5076
800-747-4457
e-mail: humank@hkusa.com

Canada: Human Kinetics
475 Devonshire Road Unit 100, Windsor, ON N8Y 2L5
800-465-7301 (in Canada only)
e-mail: hkcan@mnsi.net

Europe: Human Kinetics
Units C2/C3 Wira Business Park, West Park Ring Road, Leeds LS16 6EB, United Kingdom
+44 (0) 113 278 1708
e-mail: hk@hkeurope.com

Australia: Human Kinetics
57A Price Avenue, Lower Mitcham, South Australia 5062
08 8277 1555
e-mail: liahka@senet.com.au

New Zealand: Human Kinetics
P.O. Box 105-231, Auckland Central
09-523-3462
e-mail: hkp@ihug.co.nz

Sports Talent

Contents

Part III
Evaluating Talent by Sport

Preface

Sports talent often depends on the eyes of the beholder. Millions of parents and thousands of youth coaches see their star athletes on a can't-miss path to full scholarships at major universities or even to careers in professional sports. As a result of this farsighted, though sometimes biased, vision, these parents and coaches commit huge amounts of money, time, and energy to reach these goals.

In the eyes of trained coaches, recruiters, and scouts, however, sports talent is more difficult to assess. People who make a living recognizing and developing athletic ability understand that the potential to excel in sports depends on a combination of physical, environmental, mental, and emotional factors. Talent, even when it is present and accounted for, does not guarantee athletic excellence.

Although recognizing athletic talent is difficult, it's not impossible. Even the most uninitiated parent or inexperienced coach can observe signs of outstanding ability (or the lack of it). These indicators—present at every stage of a child's development—include more than just wins, losses, and personal statistics. If you are not sure about what to look for or what you are seeing, there are resources out there to give you a clearer view. This book is one of those resources.

Sports Talent was written for several reasons. Whether you are a parent, teacher, playground director, or coach, this book can help you to

- identify and develop young people with athletic ability;
- tell the difference between average and exceptional athletic talent;
- support young athletes in ways that are productive and consistent with their abilities;
- objectively measure sports ability;
- enhance the developmental process;
- avoid burnout;
- be patient with the late bloomer;
- make good decisions about young people's lives, not just their sports futures; and
- decide what to do next.

In addition to the preceding, *Sports Talent* gives you an inside look at what the professional evaluators of talent are seeking. What do high school coaches, college recruiters, and professional scouts look for in baseball, basketball, football, golf, gymnastics, hockey, soccer, softball, swimming, tennis, track and field, volleyball, and wrestling? How do experts know before everyone else that some players will be average and some will be good, while others are destined for greatness? And how do some athletes achieve excellence in sports without the superior skills of blue chip players?

Perhaps most important, *Sports Talent* provides insights into discovering and developing talented athletes who can enjoy sports at whatever level they are capable of reaching. They may not play at a Division I university or in the big leagues, but they can develop their skills, make teams, represent high schools and colleges, and have experiences that will make a lasting, positive impact on their lives and the lives of others.

Acknowledgments

I thank my wife, Arlene Pendas Brown, for everything she has done to make this book possible.

Part I

Identifying
Talent

Chapter 1

Profiling the Talented Athlete

Brad is what baseball people call a "five tool" athlete. He can hit, hit with power, run, catch, and throw. He can also kick a soccer ball, shoot a basketball, and pass a football. He can do things with his body that his friends can't. His parents, to their credit, are quietly curious and keeping a wait-and-see attitude. His grandparents are convinced that his sports skills are exceptional.

The recruiters and scouts haven't discovered Brad yet, but it won't be long before they do. Most of his hitting, running, catching, and throwing happens in his backyard with his mom and dad. Brad is four years old. Don't laugh. By the time you read this book, the Brads of this country and their athletically precocious sisters will have enrolled in sports camps, participated in tryouts, undergone evaluations by coaches, and been "drafted" long before they can spell the word. They will be declared talented athletes, and that declaration will determine how a lot of time, money, and energy are spent for at least the next decade.

If sports talent is that desirable and that important, what exactly is it? Two dictionaries define talent as "a special, natural ability" and "a capacity for achievement or success," but they do not define talent as it relates to sports. An athlete, says *Webster*, is "a trained competitor in a sport." A person who is athletic, however, is merely "physically active and strong."

ONE-DIMENSIONAL TALENT

None of the preceding definitions is accurate. Sports talent is as narrow as the ability to run fast in a straight line and as broad as the ability to play quarterback. Michael Johnson and Marion Jones, two people who run very fast for a living, are Olympic track champions. They represent the upper end of sports talent, even though their skills are rather one-dimensional.

At the highest levels, sprinting from one point to another is a considerable athletic achievement. Sprinting requires speed, quickness, coordination, flexibility, strength, and power, six of ten physical qualities found in talented athletes, not to mention the emotional characteristics that gifted athletes possess. But these skills are one-dimensional in the sense that they all contribute toward one goal—running fast.

One-dimensional talent can be just as demanding, satisfying, and potentially lucrative as multidimensional talent. Some place kickers in football would not meet all of the criteria for playing another position. They can't even punt the ball. But they can make extra points and field goals when big, fast defenders are trying to knock them down while thousands of people in the stands and millions on television are watching. Some "closers" in baseball can't run, field, or hit, but they can pitch one inning or less and get batters out at the end of a game. For this they are famous, and they make millions of dollars.

MULTIDIMENSIONAL TALENT

Sports talent is also as broad as the ability to play quarterback in football or point guard in basketball. Peyton Manning, a quarterback in the National Football League, and Allen Iverson, the leading scorer for the Philadelphia 76ers, have to combine physical, emotional, and intangible skills every minute they are in the game. They seldom run fast in a straight line but instead have to make decisions, call plays, handle a ball, run, change directions, avoid defenders, and react to teammates and opponents. Their sports talent is multidimensional.

ONE-SPORT TALENT

Because of early specialization, competition, and the huge amounts of money paid to professional athletes, most of them are proficient in only one sport. Ken Griffey Jr. may be skilled in other sports, but he is world class only in baseball. Mia Hamm plays soccer, period. Tiger Woods is a professional golfer, not an all-around athlete. The one-sport athlete is not as prevalent at the elementary, middle, and high school levels, but the trend is certainly going in that direction. Although most of the coaches and sports officials

© Joe Robbins Photography

Athletes such as Peyton Manning have multidimensional talent because they rely on physical, mental, and intangible skills during each game.

interviewed for this book agree that the one-sport-athlete trend is a fact, they also think that the trend is a mistake.

MULTISPORT TALENT

Jim Thorpe won the 1912 Olympic decathlon and pentathlon and was a two-time All-American running back at the Carlisle Indian School. Besides playing professional football and baseball, he was a standout in basketball, lacrosse, tennis, handball, bowling, golf, swimming, billiards, gymnastics, rowing, hockey, boxing, and figure skating. Thorpe may have been the most talented all-around athlete ever. He was able to play just about any sport. When he was in his 50s, he was still talented enough to drop-kick field goals from the 50-yard line during exhibitions at high school football games.[1]

On July 16, 1932, 18-year-old Babe Didrikson of Beaumont, Texas, entered the national AAU track and field national championships. At 5-2 and 105 pounds, she won gold medals in the shot put, baseball throw, long jump, 80-meter hurdles, high jump, and javelin. Babe, who got her nickname after hitting five home runs in one game, was an astonishing athlete. She began as a basketball All-American, then won two track and field gold medals at the 1932 Olympics. Next, she turned professional and began touring the country, exhibiting her prowess in track, swimming, tennis, baseball, and even billiards. In 1935 Didrikson-Zaharias took up golf and excelled at that too, winning 82 tournaments in a 20-year career.[2]

Thorpe and Didrikson represent the upper end of multisport talent. They could play just about any sport at the elite level. While there are some great multisport athletes out there today, they are becoming an endangered species. Such athletes should be encouraged to play as many sports as their schedules and academic responsibilities will allow. The experience will help them if and when they finally do specialize in one sport.

TALENT IN PROGRESS

A final dimension of sports talent is talent in the process of development. Talented athletes who excel in their sports or perhaps even dominate their peers exist at every age level. They may be bigger, stronger, faster, or simply better than other children. Such children are great age-group athletes, nothing more and nothing less. They are good at what they do right now. There is no guarantee that because an athlete is good at 10 he or she will be good at 14, 16, or 18.

Researchers in the department of kinesiology at Michigan State have been studying motor development, including sprinting and jumping, in children for more than 30 years. One of the things they have looked at is the percentage of adult performance already in place by the age of five. The investigators found that boys display 20 to 40 percent of their adult performance on a given task at age five. Girls tend to have 40 to 60 percent of their adult performance as five-year-olds. They concluded that girls are closer to their adult performance at younger ages than are boys.[3]

PREDICTING ATHLETIC SUCCESS

"Everybody wants to predict future athletic success based on present achievement or physical makeup," says Robert Singer, PhD, professor and chair of

© EMPICS/Topham Picturepoint

Babe Didrikson may have been the greatest multisport athlete of the 20th century.

the department of exercise and sport sciences at the University of Florida. "But predicting success is much more difficult than most people think. There are too many variables, even if certain athletes have a combination of genes that favors long-range talent. A person's genetic makeup can be expressed in many different ways, depending on environmental and situational opportunities. Variables such as motivation, coachability, and opportunity can't be predicted.

"If one wants to say that you are much more favored than I am to be a world-class champion due to genetic composition at birth, I can't argue the point. You can determine that one eight-year-old gymnast is more advanced than another," continues Singer. "But to project that talent 10 years forward and say that the child will be a world-class athlete is impossible."[4]

Little or no research correlates gifted status as a child with gifted status as an adult. However, a study in Sweden tracked two groups of elite junior tennis players from the time they were in the 12 to 14 age group until they were in their 20s. Some became successful adult players, and others did not. The successful group had three things in common: (1) they seemed to enjoy playing tennis more than the less successful players, (2) they were less pressured by their parents, and (3) they played other sports as well as tennis.

The message for parents and coaches of developing athletes is to enjoy the moment and help the children prepare for the future, but do not demand or expect equal success at each level during the children's development. If it happens, consider it a bonus.

Does a child have to be a star at 8 to be a star at 18? No. Does a child have to be involved in competition at 8 to be outstanding at 18? No. Earlier is not necessarily better in terms of sport-specific training. Sooner or later, lasting sports talent shows up.

This book is not about the average youth athlete who plays a sport for fun and fitness, although those two goals may be the most honorable of all. Instead, it is about identifying (not predicting) and developing outstanding ability among children up to the age of 18 in one or more sports. Outstanding talent means clearly above-average sports skills compared with other participants of the same general age, as well as the potential to be successful at a higher level of competition. In some sports, enduring talent may be arbitrarily defined as the ability to compete some day at the Division I college level.

All young athletes occupy positions somewhere on the sports talent continuum between Brad (and his sister) and Jim Thorpe or Babe Didrikson. Some of them will move forward, others will get stuck or slip back, and a third group—as many as 70 percent—will fall off before they become teenagers. The ones who are truly talented will possess many of the physical, emotional, and intangible qualities described in the next three chapters. To determine whether your young athletes have sports talent, where they are on the continuum, and how to move them forward or keep them from falling off, start with chapter 2, "Identifying Physical Attributes."

Chapter 2

Identifying Physical Attributes

We use many words to describe the physical abilities of athletes: *size, speed, quickness, strength, power, agility, flexibility, coordination, endurance,* and *vision.* Because people have their own definitions of these words, however, this presents a problem. Strength to one person, for example, may mean power to another.

Mark McGwire can hit towering home runs because he is powerful. Warren Sapp's strength (and power) is evident when he throws blockers out of his way while trying to sack a quarterback. Shaquille O'Neal is said to be strong because he can grab 20 rebounds, and powerful because he can dunk a basketball with force.

Physical characteristics of talented athletes become more important at higher levels of competition. For example, relatively short high school or college quarterbacks can be very successful, but lack of height will probably be an obstacle at the professional level. Nevertheless, some players are exceptions to generally accepted physical prerequisites in every sport. Muggsy Bogues is 5-3, but he played basketball for Wake Forest and has had a productive career at the professional level.

DEFINING THE PHYSICAL ELEMENTS OF TALENT

Following are some lay definitions that describe the attributes of talented athletes. The definitions are followed by subjective comments regarding the importance of each attribute to the 13 sports addressed in this book (see table 2.1 on pages 12-18). The comments are given to help coaches, parents, and athletes evaluate potential for success and are categorized into these three groups:

- Not a factor (attribute not needed to achieve high performance levels)
- Advantage (attribute contributes, but is not essential, to achieving high performance levels)
- Prerequisite (attribute is necessary to achieve high performance levels)

Size

Size—the characteristic of athletes that is easiest to describe and observe—is simply the person's height, weight, or combination of both. This characteristic (and all of the other characteristics), however, must be considered in the context of the individual sport. It is also important to note that, although athletes in almost every sport are getting bigger, a tall tennis player wouldn't necessarily be a tall basketball player. Finally, height is an advantage in some sports (basketball, for example), but can be an obstacle in others (such as gymnastics).

Speed

In the minds of most coaches and athletes, there is a difference between speed and quickness. An athlete is quick if he or she moves quickly during the first four or five steps. Speed is the ability to move from one point to another after those first few steps. Michael Johnson and Donovan Bailey, both Olympic sprinters, have speed and they may also have quickness (though we don't know for sure). Basketball's Allen Iverson is quick, but he may or may not have speed at longer distances.

Quickness

Coaches in every movement sport are looking for athletes who have quick feet. Quickness, by their definition, is the ability to explode toward an opponent, the ball, or an area of the field or court. Quickness, frequently related to lower-body power, refers to how fast an athlete moves over distances of 10 yards or less.

Strength

Exercise scientists can point out complex relationships among characteristics such as strength, force, and power. These relationships involve the speed at which muscles contract and the resistance that they contract against. But most of us are correct when we define strength as a muscle's ability to produce force. Keep in mind that muscle strength is different from muscle endurance. Some sports require strength for short periods. Muscle endurance, however, requires strength over an extended period.

Power

Power is one of the most important elements in sports and is defined as the ability to exert maximum force in the shortest period. It is the coordinated combination of both strength and speed. Eddie George of the Tennessee Titans runs with explosive power. Tiger Woods unleashes a powerful swing off the tee. Oscar de la Hoya packs a powerful punch.

Tiger Woods' powerful swing combines strength and speed.

Table 2.1   Importance of Physical Attributes

Sport	Size
Baseball	
Pitchers	Height an advantage
Catchers	Height not as important as overall size
Middle infielders	Overall size an advantage, not prerequisite
1st–3rd basemen	Height an advantage, especially for 1st basemen
Outfielders	Not a factor
Basketball	
Perimeter players	Relative to forwards/post, not important
Inside players	Size, particularly height, prerequisite
Football	
Quarterbacks	Height an advantage
Running backs	Height not a factor, but weight with speed is
Offensive linemen	Height an advantage
Wide receivers	Height an advantage, but not prerequisite
Tight ends	Overall size an advantage, perhaps prerequisite
Defensive linemen	Overall size a prerequisite
Linebackers	Overall size important if combined with mobility
Defensive backs	Overall size an advantage
Golf	Overall size an advantage
Gymnastics	Height possibly a disadvantage
Ice hockey	Overall size an advantage combined with mobility
Soccer	
Position players	Overall size an advantage combined with mobility
Goalies	Height an advantage
Softball	Depends on position; see baseball
Swimming	Height, limb length advantages
Tennis	Not prerequisite
Track	
Sprinters	Not prerequisite
Hurdlers	Height an advantage
Cross country/distance	Not a factor
Field	
Throwers	Overall size an advantage, perhaps prerequisite
Jumpers	Height an advantage, perhaps prerequisite
Volleyball	Height an advantage, perhaps prerequisite
Wrestling	Because of weight categories, not a factor

Speed	Quickness
Not a factor	Not a factor, except in fielding position
Not usually a factor	Not a factor, except in setting up to making throws
Advantage in covering position and running bases	Advantage, if not prerequisite
Not usually a factor	Advantage
Advantage; prerequisite for centerfielders	Prerequisite to get a jump on the ball
Prerequisite	Prerequisite
Not usually a factor	Advantage, possibly prerequisite
Advantage, not prerequisite (depends on system)	Advantage, depending on the system
Advantage, but not as important as quickness	Prerequisite
Advantage	Becoming prerequisite
Prerequisite	Prerequisite
Advantage	Advantage
Advantage	Advantage
Advantage, if not prerequisite	Becoming prerequisite
Prerequisite	Prerequisite
Not a factor	Not a factor
Advantage, but not as important as quickness	Prerequisite for explosive movements
Skating speed an advantage, perhaps prerequisite	Prerequisite for explosive movements
Prerequisite	Prerequisite
Not a factor	Prerequisite
Depends on position; see baseball	Depends on position; see baseball
Not applicable	Not applicable
Advantage, but not as important as quickness	Prerequisite
Prerequisite	Prerequisite
Prerequisite	Prerequisite
Relative to sprinters, hurdlers, not a factor	Not a factor
Not a factor	Advantage, perhaps prerequisite for javelin
Prerequisite for long and triple jumpers, vaulters	Advantage, not prerequisite
Not a factor	Prerequisite
Not a factor	Total body quickness (not foot speed) prerequisite

(continued)

Table 2.1 *(continued)*

Sport	Strength
Baseball	
Pitchers	Prerequisite for throwing
Catchers	Prerequisite for many aspects of the position
Middle infielders	Advantage, not prerequisite
1st–3rd basemen	Prerequisite for hitting and throwing
Outfielders	Prerequisite for hitting and throwing
Basketball	
Perimeter players	Relative to forwards/post, not a factor
Inside players	Prerequisite in positioning and rebounding
Football	
Quarterbacks	Prerequisite for throwing
Running backs	Advantage, perhaps prerequisite
Offensive linemen	Prerequisite
Wide receivers	Advantage
Tight ends	Prerequisite
Defensive linemen	Prerequisite
Linebackers	Prerequisite
Defensive backs	Advantage
Golf	Advantage
Gymnastics	Prerequisite for certain movements
Ice hockey	Advantage
Soccer	
Position players	Lower-body strength prerequisite; upper-body not a factor
Goalies	Advantage
Softball	Depends on position; see baseball
Swimming	Prerequisite
Tennis	Advantage or prerequisite, depending on style of game
Track	
Sprinters	Lower-body strength prerequisite
Hurdlers	Lower-body strength prerequisite
Cross country/distance	Not a factor
Field	
Throwers	Prerequisite
Jumpers	Lower-body strength prerequisite
Volleyball	Advantage, perhaps prerequisite in strikers
Wrestling	Prerequisite

Power	Agility
Prerequisite for throwing hard	Advantage by definition 2
Prerequisite for throwing and hitting	Prerequisite
Advantage for throwing and hitting	Prerequisite
Prerequisite for hitting and throwing	Prerequisite for 3rd basemen; advantage for 1st basemen
Prerequisite for hitting and throwing	Prerequisite
Prerequisite for explosive movements to basket	Prerequisite
Prerequisite for explosive movements near basket	Prerequisite
Prerequisite for throwing	Advantage or prerequisite, depending on system
Advantage, perhaps prerequisite	Prerequisite
Prerequisite	Prerequisite by definition 2
Advantage	Prerequisite
Prerequisite	Prerequisite
Prerequisite	Relatively speaking, a prerequisite
Prerequisite	Prerequisite
Advantage	Prerequisite
Advantage	Not a factor
Prerequisite for explosive movements	Prerequisite
Prerequisite for explosive movements	Prerequisite
Prerequisite for explosive movements	Prerequisite
Prerequisite for explosive movements	Prerequisite by definition 2
Depends on position; see baseball	Depends on position; see baseball
Prerequisite for explosive movements	Prerequisite for some strokes and turns
Prerequisite for explosive movements and shots	Prerequisite
Prerequisite for explosive movements	Not a factor
Prerequisite for explosive movements	Prerequisite by definition 2
Not a factor	Not a factor
Prerequisite for explosive movements	Prerequisite by definition 2
Prerequisite for explosive movements	Prerequisite by definition 2
Prerequisite for explosive movements	Prerequisite by definition 2
Prerequisite for explosive movements	Prerequisite by definition 2

(continued)

Table 2.1   *(continued)*

Sport	Flexibility
Baseball	
Pitchers	Advantage
Catchers	Prerequisite
Middle infielders	Prerequisite
1st–3rd basemen	Advantage
Outfielders	Advantage, perhaps prerequisite
Basketball	
Perimeter players	Prerequisite
Inside players	Advantage
Football	
Quarterbacks	Advantage
Running backs	Prerequisite
Offensive linemen	Advantage, perhaps prerequisite
Wide receivers	Prerequisite
Tight ends	Advantage, perhaps prerequisite
Defensive linemen	Advantage
Linebackers	Advantage
Defensive backs	Prerequisite
Golf	Prerequisite
Gymnastics	Prerequisite
Ice hockey	Prerequisite
Soccer	
Position players	Prerequisite
Goalies	Prerequisite
Softball	Depends on position; see baseball
Swimming	Prerequisite
Tennis	Prerequisite
Track	
Sprinters	Advantage
Hurdlers	Prerequisite
Cross country/distance	Advantage
Field	
Throwers	Prerequisite, relatively speaking
Jumpers	Prerequisite
Volleyball	Prerequisite
Wrestling	Advantage, perhaps prerequisite

Coordination	Cardiorespiratory fitness
General and hand-eye, prerequisites	Not a factor
General and hand-eye, prerequisites	Not a factor
General and hand-eye, prerequisites	Not a factor
General and hand-eye, prerequisites	Not a factor
General and hand-eye, prerequisites	Not a factor
General and hand-eye, prerequisites	Prerequisite for continuous play
General and hand-eye, prerequisites	Prerequisite for continuous play
General and hand-eye, prerequisites	Not a factor
General a prerequisite	Not a factor
General an advantage, perhaps prerequisite	Not a factor
General and hand-eye, prerequisites	Not a factor
General and hand-eye, prerequisites	Not a factor
General an advantage, not prerequisite	Not a factor
General a prerequisite	Not a factor
General and hand-eye, prerequisites	Not a factor
Hand-eye a prerequisite	Not a factor
General a prerequisite	Not a factor
General and hand-eye, prerequisites	With frequent rotations, advantage for position players
General and foot-eye, prerequisites	Prerequisite for continuous play
General and hand-eye, prerequisites	Not a factor
Depends on position; see baseball	Not a factor
General an advantage	Prerequisite for distance events
General and hand-eye, prerequisites	Not a factor
General a prerequisite	Not a factor
General a prerequisite	Not a factor
General an advantage	Prerequisite
General a prerequisite	Not a factor
General a prerequisite	Not a factor
General and hand-eye, prerequisites	Not a factor
General a prerequisite	With 3-minute periods, an advantage

(continued)

Table 2.1 *(continued)*

Sport	Vision
Baseball	
Pitchers	Advantage
Catchers	Prerequisite to handle pitches
Middle infielders	Advantage in hitting
1st–3rd basemen	Advantage in hitting
Outfielders	Advantage in hitting
Basketball	
Perimeter players	Prerequisite
Inside players	Advantage
Football	
Quarterbacks	Advantage, perhaps prerequisite
Running backs	Advantage, perhaps prerequisite
Offensive linemen	Not a factor
Wide receivers	Advantage, perhaps prerequisite
Tight ends	Advantage, perhaps prerequisite
Defensive linemen	Not a factor
Linebackers	Advantage, perhaps prerequisite
Defensive backs	Advantage, perhaps prerequisite
Golf	Advantage, perhaps prerequisite
Gymnastics	Not a factor
Ice hockey	Advantage, perhaps prerequisite for position players; prerequisite for goalies
Soccer	
Position players	Not a factor
Goalies	Prerequisite
Softball	Depends on position; see baseball
Swimming	Not a factor
Tennis	Advantage, perhaps prerequisite
Track	
Sprinters	Not a factor
Hurdlers	Not a factor
Cross country/distance	Not a factor
Field	
Throwers	Not a factor
Jumpers	Not a factor
Volleyball	Advantage
Wrestling	Not a factor

Agility

Agility can be defined in two ways. First, it is the ability to change directions while moving. Some great athletes, believe it or not, are not agile. That physical skill is just not part of their job descriptions. A sprinter who runs in a straight line has to be fast, not agile. Agility does not always involve running, however. It is also the ability to make rapid changes in body position, which is essential in sports such as gymnastics and wrestling. Although some consider balance as a separate skill category, we include it with agility in this discussion. Being fast and agile in sports such as soccer, football, wrestling, and gymnastics is not an advantage if the person keeps falling down.

Flexibility

Flexibility is the ability to move the parts of the body through a wide range of motion. In all sports, flexibility is an advantage; in some, it is a prerequisite. Wrestlers, divers, and gymnasts must have great flexibility to be talented. Runners don't necessarily have to be flexible to compete, although it makes movement more fluid and probably makes an athlete less susceptible to injuries.

Coordination

Coordination comes with the territory of being a gifted athlete. If a person is not coordinated, he or she will not likely achieve success in sports. Some sports, however, require more coordination than others.

Just as there are different movements required of outstanding athletes, there are different kinds of coordination. The coordination of hands, arms, and eyes is usually called hand-eye coordination. Greg Maddux exhibits hand-eye coordination in pitching a baseball. When Steve McNair completes a pass, he shows hand-eye coordination.

Foot-eye coordination is needed by kickers in football and every player on a soccer team. Total body (or general) coordination is required by gymnasts, pole vaulters, receivers, and basketball players, to name just a few.

Aerobic Fitness

Aerobic fitness is the maximal capability to take in, transport, and use oxygen. Athletes who demonstrate aerobic fitness are those who run, walk, swim, or ski long distances. Many exceptional athletes have high levels of cardiorespiratory fitness, although it is not needed to perform the skills in their respective sports.

© iPhotoNews.com/Clark Brooks

Foot-eye coordination is just one of at least 10 physical skills demonstrated by superior athletes.

Vision

Sports vision is an emerging science that encompasses elements such as acuity, tracking, contrast sensitivity, peripheral vision, depth perception, and color vision. Generally speaking, quarterbacks need good vision to see the whole field. Point guards use peripheral vision to see the entire court. Good hitters in baseball usually have better than average ability to pick up and track a pitch moving at high speed.

Vision

Great hitters in baseball, quarterbacks and running backs in football, and point guards in basketball, among others, have great vision. And it's not just the 20-20 kind of visual acuity that most people have checked periodically. Exceptional sports vision includes the five components listed here, all of which are measurable. Not all outstanding athletes are above average in each category, but those who are have a great advantage.

• **Acuity.** If an athlete's eyes have the ability to see the detail of an object clearly at a distance against a background that is different from the object, he or she has good visual acuity. If a person can read the 20-foot line of letters or objects on an eye chart at a distance of 20 feet, that is average. If that person can read the 15-foot or 10-foot lines at a distance of 20 feet, that is outstanding. Baseball players Ted Williams and Wade Boggs were reported to have 20-15 or better visual acuity.

• **Contrast sensitivity.** Athletes have to perform under a variety of lighting conditions. Those who can discriminate detail regardless of the amount and kind of light have great contrast sensitivity. A hockey player who can pick up a puck on ice and an outfielder who can see a ball against a blue sky or a stadium background are examples.

• **Peripheral vision.** Peripheral vision is the ability to see things outside the central area of focus, both side to side and up and down. It is one of the most valuable visual skills an athlete can possess. Seeing beyond 180 degrees to either side is not physically possible, but legendary athletes such as Pete Maravich had amazing side vision. Athletes with exceptional peripheral vision can see more of the playing area, the movement of other players, and the ball, all at the same time.

• **Depth perception.** Depth perception—the ability to quickly process an object or person in space—is necessary for judging fly balls, shooting jump shots, and passing or catching footballs. Although this is an area of controversy, there is little evidence that depth perception, peripheral vision, contrast sensitivity, or acuity can be improved. You either have those skills or you don't.

• **Tracking.** In many sports, athletes have to not only see players and objects under a variety of conditions, but also follow things that move very rapidly. This visual skill, called dynamic acuity or tracking, is of great interest because evidence suggests that it can be improved.

Joan Vickers, PhD, a professor and researcher at the University of Calgary, has developed a way to measure the ability of athletes to track.

(continued)

Vision *(continued)*

It involves three cameras, one that follows the eyes, another that follows what the eyes see, and a third that records the entire playing area. All three camera targets are locked together in time and transferred to a videotape.[1]

What Vickers has learned is that elite athletes possess what she calls a "quiet eye." A world-class volleyball player waited almost 400 milliseconds before moving. When he made his first move, it was decisive. He knew where the ball was going and what it was doing. Less skilled players were too active before moving toward the ball. Their eyes moved with the movement of their bodies, and they tracked the ball for shorter periods. The same kind of test has provided similar results in several other sports.[2]

Two things make the Vickers research especially intriguing. First, no significant physical differences existed between elite athletes and those at a slightly lower level. The difference in performance was in perception, tracking, and attention. Second, Vickers and her colleagues have developed drills that can improve the ability to track objects in several sports. The possibility of enhancing a key component of sports vision separates it from other visual skills and opens new areas of training for coaches and athletes.

ASSESSING PHYSICAL ATTRIBUTES

Athletes can do something to improve or change almost every physical characteristic. If they come up against characteristics they cannot improve, they can find sports that are a better match for what their bodies are capable of doing. Following is a Physical Skills Checklist exercise. Complete the form (or have an athlete complete it) by circling the number that best matches each physical attribute. Depending on who completes the form, the results can be discussed with a parent, coach, player, or friend. Write or discuss at least one action plan for each skill that needs improvement.

ADDRESSING PHYSICAL DEFICIENCIES

The boundaries of physical ability may be established by genetic considerations, but how much improvement or enhancement takes place within those boundaries is up to the athlete. A dedicated athlete can do something about each of the 10 physical attributes already described, starting with size.

• **Size.** Parents, coaches, and athletes can do three things about size or the lack of it. The first is to be aware of family growth patterns and to monitor growth. A pediatrician can provide information about normal and abnormal

Physical Skills Checklist

- Circle the number that applies to you (5 is high).
- Determine one action to address weakest areas.
- Discuss privately with friend, parent, coach, or group leader.

---

1. **Size** (body size and type match sport)   1 2 3 4 5
   Action plan: _____
   _____

2. **Speed** (meets basic requirements for sport or position)   1 2 3 4 5
   Action plan: _____
   _____

3. **Quickness** (has quick feet; is always in position)   1 2 3 4 5
   Action plan: _____
   _____

4. **Strength** (is strong enough to play position or sport)   1 2 3 4 5
   Action plan: _____
   _____

5. **Power** (combines strength with explosiveness)   1 2 3 4 5
   Action plan: _____
   _____

6. **Agility** (changes directions or body position while moving) 1 2 3 4 5
   Action plan: _____
   _____

7. **Flexibility** (has fluid, full range of motion in each part
   of body)   1 2 3 4 5
   Action plan: _____
   _____

8. **Coordination** (hand-eye, foot-eye, general)   1 2 3 4 5
   Action plan: _____
   _____

9. **Cardiorespiratory fitness** (can use oxygen for long periods) 1 2 3 4 5
   Action plan: _____
   _____

10. **Vision** (can see entire court, field, area)   1 2 3 4 5
    Action plan: _____
    _____

growth patterns, and he or she should be consulted when questions or concerns arise about the size of a young athlete. Table 2.2 illustrates the height of children ages 8 to 18 in the United States at the 25th, 50th, and 75th percentiles. If, for example, an eight-year-old girl or boy is four feet, four inches tall, both would be as tall or taller than 75 percent of the children at that age.[3]

Predicting growth is not an exact science, but there are charts to help you determine the percentage of adult height that is normally reached at each age. One of those charts is presented in table 2.3. Even though full adult height is supposed to be reached by 100 percent of the population by the age of 18, a very small percentage continue to grow after that age.[4]

The second thing that parents and coaches can do in regard to size is to provide direction and support for an age-appropriate resistance training program. Resistance training cannot make a child taller, but it can increase the size of muscles and body mass when that is desirable. Suggestions regarding when to start a program and what to do are given in chapter 6, "Speeding Up the Process."

The last thing to do about size is to not let it get in the way of athletic enjoyment and excellence. Examples exist in every sport of great athletes who performed at the highest levels even though they did not meet the established guidelines for height or weight.

Table 2.2   Height for Age Percentiles

Girls 8 years	Percentile	Boys 8 years	Girls 14 years	Percentile	Boys 14 years
4-1	25%	4-1	5-1 1/2	25%	5-2 1/2
4-2	50%	4-2 1/2	5-2	50%	5-4 1/2
4-4	75%	4-4	5-5	75%	5-7 1/2

Girls 10 years	Percentile	Boys 10 years	Girls 16 years	Percentile	Boys 16 years
4-4 1/2	25%	4-5	5-2 1/2	25%	5-6 1/2
4-6	50%	4-6 1/2	5-4	50%	5-8 1/2
4-8	75%	4-8 1/2	5-5 1/2	75%	5-10 1/2

Girls 12 years	Percentile	Boys 12 years	Girls 18 years	Percentile	Boys 18 years
4-9 1/2	25%	4-9	5-2 1/2	25%	5-7 1/2
4-11 1/2	50%	4-11	5-4 1/2	50%	5-9 1/2
5-1 1/2	75%	5-1	5-6	75%	5-11 1/2

From the National Center for Chronic Disease Prevention and Health Promotion.

Table 2.3 Percentage of Mature Height

Age	Boys	Girls		Age	Boys	Girls
1	42	45		10	78	84
2	50	53		11	81	88
3	54	57		12	84	93
4	58	62		13	87	97
5	62	66		14	92	98
6	65	70		15	96	99
7	69	74		16	98	100
8	72	78		17	99	100
9	75	81		18	100	100

From the National Center for Chronic Disease Prevention and Health Promotion.

• **Speed.** Some people are born with the ability to run fast, but that doesn't mean that speed can't be improved in others. Under the supervision of the right coach or teacher, sport-specific training to improve speed is an advantage in, if not an essential part of, athletic development. If you are working with a young athlete, record running speed occasionally just as parents informally record height on a wall or door at home. The increments will occur in fractions of seconds, but every fraction translates to ground covered on a track, field, or court.

The indicator of speed is not a great time in the 100-meter run, unless that is the specific event that the athlete is training for. Each sport has distances particular to it, and speed training should be undertaken with that in mind. A defensive back may need great speed over a distance of 40 yards. A basketball player or a gymnast needs speed mostly for a few steps. Further discussions about speed appear in chapter 8, "Testing for Talent," and in the chapters on each sport.

• **Quickness.** For most sports, quickness of feet and quickness of reaction time are as important as the ability to run fast. Both can be improved. Plyometric exercises—those that involve explosive movements such as hopping and jumping—have been proven to increase quickness of feet.

Reaction time is considered a skill that depends on experience and learning. So while some athletes may react faster than others naturally, the slowest-reacting athletes can learn to react more quickly. Individual differences will always exist, but each person can learn to reduce reaction time. Quickness and reaction time movements that are practiced in gamelike situations are the ones most likely to be used in competition.

• **Strength and power.** Strength is one of the most obvious athletic skills that can be improved. If a child is old enough to play an organized sport, he or she is old enough to begin a resistance training program. Power, which combines strength with explosive movement, is developed in the weight room as well as in sport-specific drills. The key for both is to find a qualified professional, preferably one who is certified as a strength and conditioning coach (CSCS), to develop a program that meets the needs of each athlete.

• **Agility.** Agility drills should be a part of training for every athlete who has to change directions while moving. The purpose of this book is not to prescribe drills for each sport but to remind parents and coaches that agility is an important component of athletic talent and one that can be improved with the appropriate training. Agility tests and norms are given in chapter 8 and in some of the individual sports chapters. They are to be used solely for the purpose of comparison and not to make judgments about overall sports talent or potential for success.

• **Flexibility.** Flexibility is often an underrated and underdeveloped component of talent. A comprehensive program of stretching is the best way to increase range of motion and at the same time reduce the incidence of injury. While no direct connection between stretching and injuries has been shown, athletes with greater ranges of motion are less likely to sustain soft tissue strains and sprains. In other words, athletes should stretch to increase range of motion, and increase range of motion to avoid injuries.

• **Coordination.** Hand-eye, foot-eye, and overall coordination are perhaps the distinguishing characteristics of talented athletes. While difficult to measure, coordination is definitely a skill that has innate and learned components. There are few quick-fix coordination drills. Rather, repeated and frequent contact with a bat, ball, racket, club, or other sport instrument is the way to improve coordination. Many coaches tell young athletes to "touch the ball every day."

• **Cardiorespiratory fitness.** Cardiorespiratory fitness is the most improvable of all physical skills. Yes, there are genetic limitations, but every athlete can achieve observable and measurable results through a program of aerobic training. Without any of the other nine physical skills discussed here, it is possible to be great in at least one sport by simply being more aerobically fit than the competition.

Whether aerobic fitness is necessary for every athletic endeavor is another issue. Golfers, gymnasts, baseball players, and football players, to name a few, don't require high degrees of cardiorespiratory fitness. They are seldom, if ever, required to perform at high levels of intensity for extended periods. They are basically stop-and-go athletes—no less talented, but not necessarily aerobically fit. This does not mean that their overall health would not be improved from higher levels of aerobic fitness, or that better cardiorespiratory fitness would not indirectly benefit their performance. It probably would.

• **Vision.** Vision, the last of the 10 attributes of gifted athletes, in many ways is the one that we know the least about and the one that is the most controversial. All of the dimensions of sports vision are critical in determining the success or failure of athletes in many sports. However, whether vision can be improved is a subject that still divides the sports vision professional community.

There is no evidence that visual acuity can be improved by training. An athlete cannot go from having 20-100 vision to having 20-20 vision by training the eyes. Nevertheless, growing evidence suggests that vision training may improve certain aspects of athletic performance, such as tracking an object. The methods for achieving this goal, however, are not available to most athletes. Vision specialists offer programs that address other areas of sports vision, and plenty of anecdotal accounts support those programs, but no scientific body of evidence supports their claims.

Talent is easily overrated. To many, the word itself is a synonym for physical ability. Some coaches and parents who discover a child with exceptional physical gifts assume that talent alone will ensure success in sports. They are wrong. Physical talent is just a key that opens the door to exciting possibilities. What happens after that has less to do with physical skills than with the opportunity and willingness to develop those skills.

Chapter **3**

Recognizing Mental and Emotional Skills

Membership in the club of talented athletes begins to diminish when mental and emotional skills are added to the list of requirements. It is one thing to run fast, jump high, or exhibit great strength. It is quite another to have the presence of mind to use raw physical talent in a complex competitive environment. This is not about having a high IQ. It is about understanding the larger picture of a sport and combining that information with physical skills to influence the outcome.

DEFINING MENTAL AND EMOTIONAL SKILLS

Talk with 10 sport psychologists and you will get 10 different lists of the emotional characteristics of exceptional athletes. However, almost all of them will agree with sport psychologist Jim Loehr, EdD, president of LGE Performance Systems, who says that drive is the most important predictor of exceptional athletic success. "These athletes are almost obsessed with succeeding," says Loehr.[1]

Drive

Drive can be present at a very early age, or it can develop as late as the college years. Some children become so captivated by sports or a particular sport that they become nuisances to those around them. They always want to play. They nag their parents to throw to them, hit with them, kick balls to them, or take them where someone else will do these things. If they can't find anyone, they'll play by themselves, make up games, or create make-believe situations in which they make the last big play that wins the game. These children will shoot baskets in the dark, wear out the garage door with a tennis ball, or play with a soccer ball instead of eating or doing their homework.

"All great hockey players have spent time practicing by themselves," says Bob O'Connor, national coach-in-chief for USA Hockey. "They never get enough ice time by just going to practices and games. They spend hundreds of hours handling the puck, creating situations, and imagining themselves playing the game."[2]

If your child only plays a sport during structured practices or games, he or she is probably not driven, although that doesn't mean that drive won't develop at an older age. Sooner or later, however, it has to be there for an athlete to rise above the others.

Although drive is evident in some children at preschool ages, it might not develop until much later in others. Dave Randall was a Southeastern Conference tennis champion at the University of Mississippi and later played on the professional circuit for nine years. According to his father, Jim, "Dave always had the talent, but he was not really driven until he got to college. Once he became part of a team and practiced against good competition every day, he started putting in the time and effort that made him successful."[3]

Passion

Closely related to the drive factor is a love for the game. Greg Patten, national junior coach for the United States Tennis Association, says, "The first thing I look for in an exceptional player is a childlike sense of play. Great players abandon themselves to playing the sport. Even if they don't have great physical talent, they have an intangible ability to compete that sets them apart from other players."[4]

Shane Murphy, PhD, a private-practice sport psychologist who spent eight years on the Olympic Training Center staff in Colorado, comments on the devotion he has observed in talented athletes. "I really can't see putting in the hours that some of these young kids spend in their sports. You can't keep them away from the game. In fact, unless someone helps them understand the important of balance in their lives, the pursuit of excellence can become a negative experience."[5]

John Heil, a Roanoke, Virginia, sport psychologist, warns that great athletes who have such a passion for the sport run the risk of having it define who they are. "Their interest is so one-dimensional that they can never take that passion to anything outside of the game."[6]

"Drive is the most important predictor of exceptional athletic success." —Jim Loehr, sport psychologist

Fortunately, others can transfer their passion for sports to other areas of life. Former New York Knick Bill Bradley and U.S. Congressman J. C. Watts, who played quarterback at Oklahoma, moved easily from sports to politics. ESPN's Robin Roberts played basketball at a relatively obscure college, then became a broadcasting superstar. Roger Staubach went from the NFL's hall of fame to being one of the most successful businessmen in the country.

Stability

Talented athletes tend to be emotionally stable. Loehr reminds us that sport is demanding. "A person who has a limited tolerance for the stress associated with training and competing is not as likely to be successful. The one who has a tolerance for stress in life and in sports has a better chance of making it. They can adapt to obstacles, and they don't seem to be always pushed to the limits of the ability to adapt. Sport has a way of washing away those who can't deal with stress."

Heil calls this quality "emotional resiliency." It is the psychological version of flexibility. "Even with all of the ups and downs that any athlete encounters, the great ones manage to survive and come out of adversity with renewed enthusiasm for the game. They always seem to be composed and rested, with plenty of energy reserves."

There are many exceptions to the emotionally stable characteristic, of course. Former Giants linebacker Lawrence Taylor, for example, did not demonstrate that quality, as his postcareer record shows. John Daly, the golfer, always seems to be in trouble and yet plays at a very high level. John McEnroe and Jimmy Connors appeared to live on an emotional edge from which they were always about to fall. Yet they used this semicontrolled rage to reach heights that other players could not approach. Unfortunately, their behavior influenced an entire generation of young players who grew up thinking they had to behave in the same way to be great.

Mental Toughness

Mental toughness has become part of sport vocabulary, but it means different things to different people. Loehr thinks it encompasses both drive and stability, as well as self-esteem and the ability to control confidence.

Exceptional athletes have to feel good about themselves, or at least feel good enough to think they can perform well. George Brett, the Kansas City third baseman, said he played well because he was afraid of failing or looking bad. Although most athletes are partially motivated by the fear of failure, outstanding ones know deep down inside that they are good.

Quarterbacks have a sort of swagger that can be irritating or offensive off the field. But in practice and in competition, it is a necessary requirement of the job that tells teammates and opponents, "I know what I'm doing, I'm going to do it, and you can't stop me." Quarterbacks must take charge of situations. If they don't have that attitude, they probably won't succeed.

Regarding cockiness among golfers, one teaching professional, who preferred to remain anonymous, said, "You have to think you can take somebody else's money."

Positive Attitude

Along with confidence, exceptional athletes often have a positive attitude. Again, a star quarterback has to think he can take a team 80 yards in less than two minutes against the wind, a good defense, and a hostile crowd. The odds are not good for that to happen, but he thinks it can. A gifted golfer who is down seven strokes with seven holes to play still thinks he can pull everything together in time for a win. To a star volleyball player, losing the first game in a two-out-of-three match means nothing.

"Athletes who are on the negative or pessimistic side rarely achieve a high level of success," says Loehr. "The fuel for their success is positive."

Realism

While great athletes have to be confident and positive, they also must be realistic about their ability. They acknowledge their limitations or weaknesses and attack them. LSU head football coach Nick Saban discussed football talent in an interview on radio station WWL in New Orleans. "That number one NFL draft choice, a player who is about to make six million dollars a year, is not a perfect player. There is some part of his game that needs improving or that can be exploited by other teams if it is not corrected."

If athletes' egos are too big, or if they are surrounded by entourages that shield them against things they don't want to hear (several boxers come to mind), they are not likely to succeed. "An athlete can be gifted," says Loehr, "but problems with ego, anger, and temper make them more susceptible to failure."

Says Heil, "Great athletes learn from experience. Whether an experience is positive or negative, they have a way of using it to make themselves better." Following are some examples:

- Pitchers who learn to vary velocity, location, and delivery when they can no longer throw heat
- Golfers who develop short games to make up for lost distance
- Linemen who use technique rather than brute strength to block or get past an opponent
- Tennis players who use the whole court and a variety of shots instead of depending on a serve-and-volley game

Focus

Early on, parents and coaches can observe the ability of some children to block out all distractions. It is both a mental and visual phenomenon. The gifted athlete is totally absorbed in the moment and can hold that concentration level for long periods of time. Watch their eyes. They are not looking in the stands, searching for friends, or trying to find their parents. Neither cars, crowds, noise, nor opponents can break them out of their almost trancelike state. Whether it is a God-given ability or a learned trait, exceptional athletes can focus. The now-famous eyes of former Chicago Bears linebacker Mike Singletary immediately before a snap illustrate a perfect example of mental and visual focus. Fortunately, those who don't have this quality naturally can acquire it.

Effort

Tom Osborne, the great Nebraska coach, said that he wanted high school players who finished blocks, ran pass patterns out although they knew the ball wasn't going to be thrown their way, and played hard even when their team was 30 points behind in a game.[7]

Dr. Osborne was talking about effort. Outstanding players work hard in practice and on the field. It is easy to find athletes who will give 100 percent during a game. Not as many are willing to give the same amount of effort to prepare for a game.

Many of the great athletes in the National Basketball Association who are poor shooters (and shooting percentage is down from 10 years ago) still don't get it. They have heard the stories about Larry Bird shooting by himself for three hours before game time, but the lesson has not been learned. Michael Jordan, who could have come and gone when he pleased, was frequently the first in the gym for practice and the last to leave.

That kind of work ethic is not restricted to any one sport. Mickey Sullivan, the head football coach at Fort Union Military Academy in Virginia, remembers Tennessee Titans running back Eddie George. "He was the first one on the field and the last one off. The first one in the weight room, the last one out."[8]

Joe Dumars, the former Detroit Piston star, got it. Even after he was an established star in the NBA, he used the summer months to develop what he perceived to be weaknesses in his game. He spent four to five hours a day, usually alone, improving his free throws, jump shots, left-hand skills, or other aspects of an already well-rounded set of basketball tools.

Tiger Woods demonstrated his work habits after winning his first Masters. He went back to his teaching pro and completely retooled his swing. Many players would have been content to ride a win in the Masters for the rest of their careers rather than, in effect, start over.

Whatever the sport, being exceptional takes time, practice, and persistence. Very few athletes, if any, can turn their athletic ability off and on without putting in the time and effort to prepare for competition.

Persistence

Even when things are going poorly, good athletes keep on doing whatever it is they are supposed to do. They trust themselves to perform at a high level, even when it looks as though they never will. That is why shooters keep on shooting in basketball, why quarterbacks continue to think that their passes will be on target, and why great tennis players stay with their strokes. Sooner or later, talent will prevail, and they trust their talent.

Talented athletes learn that mistakes happen and that they can adapt to the situation. They cannot expect perfect performances from themselves or from their teammates. Although many good athletes struggle with perfectionism, sooner or later they learn to cope with their shortcomings and those of their teammates.

The gifted athlete can become totally absorbed in the moment.

Competitiveness

Don't be surprised if the exceptional athlete makes you keep on playing until he or she wins. These people like to play and don't like to lose. They have a fighter's mentality. Said Nick Bollettieri, the famous tennis coach, "Talented players like the battle."[9] He was talking about players like John McEnroe, who thought the value of sports camps was not so much the instruction as the chance to compete against other players every day.

Exceptional athletes are competitive to the point of distraction. Those who play more than one sport, whether or not they are skilled, are frequently just as competitive in the second or third sport. They are competitive in competition and competitive in practice. If they get in trouble with a coach, it is frequently because they are pounding their teammates in a way that hurts their confidence, if not their bodies.

INNATE VERSUS LEARNED EMOTIONAL SKILLS

The emotional makeup of great athletes is a mix of inherited and learned characteristics. The father of an elite Canadian tennis player said that his son just seemed to have qualities such as drive, focus, and confidence at a very early age. "We didn't do anything as parents to foster those qualities. They were simply there from the start."[10]

© EMPICS / Heading

Athletes with exceptional talent like the battle and have a fighter's mentality.

Some people are naturally enthusiastic and energetic about sports, but those qualities can get derailed at a very young age. One or more negative experiences can make a difference. "That is why," concludes Heil, "it is so important for young athletes to have supportive coaches and parents who do not push too much and too soon. Strict coaching at the wrong time can destroy enthusiasm. The best coaches are the ones who can cultivate a framework in which the athlete can grow emotionally as physical skills develop."

Loehr emphasizes that psychological skills are honed and developed in the same way that physical skills are. Exceptionally talented athletes have to practice, work on, and plan how to use their psychological skills just as they do their physical skills.

Are there ways to measure these emotional qualities in sport-specific situations? Not many. But there are activities that give players, parents, and coaches an indication of where athletes think they are in regard to the 10 characteristics discussed in this chapter.

On page 38 is the Emotional Talent Checklist. Athletes who are mature enough to evaluate their emotional characteristics related to sports can use it themselves, or parents or coaches can use it to assess athletes' emotional attributes. The checklist is intended to be used as an informal activity, not as a psychological test, and it should not be used in a group session. Who wants to reveal weaknesses to a potential opponent?

Respond to each of the 10 characteristics by circling a number from 1 to 5. Five is high, indicating superior drive, focus, competitiveness, and so on. After completing the form, write down one action plan to address an area of concern.

ADDRESSING WEAKNESSES

Athletes should work with someone who can suggest ways to address weaknesses. If, for example, an athlete lacks confidence in certain situations and doesn't know what to do about it, a coach—or someone in a coaching role—should be qualified or mature enough to suggest some alternatives that would improve confidence. Following are examples of possible strategies (action plans) that correspond with each of the emotional characteristics on the checklist.

• **Drive.** With regard to drive, some people are tempted to say, "Well, either he or she has it or doesn't have it. It has to come from within." While this may be true generally, parents and coaches can put young athletes in situations in which drive can develop. Pete Sampras gives credit to his first coach, Pete Fisher, for giving him drive. "I had the talent," Sampras told an ESPN interviewer, "but he helped me to realize what I could do with it. He pushed me to become good until I saw what he was trying to do. Then I drove myself."

Sometimes exposure to other athletes and coaches is enough to trigger a response that becomes a drive to succeed. A person who thinks he or she is not good enough to compete at a high level suddenly realizes that it is possible. Although sports camps seldom result in significant technical changes, they do place athletes in competitive situations in which the drive to succeed is nourished.

Finally, some athletes just mature late, physically and emotionally. Those who may have appeared to be lazy, uninterested, or distracted early in their athletic lives can grow to become people that exhibit the drive necessary to become champions.

• **Passion.** When good athletes say they have no passion for the game, take it seriously, but ask why. If they don't like to play, they may simply not be ready for the emotional and physical commitment that it takes. Russ Rose, coach of the 1999 NCAA women's volleyball champions at Penn State says, "Some players just don't want to work very hard. They want to be good, but not that good."[11]

Others may be burned out. If a child has played a sport from the age of five or six and has been pushed pretty hard along the way, burnout is common. Taking time off during the year or even taking a year or more off from the sport may be necessary. Some of them will never come back, and those around them have to be prepared for that possibility. Others realize

Emotional Talent Checklist

- Circle the number that applies to you (5 is high).
- Determine one action to address weakest areas.
- Discuss with friend, parent, coach, or sport psychologist.

1. **Drive** (overwhelming desire to succeed; has something to prove)   1 2 3 4 5
   Action plan: _____

2. **Passion** (loves the game; can't stay away from it)   1 2 3 4 5
   Action plan: _____

3. **Stability** (can handle stress; resilient)   1 2 3 4 5
   Action plan: _____

4. **Toughness** (good self-esteem; confident)   1 2 3 4 5
   Action plan: _____

5. **Positive attitude** (enjoys challenges; avoids negative thinking) 1 2 3 4 5
   Action plan: _____

6. **Realism** (works on limitations; learns from experience)   1 2 3 4 5
   Action plan: _____

7. **Focus** (blocks out distractions; absorbed in the game)   1 2 3 4 5
   Action plan: _____

8. **Effort** (first on and off the field/court; keeps improving)   1 2 3 4 5
   Action plan: _____

9. **Persistence** (can manage desire to be perfect; keeps coming) 1 2 3 4 5
   Action plan: _____

10. **Competitiveness** (refuses to lose; likes the battle)   1 2 3 4 5
    Action plan: _____

how much they miss the game and return to the sport with a new appreciation of what they missed and a renewed sense of energy.

• **Stability.** Assuming there is not some emotional illness that should be handled by medical or psychological professionals, emotional stability in a sports context can be learned.

Says Shane Murphy, "Parents shouldn't back off from the willingness to discipline children on emotional issues. If a child or adolescent is out of control, that tells me that several things could be going on. The child could be testing the limits imposed by parents. Or it could be that a player's physical talent exceeds his emotional maturity. Unacceptable behavior could also indicate that the person is not ready for this level of competition."

Whatever the reason, these emotional displays have to be addressed early or they can destroy an athlete's career as well as the relationship among the player, parents, and coaches. How do you do it? "Take the sport away," suggests Murphy. "Explain to the child that there will be no more football, basketball, soccer, whatever, until that kind of unacceptable behavior is stopped. Force the athlete to change or give up something that is very important."

• **Mental toughness.** Few athletes are likely to admit, especially to someone close to them, that they might not be tough enough to compete at a high level. But if there is any indication that the problem exists (such as not performing well in pressure situations, never coming from behind to win or play well, giving up when things are not going well), there are ways to handle it.

Place the athlete in a position to succeed. While playing up in age or size levels can benefit some athletes, it can destroy others. Getting beaten down by good competition has limited benefits.

Developing pressure drills and simulated game situations can help athletes become mentally tough. Kurt Warner, the St. Louis quarterback, had a ninth-grade coach who invented the "Kill Kurt Drill." In it, there was a center, two receivers, and Warner on offense. On defense, there were two linebackers who wore arm pads. Instead of running when he saw the linebackers coming, Warner was instructed to pass the ball and take the hit. His coach told him that it would hurt less if he completed the pass, and Warner learned to stay in the pocket and make the play. This is not a drill recommended by most coaches, but it does illustrate one way of developing mental toughness under difficult circumstances.

Basketball coaches have long used seven- or eight-against-five drills to teach players to get the ball up the court against the press. Tennis coaches have their players begin a game down 0–40 or begin a set behind 0–5 to test their ability to perform under almost impossible odds.

• **Positive attitude.** What can you do to help an athlete who has a negative attitude? Psychologists sometimes suggest that people practice positive self-talk. Instead of complaining or whining, they can say positive things to themselves. Expressions such as "Good shot," "I can make this play," "We can win this game," and "We are going to play better in the second half" can become self-fulfilling prophecies.

Ask athletes what they like about the game. What is fun about the sport? What can they do to make it enjoyable? If they are not having fun, what can they do to eliminate the negative parts? Suggest working on visualizing plays, game, and events that go well, or imagining themselves performing at a high level. It can also help to mentally practice the things they have to do to succeed.

Remind pessimists that this is a game. Tell them there are worse ways in life to be spending their time and that lots of kids would love to trade places with them. What they are doing is a privilege, but they are making it out to be punishment. While there is a temptation to be preachy in these situations, remember that the right person at the right time can sometimes say something that can change a negative attitude into a positive one.

Families that emphasize service to others go a long way toward heading off negative attitudes among their children. People who help others who don't have the luxury of playing a sport are less likely to complain about the relatively trivial things that go on in a ball game.

• **Realism.** Getting a "big head" is pretty common among exceptional athletes, but it can be a terminal condition if not kept in check. Athletes who are great at one level discover that they are not so great at the next. How do you help them keep things in perspective?

Parents should make sure that the home life stays the same, regardless of how good someone is in a sport. Duties should be distributed equally among all siblings, athletes and nonathletes. Family conversations should revolve around things other than sports, especially when brothers and sisters are involved in other activities. Homework and grades should always take precedence over practices and games.

Coaches should not overlook physical and emotional weaknesses. As mentioned earlier, there are no perfect athletes. All of them have areas in which they can improve. Coaches and parents shouldn't be afraid to point those weaknesses out and to encourage the person to work on them. As great as Shaquille O'Neal is as a basketball player, he can't shoot free throws. Just think how much more he could accomplish by getting better at a relatively simple part of the game. It can happen. Sacramento's Chris Webber went from being a 45 percent free throw shooter in 1999 to being a 75 percent shooter in 2000.

Finally, there is always someone out there who can beat you. The player who unrealistically thinks he or she is unbeatable can be moved into competitive situations in which a bigger or better athlete wins. If that's what it takes to keep your player's feet on the ground, so be it.

• **Focus.** While this characteristic can be a tough one to teach, it can be developed with the right person's help. Some athletes with wandering minds and eyes have to be reminded constantly to get their heads back into the game with a string of verbal commands that keep reeling them back in. Eventually, they might be trained to block out distractions without being told to do so. Also, self-talk, even if not aloud, can keep some people focused on the task.

Dr. David Yukelson, a Penn State sport psychologist, emphasizes the importance of having a routine to block out distractions. Taking a deep breath before a shot, adjusting equipment before a pitch, and taking practice swings before a putt in golf are all examples of routines that bring an athlete into the moment.[12]

Ken Ravizza, PhD, a psychologist at California State University, Fullerton, says to watch a preschooler playing with a toy. "That child is totally absorbed in the moment, focused on the task, and oblivious to the rest of the world. The athlete playing a game has to get down to the same concentration level as the two-year-old playing with a truck. They are both playing a game."[13]

- **Effort.** A player who recognizes that his work habits are not what they should be has already taken the first step toward correcting the problem. Now it's time to actually write down and examine the practice routine and see how many hours a day or week that person is working to improve. Rising above average requires a time commitment that some are not willing or able to make. At that point, difficult decisions have to be made by the athlete, the parents, and the coach. Because of family, school, work commitments, or outside interests, the person may not be in a position to move to a higher level. The person should at least confront that reality, even if he or she can do nothing about it. Perhaps making a change later will allow the practice time needed to improve.

If the athlete is already putting the time in and improvement is not happening, the problem exists within the current practice patterns and activities. One problem may be that the athlete is practicing only the skills that he or she already excels at. Here are some examples of changes in practice that could benefit athletes who are stuck in a pattern:

- Long-driving golfers could spend more time hitting irons and putts.
- Baseline tennis players could sacrifice backcourt time to work on volleys and serves.
- Basketball players who can't go to the left could stop making all of their moves to the right.
- Power hitters in baseball could work on hitting the ball where it is pitched instead of trying to pull everything.
- Volleyball players who love to spike could learn to block and set.

- **Persistence.** It is hard to be driven and patient at the same time, but great athletes have both qualities. Putting star athletes in situations in which they cannot win in practice sessions teaches lessons in how to deal with losing. Asking them to work on selected drills with nonstarters helps them develop patience with less talented athletes. Here are some sport-specific examples of activities that can teach patience in practice sessions:

- Make hitters take at least two pitches before they swing at a ball.
- Force passers to look at two or more receivers before deciding on a target.
- Demand that players on a basketball team pass the ball at least four times before taking a shot.
- Require two tennis players to complete a six-shot rally before anyone can win a point.

- **Competitiveness.** This is the one emotional characteristic that usually shows up with or without outside help. Some players who are talented, however, may not necessarily be competitive. If that quality has to be drawn out, it may happen by challenging the person to become the best he or she can be. Better yet, it might surface when a person is challenged by peers rather than by a parent or coach. Finally, as an athlete matures, the competitiveness that may have been present in another area of life may transfer into the athletic arena. The only thing parents and coaches can do is provide the right environment for the competitive nature of a person to surface.

A WORD TO COACHES AND PARENTS

Jim Loehr concludes, "What is necessary for parents and coaches to do is give the athlete help in framing their talent in the competitive arena. Those people can teach positive adaptation skills, energy management, and goal setting. They can also influence the ability to be passionate and determined. Just as important, parents, coaches, and other role models can show gifted athletes how to portray those qualities."

Finally, remember that although basic personality traits may be established, they are dynamic in sports. It isn't just a question of having them or not having them. Confidence, for example, can change from season to season, game to game, and even from one point to another. Momentum switches often signal a loss of confidence on one side and a gain on the other. There are degrees of competence and changes in emotional skills, just as there are changes in physical capabilities. Many coaches monitor and measure the emotional qualities of their players by having them complete questionnaires following competition. Following is a competition evaluation form adapted from one used by a Big-Ten school for its volleyball players.[14]

Emotional and mental skills will overcome pure physical talent in two situations. The first is when physical skills are evenly matched, which is

Mental Skills Evaluation

Name: _____

Event: _____

Circle a number for each item (1 is low; 5 is high).

Mental preparation prior to game	1 2 3 4 5
Precompetition activity	1 2 3 4 5
Emotional readiness	1 2 3 4 5
Self-confidence	1 2 3 4 5
Quality of effort	1 2 3 4 5
Concentration	1 2 3 4 5
Consistency of focus	1 2 3 4 5
Mental toughness	1 2 3 4 5
Ability to let go of mistakes	1 2 3 4 5
Poise	1 2 3 4 5
Control of negative thoughts	1 2 3 4 5
Enjoyment	1 2 3 4 5
Communication with teammates	1 2 3 4 5

What aspects of your competition in today's event were you pleased with?

What aspects of your competition in today's event were you disappointed with?

Adapted with permission of the *Penn State Sports Medicine Newsletter*.

often the case at higher levels of competition. The second is when there is a mismatch in physical attributes, but not enough to determine absolutely the outcome of an event or an athletic career. In those cases, it doesn't matter who has the most physical talent, but rather, who has the mind-set to achieve greatness.

Chapter **4**

Spotting the Intangibles

***P**hysical skills are observable and measurable. Emotional skills are observable but hard to measure. Intangibles, something coaches like to talk about, are difficult to measure and to observe. The very meaning of the word *intangible* is "indefinite," "unclear," or "incapable of being touched."

However elusive, intangibles are as much a part of sports performance as running, jumping, catching, hitting, or throwing. They are the qualities an athlete possesses that cannot be measured with numbers. While they can't be taught, coaches and parents can discuss them with athletes so that they are exposed to the idea. By being exposed to the concept of intangibles, young athletes can slowly develop these qualities on their own.

At the highest levels of competition, everyone is talented. There, intangibles can mean the difference between winning and losing. Intangibles offer a window of opportunity for athletic success to athletes who might not make it on sheer physical talent. Nevertheless, some great athletes possess physical skills, emotional skills, and the intangibles that make for the complete athletic package. The names Woods, Jordan, Jeter, Favre, and Gretzky come to mind.

DEFINING THE INTANGIBLES

Following is a discussion of 10 athletic intangibles. Athletes who possess them are rare and gifted. Their opponents get discouraged when they realize that they need something more than superior talent to win.

Gets Most Out of Ability

Bill Clark, the veteran Reds, Braves, and Padres scout, likes to tell the story of Bob Randall. Randall graduated from a small high school in Gold, Kansas. According to Clark, he couldn't run, didn't have a great arm, and was not much of a hitter, but he somehow got a baseball scholarship to Kansas State. Later, he was signed by the Dodgers, traded to the Twins, and played in the major leagues for five years.

Clark would introduce Randall at clinics and tryout camps as "living proof that you can play in the big leagues without any ability." Randall loved the introduction. What Randall had, says Clark, was intelligence, perseverance, emotional control, a driving will to win, and enough skill to do whatever was needed to help his team.

"He was better at moving a runner than anybody in the majors," claims Clark. "He could bunt to get a man to second, and he could hit behind a runner to get him from first to third. In the field, he was always in the right place, always made the right throw, and never did anything stupid that would cost his team a run. Randall was a perfect example of using the limited skills he had to reach the highest level of professional baseball."[1]

It is a mistake to evaluate an athlete solely on appearance, technique, size, or numbers. If you had predicted success for Arnold Palmer and Lee Trevino based on their golf swings, you would have been wrong. Mike Singletary, Sam Mills, and Zack Thomas were all thought to be too small to be linebackers in the NFL. Mike Hampton is too short and Pedro Martinez too frail to pitch in the majors. Spud Webb was too small to play any professional sport, much less basketball. But all of them got (or are getting) the most out of their physical abilities.

Has Positive Influence on Teammates

Team chemistry is as important as it is hard to define. Certain players have a special ability to contribute in a positive way toward that chemistry. Some players bring energy and enthusiasm, others a calming, almost statesman-like presence, and still others carry themselves in a way that other athletes want to emulate.

Tom Glavine, Greg Maddux, and John Smoltz, the pitching trio that made Atlanta the winningest team of the 1990s, have that reputation. When not pitching themselves, they sit on the bench and watch every pitch and every hitter. Glavine says that he picks Maddux's brain. They analyze what is happening. And their influence carries over to the rest of the pitching staff as well as to the rest of the team. Mike Remlinger, a Braves middle reliever, said about being traded to Atlanta, "This is the place I always wanted to play. Guys get better when they come here. There's no doubt. Just watching Glavine, Maddux, and Smoltz, and talking to them is reason enough."[2]

Has a Nose for the Ball

Basketball has a way of showcasing players who always find the action. They dive for loose balls, take the charge, fight through screens, and pick up "trash" points around the bucket. Whether they are supposed to be there or not, find the ball and you'll find the athlete who possesses this intangible. How else could Charles Barkley, at 6-4, have dominated the boards throughout his NBA career? He may have been the best rebounder for his size in the history of the league.

"On the soccer field and in other sports, it shows up in those players who always seem to be at the right place at right time," says Dr. Ron Quinn, associate professor of sports studies at Xavier University in Cincinnati. "These players release the ball at the right moment or they are able to run off the ball and think two or three passes ahead. They have an ability to read the game and to internalize the game. We can identify this intangible, but no one has figured out how to duplicate it."[3]

Having a "nose for the ball" is not restricted to professional or elite players. Every soccer team for kids 12 and under has one boy or girl who constantly touches the ball. Baseball and softball players, usually shortstops and centerfielders, do the same thing. If it doesn't find them, they find it, just as special hockey players seem to always find the puck.

Makes Big Plays

Regardless of the sophisticated offensive and defensive systems that coaches design, most games and matches are determined by athletes who make big plays. They are the ones who want the ball "when the game is on the line," the ones who consistently produce "in the clutch," to use two sports cliches. Some players hide from the pressure; these players thrive on it. They may show ordinary skills during practices and for long stretches during games, but when their teams need a hit, a stop, a basket, a goal, or a shot, they have an uncanny ability to deliver it.

Big play makers may or may not be the most talented athletes on their teams, but talent helps. Michael Jordan became an icon for making the last-second shot in important games. The Yankees' Derek Jeter is building a reputation for hitting in the clutch. Fans expect Peyton Manning to lead his team to wins during the last two minutes of close games. The athlete who can "make a play" when it counts has a bright future.

Makes Teammates Better

"A few players will give up a good shot to give a teammate a better shot," says Paul Hewitt, men's basketball coach at Georgia Tech. "They'll make a pass that leads to a pass that leads to a bucket, or they will block out so that someone else gets the rebound."[4]

Everybody seems to play at a higher level when this player is in the game. He or she is a setter, an assist-giver, a blocker, a rebounder, a defender, a role-player; in other words, an athlete who is willing to sacrifice individual honors for the good of the team. Offensively, things flow smoothly through or around this player. Defensively, teams with this kind of player are more cohesive and tighter when the player is in the game.

Red Auerbach, who guided the Boston Celtics through their dynasty years, talks about what happened when K.C. Jones was on the court. "I believe in stats to a certain extent," Auerbach told another coach, "and K.C.'s stats weren't that good. But I also knew that if I put K.C. in when we were behind, we caught up. If I put him in when we were even, we'd go ahead. And if I put him in when we were ahead, we would go ahead further."[5]

The athlete who makes teammates better is almost always unselfish. Mark Pavlik, the men's volleyball coach at Penn State, thinks that a strong belief in the team is the antithesis of selfishness. "Understanding that one player has certain responsibilities that impact greatly on the next player is the first step of developing team belief. This has to be reinforced with constant communication—and not just on the court, but off court and in the locker room as well. I believe once the belief in team has taken hold, then a standard of accountability is accepted and reinforced by every player."[6]

Anticipates

Bill Russell, the former Celtic and now hall of famer, said that he got most of his rebounds before the ball was shot. He was talking about anticipation based on experience and information. He knew his opponents' strengths, their weaknesses, their tendencies, and what they did and did not like to do. With all of that information, he could anticipate what was about to happen and position himself to get the rebound.

Defensive backs, perhaps more than any other group of athletes, make a living by anticipating. They read receivers' routes, they predict what their teammates will do in certain situations, and they watch the quarterback's eyes. Then they make a move toward the ball that can win or lose a game.

Great passers in football, basketball, volleyball, and hockey use anticipation to get the ball or the puck to an open teammate. They need vision, timing, coordination, and ball- or puck-handling skills, but most of all, they anticipate what is about to happen before anyone else does.

Anticipation is not limited to team sports. Some tennis players start moving in the direction of an opponent's shot before the ball is hit. They understand that, in certain positions, with certain shots, and against certain players, only a few things can happen. Because they know what those things are, they start preparing for them. Older players regain a step or two they might have lost because they are always getting a head start on the ball. It drives younger players crazy.

Even talented distance runners use anticipation. They seem to know when to hold back, when to make a move, and when their opponents are likely to do the same thing.

You are not likely to observe great anticipation skills in very young athletes. Too much of it is based on experience. But as good athletes reach their teen years, some of them begin to see the game within the game. Watch for them. Their ability to anticipate can compensate for lots of physical shortcomings.

Is Coachable

Some athletes just "get it" sooner than others. "It" is the information passed on by coaches, teammates, friends, and parents. Tell these athletes what to do or show them how to do it just once, and they will grasp the idea and use it. Watch their eyes. They are able to observe a move, visualize themselves making that move, and then execute the movement. Don't ask them to explain it; just be glad that you don't have to repeat things to get the point across.

Not all gifted athletes are coachable. Some of them have gotten to the top in spite of shortcomings that could have been avoided if they had been more

A coachable athlete has a tremendous advantage over one who can't or won't listen to instruction.

receptive to coaching. Here is an easy test to prove the point. Name an NBA or WNBA player who is a poor free-throw shooter or who can't drive to the basket with the left hand. Now name a major-league baseball player who can't bunt or who swings at pitches out of the strike zone. Finally, name a professional football player who is a poor tackler. These are all basic, coachable skills, yet these athletes were not coachable enough to "get it."

Perhaps it is a generalization, but a growing number of young athletes seem to be less than coachable. They want to do it their way or no way. Basketball coaches around the world complain about players who would rather "take it to the hole" than develop their shooting, passing, rebounding, or defending skills. Some of them interpret coaching as an invasion of their privacy or as a sign of disrespect. This is unfortunate because they could become superior athletes (instead of average ones) if they could accept the instruction that coaches give. When you see a coachable athlete at any age, you have found an intangible talent that is becoming scarce.

Adjusts to Situations

Athletes who can adapt to people, to circumstances, and to the physical demands of a sport have an advantage over others who have learned to participate without having to adapt. Some teenage athletes have never played for a coach who is not their parent. Or they have had the same coach throughout their careers. They don't know what it's like to perform under the discipline or strategy or practice requirements of anyone else. This is a major disadvantage.

Other young athletes play for a different coach or under a different style of coaching almost every year. With the occasional exception of getting conflicting technical information from two or more coaches, it doesn't seem to bother them. They adapt to the person doing the coaching and to the style of play promoted by that coach. They function just as well under the leadership of a disciplinarian as they do under a "player's coach." The same attitude applies to the way they relate to their teammates. Regardless of the talent level or personalities around them, they just go about their business and keep getting better.

Not only do these athletes adapt to people, they also adapt to playing styles. If they are asked to concentrate on defense, they can do it. If they are asked to produce runs or points or goals, they can oblige. They can play in widely different systems because they have the ability adjust their talents to those needed by a coach or a team.

Finally, adaptable athletes can play in varying types of conditions. While heat, cold, wind, rain, unfamiliar surfaces, hostile crowds, tough opponents, and a hundred other variables can throw lesser athletes off their games, these people continue to perform at very high levels. Instead of seeing playing conditions as obstacles, they can turn them into advantages. Instead of complaining, they play. They are warriors.

Rises to the Occasion

"At the youth level, the most talented athletes have a way of elevating the quality or intensity of their games," says Steve Brown, an experienced youth basketball coach in Tempe, Arizona. "They are almost fearless in their approach to competition. Our team played extremely well in a big tournament here in Phoenix. But we were clearly outclassed by a team from San Diego in the finals. Most of our players kind of withdrew from the battle. But our best players upped their intensity level. They still got beat, but they didn't back down.[7]

Dave Simeone, women's national team staff coach for the United States Soccer Federation, agrees with Brown and says one continues to see it even at the professional level. "We observe this quality during national and world soccer tournaments, but I can see it in almost every sport during playoffs. Some players are able to raise the level of their games to meet a new standard that has been presented to them. They have an ability to meet the growing demand of the game."[8]

Players who continually rise to the occasion clearly separate themselves from average athletes. Early in their careers they surprise parents, coaches, teammates, and fans by their attitudes and accomplishments. It becomes evident that they are capable of doing whatever is necessary to perform well. They rise to the occasion because it is there and because they can. Others don't want to or can't.

Has Killer Instinct

In less politically correct times, talented athletes were said to be able to "smell blood" or to have the "killer instinct." Call it something else, but superior athletes know how to finish the job. When they get somebody down, they drive even harder. Instead of blowing leads, they increase leads. They don't give their opponents a chance to get back in the game. They are not trying to embarrass their opponents but rather to finish the job they have been trained to do.

When Mariano Rivera or Trevor Hoffman come into a game in the ninth inning, they know how to close. They bring an attitude with their fastballs. When Kobe Bryant or Kevin Garnett or Vince Carter stick the jumper that protects a lead in the final minute, they are displaying the killer instinct. When Karrie Webb sinks a putt that separates her from the field late on a Sunday afternoon, she leaves no doubt about who is in charge. As with all of the other intangibles displayed by gifted athletes, the killer instinct can't be taught. It's simply there in some people, absent in others.

ASSESSING INTANGIBLES

Use the Intangibles Checklist with the athletes in your house or with the ones you are teaching or coaching. Older athletes can use it as a self-assessment inventory, but only if they are mature and experienced enough to understand the concepts. The checklist is an opportunity for discussion, not a scientific method of measurement. There is no passing or failing score, merely indications of areas that can be developed.

Intangible qualities are most likely to show up in the heat of competition. When an athlete anticipates what is about to happen, makes a big play, or finishes off an opponent, it is an exciting one-time event. When that same athlete does those things repeatedly, it is not an accident. This is someone who will likely attain a level of performance that is beyond the reach of others.

Intangibles Checklist

- Circle the number that applies to you (5 is high).
- Determine one action to address weakest areas.
- Discuss privately with friend, parent, coach, or group leader.

1. **Gets most out of ability**   1 2 3 4 5
   Action plan: _____

2. **Has positive influence on teammates**   1 2 3 4 5
   Action plan: _____

3. **Has a nose for the ball**   1 2 3 4 5
   Action plan: _____

4. **Makes big plays**   1 2 3 4 5
   Action plan: _____

5. **Makes teammates better**   1 2 3 4 5
   Action plan: _____

6. **Anticipates**   1 2 3 4 5
   Action plan: _____

7. **Is coachable**   1 2 3 4 5
   Action plan: _____

8. **Adjusts to situations**   1 2 3 4 5
   Action plan: _____

9. **Rises to the occasion**   1 2 3 4 5
   Action plan: _____

10. **Has killer instinct**   1 2 3 4 5
    Action plan: _____

Part II

Assessing and Developing Talent

Chapter 5

Parenting and Coaching Talented Athletes

Now that you have confirmed that you have a talented athlete on your hands, what do you do next? There is nothing in child-rearing manuals about raising kids who have sports talent. You may be asking yourself, Who is this child? How did she get this way? Should I treat him differently from the way I treat my other children? Who coaches gifted athletes? Luckily for you, other parents and coaches have gone through the experience. What they have learned may be helpful to you.

SPORTS PARTICIPATION STAGES

Dr. Jean Côté of the School of Physical and Health Education at Queen's University in Kingston, Ontario, Canada, set out to determine the influence of the family in the development of talented athletes. Along the way, he discovered that three stages of sports participation fit the athletes in his study.[1]

Côté investigated the families of three elite rowers and one elite tennis player, all from middle-class, intact families. His conclusions may not represent patterns for other groups, but his stages of development are consistent with those reported in other sports. The stages and the roles of the families within those stages described here are not presented as the right way or the only way, but merely as illustrations. The information may be helpful to others facing similar circumstances.

Sampling Years

For the athletes in Côté's study, the first stage of sports participation occurred roughly between the ages of 6 and 13, when the emphasis was on fun and excitement. The parents were responsible for getting their children involved and allowing them to sample a wide range of activities. All of the families in the study considered participation in more than one sport an important element. All children in the same family were offered the same opportunities to get involved in sports, and all of the parents recognized a "gift" in the child athlete that led to positive reinforcement of their child's efforts.

Specializing Years

During the second phase, the specializing years between 13 and 15, there was a focus on one or two sports. Fun and excitement remained the central elements of the experience. Sport-specific skill development and practice time emerged as important characteristics. Families maintained a balance between practice and play activities. All of the families considered school achievement more important than achievement in sport.

During this period, however, the parents began to take measures to facilitate the gifted athlete's training and competition schedule. They did not expect their child to work part-time during this period. In addition, they reduced the importance of other social demands and encouraged their child to concentrate just on schoolwork and sports. The families found the necessary financial resources by making sacrifices in their own social lives. At this time the parents developed a growing interest in ways to support their child. Older brothers and sisters acted as work ethic and role models for the athlete. The siblings cooperated to create an environment that made it possible for the elite athlete to develop his or her sports skills.

Investment Years

After the age of 15, the athlete and the family became committed to achieve elite status in one sport. The level of commitment was exhibited by a tremendous amount of practice time that paid dividends but also took a toll on family members.

The number of "play activities" of the athlete was either eliminated or greatly reduced. The parents showed an even greater interest in the child athlete's support. They helped their child deal with setbacks, such as injuries, scheduling, and schoolwork, that hindered training. It is notable

During the sampling years, children should be involved in sports to have fun and to get exposure to different sports.

that the parents demonstrated different behaviors toward each of their children. In some cases, siblings showed bitterness or jealously toward the athlete.

Perfection Years

Because all three of these stages occur before the age of 18, Côté identifies a fourth stage (age 18+). He calls it a "perfection" or "performance" stage that is marked by the maintenance and perfection of skills.

DECIDING WHEN TO SPECIALIZE

While the Canadian families in Côté's study represent a rather middle-of-the-road approach to the stages of development of gifted athletes, the developmental stages vary widely in both directions in the United States and other countries.

Although the trend in the United States appears to be for parents to encourage early specialization, sometimes before the age of 10, expert opinion is overwhelmingly in support of the "sampling years" demonstrated by the Canadian athletes. Randy Hill, a sport physiologist and research assistant for the United States Olympic Committee, reflects that position. "The worldwide common denominator for reaching elite status is multilateral development—putting young children in as many different sports as possible. But the U.S. is the worst country in the world in this respect. Parents and coaches force children to specialize too early. What they should be doing is working on things like agility, coordination, balance, and speed that will help them develop as athletes. We shouldn't ask them to specialize until after sexual maturity when their bodies normalize."[2]

Waiting to specialize appears to favor the development of carryover skills. A former college soccer player and now an NCAA Division I coach said that playing basketball and running cross country helped her develop the skills and discipline that she would not have had by playing only soccer at an early age. A well-regarded Indiana club swim coach requires participation in a second sport. An NCAA Division I volleyball coach says his best players all start in other sports.

PARENTAL INVOLVEMENT

The role that parents play in the development of their children's interest in sports ranges from too little to too much. Parental involvement and expectations are associated with success and enjoyment as well as with pressure and stress.

In 1987 J. C. Hellstedt described parents' behavior on a continuum from underinvolved to moderate to overinvolved. The moderate level of parental involvement, concluded Hellstedt, is usually the course that is in the best interest of their children.[3] In a later study, Hellstedt suggested that to avoid delays and obstacles in the development of athletes, families with young children should emphasize fun and skill rather than competitive stress.[4]

In 1985 B. S. Bloom edited a book titled *Developing Talent in Young People*, which became a landmark publication on the subject. Bloom and his colleagues reported that parents tend to be supportive during the early years of their children's participation in sports (and other performance endeavors), allowing them to decide whether or not to practice. During the middle years, both the parents and the athletes demonstrated a period of increased dedication. In the later years, the athletes became fully committed in time and effort to improving performance, while their parents' roles were more restricted, consisting primarily of financial support.[5]

Table 5.1   Characteristics of Talented Athletes, Coaches, and Parents

	Early years	Middle years	Later years
Athlete	Joyful	Larger perspective	Obsessed
	Playful	Committed/hooked	Responsible
	Excited	Identity linked to sport	Consumed
Coach	Kind	Strong leader	Successful
	Cheerful	Knowledgeable	Respected/feared
	Focused on process	Demanding	Emotionally bonded
Parents	Model work ethic	Make sacrifices	Limit roles
	Encouraging	Restrict own activities	Provide financial support
	Supportive	Child-centered	
	Positive		

Bloom also described the characteristics of athletes, their coaches, and their parents during the three stages.[6] Table 5.1 presents some of his descriptions as they apply to athletes.

Dr. Robert Malina, director of the Institute for the Study of Youth Sports, offers several recommendations for parents of elite athletes.

- Let your child participate in the decision-making process, including the freedom to withdraw from a select program.
- Select a coach who will challenge and improve the abilities of your child while keeping the sport fun.
- Be aware that there are social and emotional problems associated with progressing too rapidly in a sport.
- Monitor elite training programs to guard against potentially harmful training methods, conditioning demands, and nutritional practices.
- Do not become overinvolved in your child's athletic activities.
- Consider the consequences of the developmental process for the athlete and the rest of the family.[7]

DEVELOPING BOYS, DEVELOPING GIRLS

Dr. Carol Wood, an associate professor in the department of physical education at Salisbury State University in Maryland and a child development expert, shares some thoughts with parents regarding the athletic development of boys and girls. "At young ages, there is not a big difference in boys and girls in physical skills unless their experiences have been different. The more active the parents are in sports, the more likely the child will be, also. The girl who is interested in soccer at the age of six will naturally be just as skillful as a boy. That will change at puberty (9–12 for girls; 12–14 for boys), when boys will begin to develop more strength while girls' strength levels off."

Wood thinks there is a big difference in boys and girls when it comes to team play. "Probably because of cultural influences, a coach can chew out a boy and he'll probably shrug it off. But if the coach says the same thing to a girl, there is research to show that it is likely to have an impact on her self-esteem." Wood suggests that parents make sure that whoever coaches their children has some experience and training in how to communicate with each gender.[8]

ESTABLISHING A PLAN

There are two ways to approach the development of a talented athlete. One is for the athlete, family, and coach to let the development process unfold with little planning. If the person has knowledgeable parents or other family members, competent coaches, and exposure to challenging competition, this laissez-faire approach can work. Thousands of college and professional athletes have achieved greatness without a master plan. However, if all the pieces do not fall into place, a gifted athlete's talent may be overlooked, misused, or squandered.

Nick Saviano, director of technical development for USA Tennis Player Development, recommends a developmental plan—a blueprint for long-term success.[9] Although he had tennis players in mind, the plan is applicable to athletes in other sports, particularly individual sports. "A well-devised plan," says Saviano, "provides focus and clarity to the coach and athlete on exactly what needs to get done and how it is to be accomplished. The plan also serves as a tremendous source of motivation and inspiration to a player on a daily basis to work hard to achieve his or her goals."

Saviano says that the developmental plan (the term *master plan* might be easier to sell to the athlete) should be established when a young person starts to exhibit a strong interest in becoming the best athlete possible. But this is a tricky situation. Some eight-year-olds will tell everyone that they want to be professional athletes when they grow up. And some parents buy into that thinking along with their children. That is a huge mistake. Every sport psychologist and most elite coaches say that children should play sports because they are fun, exciting, promote fitness, and teach lifetime skills. This theme is repeated by the most successful coaches in the country throughout this book. The parents who push their kids into a master plan too early are setting the child up for failure by, in effect, creating "professional" child athletes.

However, between the ages of 13 and 15, the plan can become the cornerstone for implementing a systematic training program instead of a more or less random commitment to the sport. The basic plan can be put together in a relatively short period, but it should be updated periodically.

Team Leader

Each athlete should have a developmental team leader. This person is responsible for taking the lead role in ensuring that the player's developmental needs are being met on a daily basis. The leader can be a coach, parent, or friend. If he or she is not a coach, one should be found. This is essential in individual sports, but not as important in team sports where school or club coaches assume the responsibility.

The developmental team leader should monitor all coaching information that is passed on to the player in order to ensure continuity and to see that it fits into the systematic training objectives. Says Saviano, "History has clearly shown that virtually every top 10 player over the last 15 years has had one key person that closely monitored every aspect of his or her development. This role is significant and time-consuming."

Long-Term Vision

A long-term vision "is by far the most important aspect of a successful developmental plan," continues Saviano. "It is one of the best ways of cultivating and stimulating the motivation of a player. The coach should guide the player in helping to develop a vivid and comprehensive vision of the ultimate player he or she wants to become."

The vision should be that of the player, put together with the help of others. It should cover every aspect of the game, including goals, style of play, weapons, conduct, physical condition, nutrition, and so on. It should maximize the physical and mental skills of the athlete and should incorporate the player's personality into the equation. Everything else emanates from this long-term vision or mission statement, which will probably evolve over time.

Strategy

Once the mission or vision is in place, the coach and player can begin building a structure to support it. One of the first tasks is to discuss what strategy and patterns need to be mastered, as well as the weapons that need to be developed in order to make the athlete's vision a reality. These strategies should take advantage of strengths and minimize weaknesses. The coach should be able to anticipate where future strengths and weaknesses will appear.

Tactical Considerations

The ability to make sound tactical adjustments and good decisions within the context of overall strategy is an important part of successfully working toward the player's long-term vision. For the purposes of setting up a developmental plan, tactical discussions should come after talks about strategy. A golfer, for example, may have an overall strategy for every round or tournament but supplements that strategy with contingency plans for things that might happen during play. A tennis player may have to consider different tactics depending on playing conditions or court surfaces. Tactical decisions made in the absence of a clearly defined strategy can result in a lack of direction when competing.

Technical Development

Saviano thinks that discussions of technical development should come only after the issues of vision, strategy, and tactics have been established. Then the technical needs of the athlete become clear. At this point it is also easier to prioritize what should be worked on and when it should be addressed. Then the athlete will be more open to making changes and the sacrifices they require. A basketball player who can handle the ball but is a poor shooter can allot more individual practice time to work on shooting skills. A good defensive catcher in baseball may need to spend more time in the batting cage. The coach of a running back in football may determine that the player should devote more time to blocking technique.

Emotional/Psychological Development

Emotional and psychological development addresses the issues of how the athlete approaches competition, competes, and conducts himself or herself before, during, and after competition. One of the objectives is to develop good practice habits and self-discipline. Players who tend to lose concentration during a game, match, or race, need someone to work with them on refocusing skills. Athletes who let their tempers interfere with their performances can develop anger management skills.

Scheduling/Periodization

The coach, the athlete, and the parents or guardians should discuss an annual training and competition agenda. This includes the total number of events, the number of consecutive events, the volume and intensity of training, and the amount of rest time needed for maximal performance. Elite coaches in almost every sport worry about burnout. Rather than simply reacting if the situation develops, coaches and athletes can address burnout as part of a master plan and thereby establish ways to prevent it.

Physical Development

One of the most common observations of college coaches is that too many recruits do not understand the level of training intensity required to compete at that level. There are no perfect athletes. No matter how gifted they may be, they all have deficiencies. In Saviano's model, the developmental team relies on the coach to explain the importance of what the athlete has to do to get the most out of his or her physical skills. The coach then develops a program consistent with the master plan to address the athlete's weaknesses.

Goal Setting

After all of the preceding areas have been discussed and outlined, the coach, the family, and the athlete can establish short-term and long-term performance goals. Instead of referring to them as goals, educators would probably call them objectives. They are concise, precise, observable, and measurable statements of performance expectations. Examples of goals (objectives) might be a state, regional, or national ranking; being chosen for a select or elite team; or becoming good enough to play at the collegiate level. Again, goal setting or objective setting happens only when a master plan is in place. If you don't know where you're going, it doesn't make sense to plan how to get there.

COACHING TALENT

In chapter 14, William Sands, PhD, director of research and development for USA Gymnastics, makes a point worth repeating here because it applies to athletes and coaches in every sport: Talented athletes go through the three stages of development outlined by Côté, Bloom, and others, and athletes usually need a different coach at each stage.[10]

At the first level, the coach makes the sport fun and shows the child how to fall in love with the activity. Sands even calls it the "love level." The coach is not usually a sophisticated technical or tactical expert, but one who knows how to work with children and how to communicate whatever technical knowledge he or she does possess. These coaches are a vital component in developing exceptional talent and should be given all the respect and rewards that coaches at higher levels command. They have a degree of teaching and organizing skills that many college and professional coaches never approach.

At some point, most gifted athletes move on to another coach. The second-stage coach is a strict technician who teaches the nuts and bolts of the sport. Make no mistake. This is not a "love level" coach. This person is more like a drill sergeant or perhaps a dictator. This coach knows the sport, knows the price that has to be paid, and is very comfortable pushing the athlete harder than he or she has been pushed before. Under the second-stage coach the athlete puts more distance between himself or herself and average athletes through dedication, sharpened skills, performance, and expectations.

But there is still another coach in the lives of most talented athletes. The third-level coach takes the athlete to the pinnacle of success. This coach has the experience and vision to bring out the best at the highest level of competition. At the very highest level, Bloom says that there may be only eight to ten master coaches per sport in the country.

Top-level gymnastics coaches bring an artistic quality to athletes by allowing their personalities to show in their performances (Bela Karolyi is a good example). Tennis coaches, such as Nick Bollettieri, may travel with or train professional players. Tiger Woods' third-level coach is the swing coach Butch Harmon. Why does the greatest golfer in the world need a coach? "Every athlete needs another set of eyes," explains Tiger.

It's one thing to recognize that athletes have different coaching needs at different developmental levels, but quite another to know if and when to make the change. The first-level person may be a recreation or city league volunteer, schoolteacher, middle school coach, or volunteer parent. At the second level, there are elite, travel, club (including golf and tennis pros), or high school coaches. The third-level coach could be a college or professional sports coach or a highly respected full-time coach such as Bela Karolyi in gymnastics. This may seem very cut and dried, but sometimes the transition from one coaching level to another is complicated and stressful.

Typically, the first-level coach likes what he or she does, has no interest in coaching at another level, and is very comfortable in letting go of a great athlete. A few coaches can change roles, but most of them who try get stuck at the dictator level. And some of them have a difficult time acknowledging that it's time for an athlete to move on to someone else. After all, they are the ones who have spent countless hours developing the skills of gifted athletes, and they are reluctant to let someone else get the credit and the money that goes with sports stardom. Third-level coaches seldom have to recruit athletes, but it happens. They are well known and sought out by talented athletes whose families are willing to pay the price in time and money for their services.

In helping your athlete through the developmental process, don't rush into coaching changes. This is not an emergency. Sometimes an athlete has the physical skills to play up or to move up to another level of coaching, but is not emotionally mature enough to make the move. Athletes who repeatedly bounce from one coach to another in search of some secret success formula never find it.

Talk with others who have gone through similar experiences. Get second opinions. People who evaluate talent for a living can, at times, observe an athlete for five minutes and know if they are looking at talent. They can also miss late bloomers. Talk with coaches and teaching professionals about your child's development. Ask them about other athletes they have coached. Ask them what goes on during training sessions. Ask them if they travel to out-of-town competitions with outstanding athletes and if that is included in the price of instruction.

Coaches such as Bela Karolyi encourage their athletes to infuse personality into their performances.

    If you think your athlete is ready for the third level, ask a prospective coach if he or she has ever developed a long-range plan for an athlete. If they don't know what you're talking about or if your child is the first one, move on. Be wary of the one who tells you that your athlete is going to be a world-class performer and he is the one who can take her there. No one can or should guarantee that kind of success.

TAKING THINGS SLOWLY

Finally, it is important to understand that the process of developing talent is interesting, exciting, and fun, but it can also be long, difficult, costly, and unpredictable. The athletes in Bloom's study worked eight to ten years to reach world-class status. This is not pre-1990 Eastern Europe or present-day China, where athletes were or are selected at young ages and placed into regimented training tracks.

For all of the sophistication of modern day sports, identifying and developing talent in most countries is as much a random chain of events as it is a well-planned process. No book exists (with the possible exception of this one) that tells you what to do.

Gifted athletes may start showing signs of exceptional talent during the first few years of life, or they may not excel until later. Out of 120 athletes in Bloom's study, only a few were regarded as child prodigies. No world-class volleyball players were identified at the age of six, and no correlation exists between "wee-ball" success and getting a college baseball scholarship. You don't have to play in a football bowl game as a child to become an NFL star 20 years later.

If you suspect you might have a preschool athlete on your hands, look for early indicators such as coordination; balance; reaction time; attention span; and the ability to catch, throw, and kick. Almost every great swimmer was observed to have "a feel for the water" from the beginning. Enjoy the experience for however long it lasts. Don't get excited about speed, strength, and size if they are present, and don't worry about them if they are missing. Those things are pretty much out of your hands for right now.

Good athletes are good imitators. They can see another person perform a skill and come surprisingly close to mimicking the movement. Some of them, even at early ages, can take instruction and make changes in the way they are executing a skill.

When you see these markers, don't sign them up for anything just yet. Give them as many opportunities to develop their skills around the house and in the yard as possible. Make up games and activities that challenge some of the skills they are demonstrating and some they haven't yet discovered. Time spent playing catch or kicking a ball back and forth or doing simple tumbling tricks is far more beneficial than entering the world of organized sports too early. Sacrificing personal enjoyment for the sake of the team is not a concept held in favor by most four- and five-year-olds.

Until your child reaches the investment years (15+), don't start dreaming about college scholarships and professional contracts, if then. Gifted athletes can dominate their peers at one age level and drop back into the field at the next. Less talented athletes can catch up with true talent because they work harder. Kids who are big at 10 can be average in size at 12, 14, and 16. Growth spurts and growth slowdowns in the early teen years can make or break previously successful athletes. Superior athletes can demonstrate all of the signs of greatness before they become teenagers and then discover that there are other things in life, such as cars, friends, studies, and the opposite sex (not necessarily in that order).

If you have a potentially great athlete, allow the developmental process to take its own course for the first few years. During Côté's specializing and investment years, get involved enough to put together a developmental team that will allow your child to grow athletically, socially, and emotionally. The message to parents from those who have studied talent is: Support, but don't push, interfere, or make predictions that put unnecessary pressure on you or your child.

Chapter 6

Speeding Up the Process

Most parents allow their children to develop sports skills by taking advantage of programs that are available at each grade, size, ability, or age level. It is a sensible approach and a proven way to develop athletic talent.

But there is the temptation, especially if a child has outstanding talent, to look for ways to put him or her on a fast track to sports success. Some young athletes benefit by intensified training and competition, while others suffer. The idea of speeding up the process may not be appropriate for every athlete, but it is becoming more common. In some cases, it's absurd. You will read in the chapter on golf about parents who called a national organization to ask about lessons for an 18-month-old baby.

Earlier is not necessarily better in regard to organized sports participation. One veteran baseball scout was asked if Little League is too late to get a player started. He replied, "Little League might be too early."

WHEN TO START

There is no "right" time for every child to get involved in organized sports. Individuals are ready at different ages. Consider your child's physical and emotional readiness before signing up for instruction or play in any sport. Organized sports expose children to physical and emotional demands that they may or may not be ready to handle. Ask yourself these questions about your child:

- Will he or she be willing to attend regular practices?
- Is he or she mature enough to understand and play by the rules?
- Is he or she ready to conform to team goals rather than individual wishes?
- Is he or she willing to accept coaching and discipline from someone other than you?
- Can he or she keep up with schoolwork and participate in organized sports?

Parents should discuss, or at least consider, these questions before making commitments for their children. It is easy for the child to say yes to an activity that is new, exciting, and popular with friends. It is another matter for a child to follow through on those commitments when he or she is tired, is irritable, is not getting to play, doesn't like the coach, or is playing on a losing team.

Encourage your child to get involved in sports, but consider the impact on the whole family. Include everyone in the process of making decisions, but reserve the right to make the final decision yourself. That's why they call you the parent.

Most experts don't recommend organized sports before the ages of 8 to 10. In sports such as football, volleyball, golf, track and field, and wrestling, waiting another year or two is not likely to hurt an athlete's chances of success in high school or college. Also, these sports either carry a higher risk of injury or are simply too complex for younger children. Many football coaches think 13 is not too late to start playing. Peewee soccer or T-ball at ages six to eight is fun and safe, depending on how the participation is handled by the parents and coaches.

One of the consequences of early participation is early burnout. Given the fact that most children drop out of organized sports by the time they are 13, we might argue that every youth athlete has a career life expectancy of six to eight years. Start a child in highly competitive and physically demanding sports at 6 and the career is over at 12, perhaps 14. Start him or her at 10 and he or she may play all of the way through high school and perhaps beyond.

First exposure to sports does not have to be in the form of organized activity. There is something to be said for playing catch in the backyard or playing pickup games in the neighborhood where children have to make their own rules, develop their own skills, devise their own strategies, and resolve their own disputes.

If you say no to a plea to be on a team, offer an alternative activity. If not, you could end up with a child who retreats into the solitude of watching television, playing video games, or getting lost on the Internet. Try this: "You can play on a team (or take lessons) next year, but I promise that I'll play catch with you at least three times a week."

Unsupervised pickup games are valuable for developing skills, making up rules, and interacting with other kids.

MATCHING THE ATHLETE WITH THE SPORT

Kids want to play sports that are fun, sports in which they can be successful, and sports that their friends play. That's the way it should be. The elementary school, middle school, and early high school years are the times when they should be experimenting with many different sports, developing basic physical skills, and learning to compete and train in a variety of sports environments.

At some point, parents, coaches, and athletes have to face the reality that certain sports require certain physical attributes if the person is to get beyond the recreational level. A 5-7 high school player who can shoot but can't run, jump, or play defense is not going to be a college basketball player. A young man with the body of a tight end is not going to be a college gymnast.

The sooner a good match between physical skills and sport of choice is found, the greater the likelihood for success. Dr. Tony Grice of Lambuth College in Tennessee has developed a tool called the KidTest TIDESGRAM to help parents, coaches, and physical education teachers find the right sports match for elementary-age children. The process produces a talent identification evaluation score.[1]

For the KidTest TIDESGRAM, norms were established for K–5 students based on various tests. These test results are combined to measure aerobic power, motor skills, and coordination. On the basis of test results, Grice then assigns composite scores for the three variables on a scale of 1 to 5 and displays the results on a Talent Identification Evaluation Score graph. A typical score might read 4-4-5, the first two numbers referring to high scores in aerobic power and motor skills and the third, the highest score possible in coordination.

Grice goes a step further with the KidTest TIDESGRAM and offers a sheet that lists 20 sports in one column and the aerobic power, motor skills, and coordination values (again, on a five-point scale) that have been subjectively determined to be required by each sport. For example, golf requires 1 on aerobic power, 3 on motor skills, and 4 on coordination. The closer a child's numbers are to matching the values required by that sport, the greater potential talent a child exhibits for success. Table 6.1 shows examples of five sports listed in Grice's KidTest Talent Identification Evaluation and their values (on a five-point scale) in terms of aerobic power, motor skills, and coordination requirements.

Says Grice, "On the TIDESGRAM, the suggested sports in which your child would seem to have the most potential for success are highlighted and recommended in order of first, second, and third choice."

Grice's talent evaluation tool has the potential for helping parents and children make data-based decisions in selecting sports. For more informa-

Table 6.1   KidTest Talent Identification Evaluation

Sport	Aerobic	Motor	Coordination
Baseball	2	4	5
Basketball	5	4	4
Football	2	4	4
Golf	1	3	4
Tennis	3	2	5

tion about KidTest TIDESGRAM, contact Dr. Grice at Lambuth University in Jackson, Tennessee.

SPECIALIZING VERSUS PLAYING TWO OR MORE SPORTS

Of all the decisions that parents and coaches have to make about their children's participation in sports, the decision regarding specializing in one sport versus playing multiple sports through the high school years is the easiest. Although little research exists on the subject, the overwhelming expert opinion from coaches, scouts, and others who evaluate talent is that playing more than one sport is an advantage that pays off in the primary sport. Listen to what these highly successful coaches and scouts have to say on the subject:

> "Playing two or three sports in high school is an advantage. Those athletes experience a variety of competition that one-sport players do not get."
>
> —*Tom Osborne, former head football coach, University of Nebraska*[2]

> "We love for our players to have played more than one sport in high school."
>
> —*Stella Sampras, women's tennis coach, UCLA*[3]

> "I absolutely think that young athletes ought to play more than one sport. Parents are making them specialize way too early."
>
> —*Bill Clark, international scouting coordinator, San Diego Padres*[4]

> "The player who has only participated in volleyball has seldom had enough athletic experience to be good."
>
> —*Mark Pavlik, men's volleyball coach, Penn State University*[5]

> "I played three sports in high school and it was great to put the ball in the closet every once in a while and get away from soccer. I think playing another sport keeps the passion alive for your primary sport."
>
> —*April Kater, head women's soccer coach, Syracuse University*[6]

The sentiment on this subject is clear. Not only does participation in more than one sport help develop a variety of athletic skills, but it also puts young athletes in pressure situations that can transfer to other sports.

At some point, talented athletes have to decide on the sport that is likely to earn them college scholarships or a professional contract. That decision is usually made during the last two years of high school, although stories abound of children who decided very early in life that they were going to be a star in a particular sport. Even when they decide on a sport to specialize in, gifted athletes continue to play a second sport at a lower competitive level during the off-season or to get a break from year-round training in the primary sport.

One other thought on this subject: Encourage your children to play one team sport and one individual sport. Those who grow up having played only on a team have no idea how to compete without the support (or protection) of teammates. It's easy to hide in the crowd of a team. On the other hand, athletes who are restricted to individual sports don't have a clue about what team-before-self means. Give them the opportunity to learn from both forms of competition.

CHOOSING A COACH

It happens two or three times a week. You load your children into the SUV, drive them to practice, and turn them over to a person you may not even know. This volunteer coach will exert a lifelong influence, positive or negative, on your children's attitudes toward sports.

Who are these people? What kind of training have they had? What do they know about sports? What do they know about children? What if they are screamers, weirdos, or worse?

If it will make you feel any better, most of them are you. Sixty to eighty percent of all youth sports coaches are parents who are coaching one or more of their own children. They are giving up a large chunk of their free time because, qualified or not, they enjoy coaching—or because no one else would do it.

So how do you tell the difference between the ones who are helping to mold lives and the jerks who are messing up our kids? While observation and common sense can help you make those judgments, there are professionals out there who know what to look for.

One of them is Keith Zembower, a youth sports consultant in Dallas, who has taught, coached, and administered programs from T-ball to the college level for more than 20 years. Here are his four Cs of coaching.[7]

Communication

"A coach should call a conference with parents before the season begins to discuss what is expected from them and their children," advises Zembower. "The content of the conference can change with the situation, but coaches should at least talk about how long practices will last, what will happen during practices, behavior on the field and in the stands, and the role of the coach versus the role of parents.

"Some coaches don't have any idea about when to tell parents to pick up their children. Good coaches limit practice sessions to one and a half hours—two at the most—and stick with the schedule. No one has to wait more than a few minutes or return home to check on dinner while practice continues."

A coach has to enjoy teaching and be good at the process of managing time and personalities. Don't expect volunteer coaches working with very young children to have a big-league knowledge of the game, but they should be able to organize practices that keep everybody busy.

Coaches should explain that they will not embarrass players on either team with their comments, and parents should follow that example. No riding the umpire. No coaching from the stands or from behind a fence. Getting instruction from several sources at the same time just confuses young athletes. Let the coach do the coaching or even the arguing with umpires. You do the parenting.

Consistency

Good coaches are consistent in the way they deal with players, parents, and problems. Bad coaches make so many rules that they can't help but bend or break some of them before the season is over.

Zembower says, "When coaches make rules or set policies, they should stick with them throughout the season. For example, coaches shouldn't tell parents and their children that playing time will be based strictly on performance, then play a favorite (like their own child) ahead of someone whose numbers are better. Neither can a coach simply focus on talented kids. It is important that all of the players on a team get individual attention."

Dr. J. Morrow, a Westchester, New York, sport psychologist and president of Sportsense, Inc., extends consistency to a coach's personality. "Look for emotional moderation, not a person who gets too high after a win or too low after a loss. Young athletes will copy what they see. If a coach is always on an emotional roller coaster, it will have a negative effect on their players' attitudes and performance."

Challenging

Good coaches challenge their players to practice hard and with a purpose. They don't use winning as the only measuring stick. They spend time teaching fundamentals, and they don't focus on the talented athletes at the expense of less gifted ones.

Drills should be directly related to game situations. What, for example, does swimming lap after lap after lap have to do with a sprint event? What does running half-speed sprints in the outfield have to do with playing baseball? Exercises should be consistent with the physical capabilities of growing athletes. Coaches should not have their peewee football players doing bridges (lying on the back, then putting the weight of the whole body on the neck, for example). Neither should they have your children doing high-intensity weightlifting before puberty.

Compassion

Good coaches recognize that children react differently to different coaching styles. The "Vince Lombardi-one-size-fits-all" coaching method has passed. Some athletes need more praise than others do. Some can take constructive criticism so that others won't wilt when it's their turn to get it.

Compassionate coaches don't say anything about players' strengths or weaknesses to parents that they don't want to be repeated. They speak directly with a player's parents if there is a problem. They meet with players after games, and they help their players take something positive away from the experience, win or lose.

CHANGING COACHES

What if you are not satisfied with a coach? If for one reason or another you feel a coach is not meeting your child's needs, either physically or emotionally, you have three acceptable options. The first is to speak with the coach privately to resolve the problem. An expression of concern or an explanation of why something is happening may be all that is needed.

The second choice is to pull your child out of the program. Think carefully before choosing this option; it should only be used in extreme situations. Otherwise, you may be teaching a lesson about quitting that is not good for your child.

Finally, let your child finish the season or instructional program, bumps and all, then look for a better coach the next time around.

PRACTICE: HOW OFTEN, HOW LONG

A total of three games or practice sessions per week is enough for preadolescent athletes, although there may be occasions when extra games or practices are appropriate. Playing for travel, select, or elite teams frequently involves daily practices, as does playing on a high school team.

Remember that the talented athlete is driven and will find time to "touch the ball" every day in the absence of organized workouts or games. Don't discourage that behavior. There is something "old school" and reassuring about your 12-year-old shooting hoops alone in the driveway at 9:00 in the evening. As long as it doesn't interfere with academic work, family routine, or the neighbor's sleep, let it go.

Practice sessions at any level that last longer than two hours are hard to justify. Sixty to ninety minutes is about right. When practices last longer than that, children and adults begin to lose concentration and energy.

RESISTANCE TRAINING

Properly designed and supervised youth strength training programs not only increase muscular strength in children and adolescents, but also can enhance skills such as sprinting and jumping as well as overall sports performance. Resistance training may also decrease the incidence of some sports injuries by strengthening muscles, tendons, ligaments, and bones.[8]

When children are old enough to participate in sports programs, they are old enough to begin resistance training. But don't confuse resistance training with competitive bodybuilding, weightlifting, and powerlifting. "Adults and children have to understand that the goal of resistance training is not necessarily to look like some of the wrestlers or professional football players," says Dr. William Kraemer, co-author of *Strength Training for Young Athletes*. "The idea is to develop a total individual fitness program."

Kraemer also warns that resistance programs for children and those for adults are not the same. "Don't start a program for kids that is designed for adults," he says. "There has to be a progressive approach that changes over as a person gets older." He also says that a child must be able to follow directions, use the correct technique, and demonstrate the ability to stick to a program before engaging in one. Some children may be physically ready but may not have the emotional maturity to participate in resistance training.

Schedule a physical exam for your child before he or she begins a resistance training program. Don't let a child try to do too much too soon. Stress the need for adherence and consistency in training. Also, try to avoid comparisons to other children. In table 6.2, Kraemer and co-author Steven Fleck offer guidelines for structuring strength training programs according to age.

CAMPS, CLINICS, LESSONS

If you are the parent or coach of a talented athlete, get ready to be overwhelmed by the choices of camps, clinics, and private and group lessons. They represent a growth industry and range in quality from excellent to terrible at prices from reasonable to exorbitant.

Camps

There are three basic kinds of camps—day camps, live-in camps that run from one to two weeks, and resident camps where athletes go for extended periods (months or even years). In most cases, camps are neither good nor

Table 6.2　Basic Guidelines for Resistance Exercise Progression in Children

Age	Consideration
7 and under	Basic exercises with little or no weight Low volume Progress from calisthenics to partner Exercises to light resistance
8–10	Gradually increase variety of exercises, load, and volume Monitor toleration of exercise stress
11–13	Introduce all basic techniques Continue progressive loading Emphasize technique Introduce more advanced exercises with little or no resistance
14–15	Progress to more advanced exercises Add sport-specific components Emphasize technique Increase volume
16 and older	Move to entry-level adult programs if a basic level of training experience has been gained

Adapted, by permission, from W. Kraemer & S. Fleck, 1993, *Strength Training for Young Athletes* (Champaign, IL: Human Kinetics), 5.

bad. The issue is whether they meet the needs of your children and whether they live up to your expectations.

Day camps are arranged so that participants show up in the morning, practice or play until sometime in the afternoon, and go home at the end of the day. Generally, athletes are given a noon meal. Most are set up to run in cycles of one or two weeks.

Day camps are particularly attractive to children in the 12 and under group, but they are also popular for high school students in sports such as baseball, golf, tennis, basketball, and football. The advantages of day camps are (1) relatively low cost; (2) a safe environment; (3) enjoyment; and (4) the opportunity to meet, play, and interact with peers. All are worthwhile selling points.

The disadvantage of day camps is that they offer mostly group instruction; individual attention is rare. If there are too many kids per instructor, not much learning will take place. It is difficult to say what an acceptable ratio is because it varies with each sport. A ratio of six or fewer to one in individual sports such as golf and tennis is good. Anything higher than ten to one in team sports is unacceptable. Ask about the student-teacher ratio before enrolling your child in a day camp, then do the math and make a decision.

If you want your child to have a good time and work on a sport under supervised conditions, day camps are a good idea. If you are expecting dramatic improvement in technique or performance, you will be disappointed.

One- or two-week camps in which athletes live in dormitories or cabins operate primarily during the summer months. They offer the same advantages and disadvantages as day camps, with the added attractions of getting away from home and having a total camp experience. The good ones offer special entertainment, field trips, and enrichment programs in addition to long hours of sports instruction.

The most controversial camps are those in which elite athletes (or those who want to be elite) live in order to participate in a sport for extended periods. Arrangements are made for athletes to attend nearby schools. These camps are most common in sports such as tennis.

The advantages to resident camps are total immersion in the sport. Hours of practice and play are part of the daily schedule. Those who attend are very focused on playing at the highest level possible. Many earn college scholarships, and a few get professional contracts. The great ones get lots of individual instruction, but those not as talented spend as much time in group drills as in personal instruction. Resident camps are great for offering opportunities to compete against top-level players on a daily basis.

The disadvantage of resident camps is that a child or adolescent is removed from his or her home environment and placed in an intense, sport-centered setting. It is not the real world. The chances to participate in the normal activities associated with each stage of child development are limited. At a time that is difficult enough when living at home, being separated from that support system is of questionable value.

Clinics

Clinics are conducted much like day camps, but for shorter periods. A typical junior development clinic lasts one to three hours and includes conditioning, drills, and competition. Look for one that has a reputation for teaching fundamentals. Too many of them consist primarily of games, which are easier to administer and neglect the fundamental skills needed at young ages.

Clinics are less expensive than day camps because they don't last as long, and they are commonly available on a year-round basis. You can sign up for a one-time-only clinic or a series of clinics that run two or three times a week for several weeks. Clinics offer good opportunities for young athletes to train during off-seasons or when they don't participate on a school team. The cost is reasonable and the quality of instruction again depends on the student-teacher ratio as well as on the qualifications of the instructors.

Ask about videotaping services as part of the camp or clinic package. They are invaluable tools for instruction in any sport, and they can be used at a later date to compare fundamental skills at different stages of a player's career.

Private Lessons

Private, one-on-one lessons have traditionally been associated with sports such as tennis, golf, and figure skating. More recently, though, the private lesson format has extended to baseball, softball, track, and other sports.

The great advantage of private lessons is individual attention that results in immediate reinforcement of good technique and performance, as well as instant diagnosis and correction of technical problems.

During the developmental stages of a young athlete's career, private lessons should be considered only as one part of the overall training program. This is especially true in tennis, golf, and baseball/softball, where bad habits developed at young ages can haunt an athlete for the rest of his or her life. In some cases, private lessons may be necessary to prevent bad habits from becoming ingrained.

While private lessons can be beneficial, remember that many great athletes never took a private lesson. Consider the great baseball players who came out of small towns and the great basketball players who developed their games on inner city playgrounds. Private lessons have several disadvantages worth considering.

First, the cost factor eliminates private instruction for a large segment of society. Private tennis and golf lessons can cost $40 an hour and up.

Second, restricting all formal instruction to private contact between an adult and a child restricts the amount of time that could be productively spent learning to interact and enjoy the company of peers. The bonds established among friends during long hours of practice are strong and long lasting. Moreover, young athletes benefit from the discipline and sacrifice inherent in group instruction.

Finally, at times the team sport player is getting private instruction that is not consistent with what is being taught by a middle school or high school coach. When this happens, the athlete or the parent should ask questions regarding the two sets of instructions. In the case of an impasse, the instructions of the team coach, not the parent or the private teaching professional, should take priority since he or she has the greater interest of the entire team in mind.

PERFORMANCE ENHANCERS

The most controversial and potentially dangerous method of speeding up the process of sports development is the use of dietary supplements. There are enough advertisements, studies, stories, and misinformation out there to confuse even the most conscientious athlete, parent, or coach.

Creatine

Of the hundreds of supplements available in health stores, by direct mail, or on the Internet, creatine is the most widely used. Some coaches even advocate its use among their players.[9]

"Creatine is everywhere," says Houston Astros strength and conditioning coach Gene Coleman, EdD, who is also chairman of the Department of Fitness and Human Performance at the University of Houston, Clear Lake. "It would be hard to find a middle school, high school, or college athlete who hasn't seen it, heard about it, or taken it."

Creatine is a natural substance that the body produces through a combination of three amino acids. Almost all of it accumulates in muscle tissue and becomes a source of energy. This energy boost allows some athletes to exercise longer and achieve better results because of the extended training capacity. All of us produce certain amounts of creatine. Those of us with naturally high levels are not likely to benefit from creatine supplements. Those with lower natural amounts, however, can make up the difference with creatine supplements.

"We do know that creatine supplementation has been shown to enhance performance that is short, intense, and intermittent," says Jeff Volek, an assistant professor at Ball State University in Muncie, Indiana, who did much of the early research on creatine while at Penn State. "There is no evidence that it is helpful in aerobic training."[10]

Typically, an athlete goes through a loading period in which he or she takes 15 to 20 grams per day for five days. Maintenance levels after the first week are 2 to 5 grams per day, but there is a lack of evidence regarding the amounts of creatine loading and maintenance in relation to body weight.

There are anecdotal reports of weight gain, cramping, and dehydration among those who use creatine, but again, little scientific evidence supports those claims. Most of those who use it report that there are no short-term negative side effects. The weight gain possibility makes creatine a less attractive choice among athletes who are concerned about adding weight or having a bulkier appearance.

The most disturbing unknown about creatine is its long-term effects. Researchers have yet to conduct studies to determine what happens to the athlete who takes the supplement for months or years. Concludes the Astros' Coleman, "Teenagers should get bigger and stronger because they eat and train properly, not because of some gimmick substance like creatine."[11]

Protein Supplements

To say that protein powders and drinks are popular with young athletes is an understatement. A perception among growing athletes is that consuming extra amounts of protein results in bigger and stronger muscles. There is just enough truth in that belief to misguide athletes, parents, and coaches and to fuel the protein supplement market.

"The growing athlete needs more protein relative to body weight than does the adult athlete to support growth requirements," according to Ellen Coleman, RD, MA, MPH, author of *The Ultimate Sports Nutrition Handbook*. "A diet supplying 15 percent of the calories as protein, or 1.2–1.7 grams per kilogram of body weight daily, should meet the needs of most children and adolescents in sports." A diet containing 12 to 15 percent of calories from protein is adequate for adults, so the 15 percent figure mentioned by Coleman represents the top of that range.

Coleman points out that these guidelines assume that the athlete is taking in a sufficient amount of calories. Total calorie intake is more important than increased protein when the goal is to increase the size of muscles. "Many athletes mistakenly emphasize protein over calories when trying to bulk up. Athletes who have difficulty gaining weight generally aren't eating enough calories," advises Coleman.[12]

If creatine and protein powders were the only controversial supplements being sold to young athletes, the problem would probably be manageable. Unfortunately, there are too many other products out there to monitor or describe here. Table 6.3 presents a summary of the alleged benefits and risks of creatine, protein mixes, and other supplements.

The process of developing an athlete can be accelerated. The question is, should you do it? The line between speeding up the process and pushing an athlete too early or too hard is not clear. Before you make a move in that direction, consider the physical, social, emotional, and academic impact on the athlete and the athlete's family. If everyone benefits, do it. If not, back off.

Table 6.3 Supplements: Alleged Benefits vs. Possible Side Effects[13]

Product	Alleged benefit	Possible side effects
Androstenedione	Testosterone production Adds muscle mass Increases power Increases strength	Aggressiveness Masculinization Mood swings Acne
Creatine	Increases strength Increases power Extends time to fatigue	Dehydration Cramps Weight gain
Ephedra (ma huang)	Expends body fat Increases energy Accelerates metabolic rate	Increased heart rate Elevated blood pressure Insomnia Irritability Chest pain
GHB	Induces deep sleep Induces euphoria	Coma Death Breathing problems Vomiting Seizures
Ginseng	Increases energy Increases resistance to stress Helps resist disease Improves oxygen delivery	Insomnia Skin eruptions Diarrhea
Protein powder	Builds muscles	Fatigue Excess protein stored as fat Energy loss

Chapter 7

Overcoming Obstacles

*D*ealing with potential obstacles is not about deciding whether to participate in a sport. There is a point well into the development of every talented athlete when the child or teenager, the parents, and the coach have to make some difficult decisions. Those decisions all revolve around the increasing commitment of time, energy, and money that enable an outstanding athlete to move to a higher level of training and competition. Although the problems facing parents and coaches of exceptional athletes are nice to have, they are problems, nevertheless.

Following is the story of Amanda, a tennis player. It offers insights into the problem with being gifted. Later in the chapter you will find a more detailed discussion of the factors that have to be considered in the development of talented athletes.

Amanda's Story

At 13, Amanda was a gifted athlete who had never taken a tennis lesson. An hour into her first lesson, she had made dramatic changes in the way she held and swung a racket. Every suggestion was understood, accepted, and put into play. Gifted athletes can do that sort of thing. Average athletes can't.

Within a year, Amanda was the best junior player in her area of the state. By the time she was 15, she was number one in Girls 16 at the state

(continued)

Amanda's Story *(continued)*

level, ranked in the top five in the open division, and ranked high in her nine-state section. Amanda was clearly an exceptional athlete and a tennis player with the potential to compete at the professional level.

Amanda's teaching professional met with Amanda and her parents to present two options—two courses of action that would lead in very different directions. First, he outlined Amanda's strengths and weaknesses and projected what it would take in lessons, time, money, competition, travel, and family impact to fulfill her potential. He explained that even with this kind of commitment, there were no guarantees of success at the professional level. On the other hand, there was a chance that Amanda could reach the highest (national and international) levels of the game and enjoy all of the benefits that go with it.

Then the pro presented the second option. It included playing high school tennis and area USTA events, living a normal family and social life, participating in a variety of high school activities, and probably earning an athletic scholarship to a Division I school. The pro asked the family to think about the options and to let him know their decision.

Although Amanda participated in the decision, her parents had the final word. They decided on option two. Amanda competed for her high school, maintained a high state ranking, and earned a scholarship that paid her way through college. Today she is happy, well adjusted, and married with three children, and is one of the best, though unknown, league tennis players in Texas.

Following are some of the obstacles that parents and coaches of outstanding athletes must face. Remember that every athlete's situation is unique, depending on the sport, the person, the family, and local circumstances. Keep in mind that in every case, the discussion is about athletes who may have the potential to go beyond interscholastic competition.

SOCIAL ISOLATION

Serious athletes have a way of becoming immersed in their sports. Because of the huge amount of time they spend developing their skills, they can become relatively isolated from those who would have been friends or acquaintances. Basketball players tend to hang out with basketball players, soccer players with soccer players, and so forth. Because of this sport-inflicted isolation, gifted athletes may miss out on an important phase of social development.

The athlete who wants to have a normal circle of friends (as opposed to other athletes, exclusively) has to work at it. If your child or the player you coach is already somewhat of a loner, that characteristic is likely to be reinforced, especially in individual sports such as golf, tennis, or skating. Athletes need some friends who are not athletes. It gives them perspective and an appreciation of the talents of others.

REPETITIVENESS

No matter how gifted the athlete, a certain amount of repetitiveness is required to refine skills in every sport. While that kind repetition in sport-related drills is understood by athletes, the concept of repetitiveness extends beyond what happens in practice.

At advanced levels, there is a repetition of daily life, of going to the gym, court, pool, field, or rink, of eating certain foods at certain times, and of the entire training/competition cycle. Sooner or later, every athlete gets tired of the routine and questions whether what he or she is doing is enjoyable. Sports are not always fun and, for some, can become a grind.

The problem of repetitiveness can be solved. Periodized (heavy, moderate, and light) training cycles, cross-training (participating in other sports), and relative rest (continuing to train at a less intense level) are three of them. Every coach interviewed for this book advised parents and coaches to make sports fun. But athletes, coaches, and parents should be aware that aspiring to higher levels demands a lifestyle that at times can be more like going to work than going out to play.

MISSED EXPERIENCES

One of the great attractions of sports is that they give young people an opportunity to travel, meet people, have experiences, and compete in places they would not normally get to visit. Every parent knows the excitement a school-age child can display in the face of something as ordinary as a field trip. Missing school is a big deal, and missing school to play a sport in some other city is even more fun.

However, the outstanding athlete who gets caught up in playing for an elite, select, or travel team in any sport misses some things that are a normal part of growing up. This was a concern of Amanda's parents in the story at the beginning of the chapter. The statement, "I can't go to the prom because I'm playing a tournament out of town," has been repeated in one form or another hundreds of thousands of times. "I'll do my homework later because I have to go to practice right now," is another. "I can't go to the family reunion because we have a game this weekend," reflects a sad but true schedule conflict for many athletes. "I never seem to have any time for myself," is a discovery athletes frequently make after investing too much to turn back.

As with other potential problems faced by the athlete, the key to sports, academic, and social success is to maintain as much of a balance as possible. Athletes should make it a point to participate in as many nonsports activities as their schedules allow. But even the most conscientious athletes and parents can expect to make sacrifices at some point.

IDENTITY FORECLOSURE

Enjoying the recognition for participating in sports is perfectly normal. In fact, some psychologists see the need for recognition as basic to all humans. Athletes, like artists, actors, entertainers, and musicians, perform their skills in front of other people. The attention they get from those people (and parents are frequently at the top of the list) is important and rewarding.

So what's the minus here? People whose identities are entirely tied to sports performance are often judged by themselves and by others according to how they do in the sport. In addition, a parent's identity can also be tied to a son or daughter's performance (such as the mother who wears a T-shirt that says "Chad's Mom"). If a good or bad performance in a sport affects the way a person feels about himself or herself or how other people act toward the athlete, there is a problem. It is called "identity foreclosure."

"You want athletes to immerse themselves in practice and in competition," explains Dr. David Yukelson, a sport psychologist at Penn State University, "then to let go when they are done and develop other aspects of their person. If everything is always athletics, they are going to get burned out. In addition, they are not prepared for life. People around athletes keep reinforcing achievement-by-identity. In school, many athletes are allowed to slide by because of their ability in a sport. At home, parents may favor the sports star over other brothers or sisters. These young athletes have been done a disservice. You can see the results in maladapted behaviors of athletes in professional sports. They don't have anything else to fall back on."[1]

Regardless of athletic talent, it is essential for athletes to have interests, friends, and hobbies apart from the sport. If at some point athletes are unable to continue playing their sport, due to age, injury, loss of interest, work, or diminishing skills, they (and their parents) need to have developed an identity that is not dependent on athletic achievement.

FAMILY DISRUPTION

Because of the commitment that a child athlete displays and the attention that success brings, some families are tempted to make the athlete the center of family life. Listen to this quote taken from a study of the families of elite athletes: "We never miss an event—it doesn't matter what it is—we're there and that's all we can do. We can't do the training for her."[2]

Family support of an athlete is admirable, but it should not be done at the expense of other children in the family. If the focus is totally on the athletic achiever, the lack of attention and resources given to their siblings will be noticed, perhaps resented, and it could lead to behavior problems.

Here is more evidence of this problem from a conversation with the younger brother of an elite rower: "I just don't get into that conversation. It's almost gibberish to me. I just sort of sit there and eat. When they are talking about rowing, I'll talk about something else and then they'll get right back into rowing. That's all that's on their minds. They're almost mental about rowing. It's almost like they don't care what I do."

Again, the way to avoid this problem before it surfaces is for parents to spread attention, time, resources, and reinforcement equally to all siblings, even those who do not participate in sports. If that is not possible, then the parents have to weigh the risks of neglecting some children against the benefit of developing an exceptional athlete. The other solution is to have only one child, which, for most parents, would be an unreasonable decision just for the sake of sports.

ABUSE

At the same time that many teenagers resist the discipline imposed by their parents, they accept and even welcome it from coaches and teachers. This gives those coaches and teachers a tremendous opportunity to have an influence on young athletes, but it is an opportunity that can be abused.

Abuse can be physical, verbal, or emotional, and it is not restricted to coaches. Grabbing a player by the helmet, throat, or jersey is not necessary to get a point across. Screaming is not necessarily coaching. Parents who grant favors or withhold privileges based on athletic performance have made it onto the discipline/abuse continuum.

The line between strict discipline and abuse is a thin one. As a parent, it is your responsibility to monitor the behavior of a coach without interfering with his or her work. It does not mean showing up at every practice or criticizing a coach in the presence of others. But it does mean communicating with the coach and your children enough so that you have a feel for what is going on at practice and in games.

One important disclaimer is necessary in regard to discipline. Athletes interpret coaching methods in different and not necessarily accurate ways. For example, a coach may have to shout at a player across a field or court to make a point immediately. He or she doesn't have time to run 40 yards and make the explanation after two or three more plays have been made. Most athletes understand the reason for the loudness, intensity, and immediacy in such a situation. But some players will go home and tell their parents, "My coach is always screaming at me." Wrong interpretation. In that case, it was coaching, not screaming.

BAD GRADES

That some gifted athletes are more interested in performing well than they are in making good grades is an understandable, but sad, story. Some lack a good academic foundation, and others come from families that don't support and demand academic excellence. A few simply aren't bright enough, don't work hard enough, or both.

But participating in sports, even at the elite level, and making good grades don't have to be mutually exclusive. Golfers, tennis players, and volleyball players have well-deserved reputations for being good student-athletes. During the 2000 season, all nine golfers on Georgia Tech's men's team had been on the dean's list the previous semester. The team was also ranked number one in the country for most of the season and finished second in the NCAA tournament.

Nevertheless, sports can interfere with grades if the parents, coaches, and athletes let it happen. Some athletes grow into being good students, but most of those who do well in school and in sports were given a solid academic foundation starting at the elementary level, along with high academic expectations. The no-pass, no-play laws that some states have adopted were instituted by families long before politicians got involved.

DIMINISHING RETURN ON INVESTMENT

"The parents who spend thousands of dollars on their children in hopes that they will earn a college scholarship are making a mistake," warns Georgia Tech head golf coach Bruce Heppler. "The money would be put to better use as a college education fund."[3] The Center for Educational Statistics backs Heppler's position. It says that about two percent of all children participating in organized sports at the eighth-grade level will eventually qualify for college scholarships. The odds are even less for female athletes.[4]

But achievement in sports can be expensive. Private lessons in golf and tennis, for example, can cost $40 to $60 per session. It's more than that for world-class teachers. Just suiting up a hockey player can run into the hundreds of dollars. Middle school basketball players are wearing shoes that range in cost from $150 to $200, although they are paying for style as much as for substance. The parents of several nationally ranked athletes in different sports conservatively estimated that it cost $10,000 to $15,000 a year to finance their child's program of equipment, lessons, travel, and fees. Athletes who enroll in residential sports academies pay far more.[5]

Other activities (track and field, volleyball, and football, for example) are not as costly. Before parents and coaches decide that the child they are working with is going to be a sports star, they should take a realistic look at the cost and then decide if they can afford it.

When funds are limited, difficult decisions that affect the entire family have to be made. When parents start taking second jobs to finance the cost of their child's participation in sports, a warning flag has been raised. Parents would be well served to reflect at this point on the costs to the entire family of such a commitment. If they decide the benefits outweigh the costs, fine, but experts agree that it is best for the child when parents do not to expect a financial return on money invested in sports activities.

LACK OF OPPORTUNITY

Like it or not, opportunities for athletic achievement are not equal for everyone. The child in Mississippi who decides she wants to be an Alpine skier needs some serious sports counseling. The golfer who lives in Minnesota has to understand that his seasons are going to be shorter than those of athletes who live in Sun Belt states.

The lack of opportunities for others may not be as obvious as the preceding, but it is real. Although the United States Tennis Association and the National Junior Golf Association have programs in place to encourage participation, minority involvement in those sports is traditionally low. Opportunities for girls and women have exploded during the past decade, but the teaching, coaching, training, and competing gaps between the genders still exist.

Access to facilities and coaching is an obstacle in many states and countries. People in the business of sports know that there are states, even countries, where certain sports are immensely popular and others are either nonexistent or offer very limited opportunities. Canada produces far more hockey players than baseball players. The Dominican Republic produces baseball players, period. Texas, Florida, Ohio, and Pennsylvania, among other states, are best known for developing football talent. California is a great state for all sports, but it has been recognized as a source of world-class tennis players for decades.

However distasteful the lack of opportunity may be, take it seriously before making a decision to specialize in a sport that doesn't provide a reasonable path to success. Your child can be a pioneer for equal opportunities, or he or she may choose instead to match interest and ability with sports in which opportunities for development exist. Both are worthy goals.

GENES

Genetic makeup can give an athlete an advantage and serve as an obstacle at the same time. Every person has a predetermined type and number of individual muscle fibers. These fibers can dictate whether a person will be more successful as a sprinter or a world-class distance runner.

Muscle fibers can be classified as Type I (slow-twitch) and Type II (fast-twitch). Long-distance runners, cross-country skiers, and other athletes usually have more motor units in the Type I category. Sprinters and other athletes who depend on quick, powerful movements are likely to have more than an average share of Type II motor units. Having a predominance of fast-twitch muscle fibers allows an athlete to run very fast but prevents that person from doing well in distance events. The more extreme the activity, the more limited an athlete may be in terms of athletic potential.

Most people fall somewhere between the 40 and 60 percent range of both slow- and fast-twitch muscle fibers. Many sports do not have extreme performance requirements that would be aided by a higher percentage of either type of fiber. Athletes can effectively train for activities that require slow- and fast-twitch fiber types. They can be successful and enjoy a sport, but they may not be able to make it to higher levels of competition.

You don't have to perform muscle biopsies to discover matches and mismatches between fiber makeup and the demands of certain sports. Both types of muscle fibers have to be trained for the demands that are specific to that sport. The message is: Don't try to make a distance runner out of a person whose body is made for sprinting, and don't expect those who have the gift of explosive speed to be successful in long-distance events.

BURNOUT AND INJURIES

Burnout is an increasingly frequent problem. In a society where "wee-ball" (baseball for three-year-olds) is an option, where 12- and 13-year-olds play 100 basketball games a year and 10-year-olds play 80 to 90 baseball games a year, burnout is not just a possibility, it's a probability. If, by the time a child is 12 years old, he or she has won, lost, had uniforms, banquets, trophies, trips, and even cheerleaders, he or she may wonder, why keep on doing it for another five or six years?

Steven Lyman, PhD, a researcher at the American Sports Medicine Institute in Birmingham, Alabama, says, "More than 50% of young pitchers suffer some kind of elbow injury or pain during their youth league play. And around the ages of 11 and 12, there are half a dozen different growth areas in the elbow that are susceptible to long-lasting damage from excessive pitching motions."[6]

The childhood years are for experimenting and developing all-around athletic ability. The early teens are for narrowing choices. And the mid to late teens are for specialization. When that pattern is not followed, the chances for burnout increase.

The consequence of too much, too soon is burnout. While this is a manageable problem, parents and coaches must have the will to limit practice and game time at the 6 to 12 age levels. They can accomplish this goal in one of four ways.

One is to avoid pushing kids into organized programs before they are physically and emotionally ready. When children begin organized sports too soon, they often drop out and never return to the sport. In many sports, eight is not too late for entering organized sports. In sports such as football and volleyball, waiting until middle school or the first year of high school is not too late.

The second way to prevent burnout is not to enroll a child in every program that is offered. Even children with outstanding athletic skills need down time. They don't have to attend every clinic, take every lesson, or play on every team. Be selective in arranging a schedule of training and competition so that the child has time for balancing sports with other life activities.

The third way to avoid burnout (and injuries) is to limit the intensity of training and play. More is not always better, and in fact it can take its toll on children's physical and mental health. Limiting the number of pitches in baseball and the number of games and practice sessions per week in sports such as football and basketball are examples.

A final strategy is to allow athletes to play other sports during the 8 to 18 years. College coaches say that playing sports other than one's primary sport is beneficial to athletes because it puts them in a variety of competitive situations. Playing a second or third sport, at times in less-than-intense circumstances, gives serious athletes a physical and emotional break from the demands of their primary sport.

Athletes, along with their families and coaches, have to find a strategy to avoid burnout that works in their particular circumstances. If they don't, they will become part of the 70 percent of youth athletes who drop out of sports by the time they are 13.

COACHING QUESTIONS

Coaching styles and access to coaching have been addressed in chapter 6, but two other factors are worth considering. An estimated 60 to 80 percent of volunteer youth coaches coach their own children. That situation presents some unique problems for both parents and their families.

Dr. Frank Smoll, professor of psychology at the University of Washington, thinks that the most serious problem is role confusion between being a parent and being a coach. "There has to be an understanding between the parent and the child that parenting behavior and coaching behavior will be different. For example, a coach will not be able to give the immediate access or personal attention that a parent would give a child at home. The coach has to make time for a group of players. A parent can concentrate on a couple of kids."

Smoll also suggests that the parent/coach first get the child's perspective on the situation. There may be a sense of undue pressure to perform, favoritism, or even reverse favoritism. He also emphasizes that a parent should reaffirm his or her love for the child regardless of athletic performance. Finally, Smoll thinks that it is not a good idea to coach your own children for more than two years in a row. "You shouldn't be the only coach your children ever have. They should learn to adjust to other styles of leadership."[7]

The second coaching decision is when to change coaches. In team sports there is not much of a choice, but athletes in individual sports who take private and group lessons can choose. The questions are why and when, and there are no absolute answers. The worst case scenario is bouncing from one coach to another, always looking for some magical piece of instruction or strategy that will vault an athlete to the legendary "next level." That is generally an unrealistic expectation.

There are good reasons to change coaches, however. In almost every sport, some coaches are good at teaching fundamental skills, others are adept at strategy, and those in a third group excel in motivation. Others are skilled at working with certain age groups. Great high school coaches don't necessarily make great college coaches, and great college coaches might not be effective at teaching young children.

There is no absolute guideline that signals when a coaching change is appropriate. The important thing is that the coach and the parent recognize how far they can take an athlete and when to let that athlete go.

PARENTAL ROLES

No parents consider themselves obstacles to the athletic success of their children. None. All of them think they have done or are doing exactly the right thing for the right reasons. Many of them believe they are willingly making great sacrifices to allow their children to go as far in sports as their talent will take them.

Most of these parents are right. Many are doing the right thing and making personal, financial, and social sacrifices for the sake of their children. That's what parents do.

But ask youth coaches if they have ever seen parents get in the way of athletic talent and they will start telling you stories. Some parents push too hard. Some hover too closely. Some verbally abuse their children, and others border on physical abuse. Some insist on being the coach. Some control every aspect of their children's lives. Some won't let go.

All of the evidence shows that most elite athletes have parents who are supportive but not interfering. They do the parenting and let the coaches do the coaching. In general, the more advanced the child athlete becomes, the more the parents should separate themselves from day-to-day involvement. They should provide the economic and emotional support that allows the child to develop, but should stay away from sport-specific technical advice.

Overcoming obstacles may, in itself, be an indication of talent. It is certainly a part of the process that tests an athlete's determination to succeed. The person who has always had it easy is not likely to be tough enough to withstand the pressure of high-level competition. The one who has had to struggle to reach the top is the one who appreciates it the most and who defends that position fiercely.

Chapter **8**

Testing for Talent

Before you declare that your children or the children you coach are superathletes, it might be interesting to learn how they compare to normal kids around the country on some basic physical tests. Young athletes don't have to perform well on independent tests of strength, speed, agility, and flexibility to play a specific sport well, but physical skills are an advantage now and an imperative later.

THE PRESIDENT'S CHALLENGE

The President's Council on Physical Fitness and Sports, through a program entitled the President's Challenge, has established a battery of tests and has provided norms for the purpose of comparison at various age levels. Before administering the tests, students should be taught the correct technique, including proper pacing and running style. There is no limit to the number of tries on the eight tests described in this chapter.

The following pages give the instructions for each test and sample percentile norms for boys and girls at ages 8, 10, 12, 14, and 16. If, for example, an eight-year-old girl performs 22 curl-ups in one minute, she ranks ahead of only 20 percent of all the eight-year-olds who have taken the test. If she completes 29 curl-ups, she is in the 50th percentile, meaning she has completed more curl-ups than half of those who have taken the test. A score of 40 curl-ups puts her in the top 10 percent of all those eight-year-olds who have taken the curl-up test. Percentiles are given for the 20th, 50th, 70th, and 90th levels.[1]

Schools and other organizations can qualify young athletes for fitness awards by participating in the President's Challenge. For more information, write to The President's Challenge at Poplars Research Center, 400 East 7th Street, Bloomington, IN 47405-3085.

Curl-Ups

Abdominal strength/endurance

1. Lie on back, knees flexed, feet 12 inches from hips; partner holds feet.
2. Cross arms placing hands on opposite shoulders, elbows close to chest.
3. On signal "Ready, Go," raise trunk up and forward so that elbows touch thighs.
4. Lower the back to the floor so that shoulder blades touch the floor.
5. Count number of curl-ups completed in one minute.

Girls 8 years	Percentile	Boys 8 years		Girls 14 years	Percentile	Boys 14 years
22	20%	23		30	20%	37
29	50%	31		37	50%	45
33	70%	36		42	70%	51
40	90%	42		49	90%	58
10 years		**10 years**		**16 years**		**16 years**
23	20%	28		27	20%	37
30	50%	35		35	50%	45
35	70%	40		40	70%	50
42	90%	48		49	90%	58
12 years		**12 years**				
27	20%	32				
35	50%	40				
40	70%	45				
47	90%	53				

Partial Curl-Ups

Option to curl-ups

1. Lie on back, knees flexed, feet 12 inches from hips, feet not held or anchored.
2. Extend arms forward with fingers resting on legs and pointing toward knees.
3. Partner cups hands under athlete's head.
4. Curl up slowly until fingertips touch knees, then down until head touches partner's hands.
5. Perform one curl-up every three seconds (in rhythm) as long as possible.

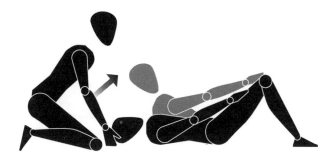

Girls 8 years	Percentile	Boys 8 years	Girls 14 years	Percentile	Boys 14 years
11	20%	11	21	20%	28
17	50%	17	30	50%	40
25	70%	25	40	70%	52
31	90%	31	51	90%	77
10 years		**10 years**	**16 years**		**16 years**
17	20%	14	19	20%	28
24	50%	24	26	50%	37
27	70%	29	32	70%	48
36	90%	38	50	90%	79
12 years		**12 years**			
21	20%	24			
30	50%	32			
40	70%	48			
56	90%	100			

Shuttle Run

Speed and agility

1. Mark two parallel lines 30 feet apart.

2. Place two blocks of wood (2 × 2 × 4 inches) behind one of the lines.

3. From starting position behind opposite line, start with command of, "Ready? Go!"

4. Run to pick up first block, return to starting line

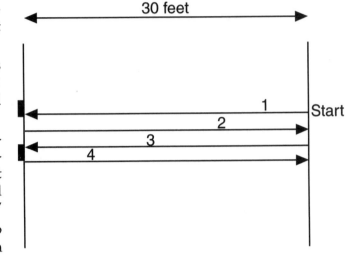

and place block behind line, run to pick up second block, and run back across finish line.

5. Record score to the nearest 10th of a second.

Girls 8 years	Percentile	Boys 8 years	Girls 14 years	Percentile	Boys 14 years
14.3	20%	13.6	12.1	20%	10.7
12.9	50%	12.2	11.2	50%	9.9
12.2	70%	11.5	10.6	70%	9.5
11.5	90%	10.9	9.9	90%	9.0
10 years		**10 years**	**16 years**		**16 years**
13.3	20%	12.7	11.9	20%	10.1
12.1	50%	11.5	10.9	50%	9.4
11.4	70%	10.8	10.5	70%	9.0
10.6	90%	10.0	10.0	90%	8.6
12 years		**12 years**			
12.3	20%	11.4			
11.3	50%	10.6			
10.8	70%	10.1			
10.2	90%	9.6			

Pull-Ups

Upper-body strength/endurance

1. Begin by hanging from bar, arms extended, feet clear of floor. (Athlete may be lifted to starting position.)
2. Use underhand or overhand grip. (Grips are shown in the illustrations.)
3. Raise body until chin clears bar, then lower body to starting position.
4. Complete and record as many pull-ups as possible.

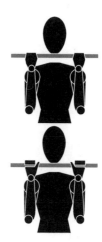

Girls 8 years	Percentile	Boys 8 years
0	20%	0
0	50%	1
1	70%	3
3	90%	6
10 years		**10 years**
0	20%	0
0	50%	2
1	70%	4
3	90%	7
12 years		**12 years**
0	20%	0
0	50%	2
1	70%	5
3	90%	8

Girls 14 years	Percentile	Boys 14 years
0	20%	1
0	50%	5
1	70%	7
3	90%	11
16 years		**16 years**
0	20%	4
0	50%	7
1	70%	9
2	90%	12

Right-Angle Push-Ups

Option to pull-ups

1. Lie face down in push-up position, hands under shoulders, fingers straight, legs straight and slightly apart, toes supporting feet.
2. Straighten arms, keeping back and knees straight.
3. Lower body until there is a 90 degree angle at elbows.
4. Partner holds hands at 90 degree point so that athlete's shoulders touch partner's hands.
5. Complete and record one push-up every three seconds (in rhythm) as long as possible.

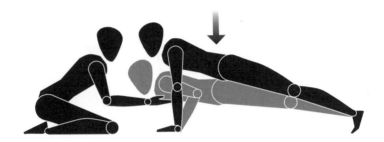

Girls 8 years	Percentile	Boys 8 years	Girls 14 years	Percentile	Boys 14 years
6	20%	6	5	20%	15
9	50%	9	10	50%	24
13	70%	13	12	70%	30
19	90%	19	21	90%	41
10 years		**10 years**	**16 years**		**16 years**
8	20%	10	5	20%	23
13	50%	14	12	50%	30
17	70%	18	19	70%	36
21	90%	25	26	90%	46
12 years		**12 years**			
3	20%	10			
10	50%	18			
15	70%	25			
21	90%	34			

V-Sit Reach

Lower back and hamstring flexibility

1. Draw a two-foot baseline on the floor.

2. Place a yardstick perpendicular to the baseline, between and parallel to the legs leaving 24 inches on each side of baseline.

3. Sit on floor, shoes off, soles of feet placed immediately behind baseline, heels 8 to 12 inches apart.

4. With one hand on top of the other, palms down, and legs held flat by partner, reach forward as far as possible four times, keeping fingers on baseline and feet flexed.

5. On the fourth reach, record, to the nearest half-inch, a plus or minus score.

Girls 8 years	Percentile	Boys 8 years		Girls 14 years	Percentile	Boys 14 years
0.0	20%	-2.0		2.0	20%	-2.0
2.0	50%	0.5		4.5	50%	1.0
3.5	70%	2.0		6.0	70%	3.0
5.0	90%	3.5		8.5	90%	5.0
10 years		**10 years**		**16 years**		**16 years**
0.5	20%	-2.0		2.5	20%	0.0
3.0	50%	1.0		5.5	50%	3.0
4.0	70%	2.0		7.0	70%	4.5
7.0	90%	5.0		9.5	90%	7.0
12 years		**12 years**				
1.0	20%	-2.0				
3.5	50%	1.0				
5.0	70%	2.0				
8.0	90%	5.0				

Standing Long Jump

Lower-body power

1. Mark a baseline on the floor, mat, or ground.
2. Start with both feet placed immediately behind the baseline.
3. You may begin in crouched position and use arms to gain momentum.
4. Jump forward as far as possible.
5. Mark and record the distance between the point where the heel(s) touch and the baseline.

Girls 8 years	Percentile	Boys 8 years	Girls 14 years	Percentile	Boys 14 years
3-5	20%	3-9	4-8	20%	5-7
4-0	50%	4-4	5-3	50%	6-4
4-3	70%	4-8	5-8	70%	6-10
4-8	90%	5-2	6-3	90%	7-6
10 years		**10 years**	**16 years**		**16 years**
3-11	20%	4-3	4-8	20%	6-3
4-6	50%	4-11	5-4	50%	7-1
4-10	70%	5-4	5-9	70%	7-6
5-5	90%	5-10	6-4	90%	8-0
12 years		**12 years**			
4-5	20%	4-10			
5-1	50%	5-5			
5-5	70%	5-10			
6-1	90%	6-4			

50-Yard Dash

1. Mark a distance of 50 yards on a track or open area.
2. Timer stands to the side of the finish line.
3. Runner starts with command, "Ready? Go!"
4. Timer starts stopwatch on "Go" command.
5. Record time to nearest 10th of a second when runner crosses finish line.

Girls 8 years	Percentile	Boys 8 years	Girls 14 years	Percentile	Boys 14 years
10.5	20%	10.1	8.7	20%	7.8
9.6	50%	9.1	8.0	50%	7.1
9.1	70%	8.6	7.5	70%	6.8
8.2	90%	8.0	7.0	90%	6.3
10 years		**10 years**	**16 years**		**16 years**
9.6	20%	9.2	8.8	20%	7.1
8.8	50%	8.4	8.0	50%	6.7
8.4	70%	8.1	7.6	70%	6.4
7.9	90%	7.5	7.1	90%	6.0
12 years		**12 years**			
9.0	20%	8.4			
8.2	50%	7.8			
7.8	70%	7.3			
7.3	90%	6.9			

Adapted, with permission, from The President's Challenge Youth Physical Fitness Program.

THE FUNCTIONAL MOVEMENT SCREEN

Gray Cook, a physical therapist and director of Rehabilitation Services of Danville, Virginia, and his colleagues have developed a series of movement tests that are being used to identify physical problems, prevent sports injuries, and predict potential for athletic success.

Cook has a database of hundreds of athletes who have participated in the Functional Movement Screen. It includes the following seven tests:

- Deep squat
- Hurdle step
- In-line lunge

- Shoulder mobility
- Active straight leg raise
- Rotational stability
- Trunk stability push-up

The Functional Movement Screen cannot be administered by untrained parents or coaches. The tests are monitored by qualified physical therapists, trainers, and strength coaches. Athletes are graded by very specific standards. A score of 3 is perfect on a single test; 21 is perfect for the battery. When the score is 1 or 2, the limiting factors are identified and a series of corrective exercises is prescribed. The therapy routines have even been written into software so that the person can follow through with a program based on the numbers posted during the screening tests. A score of 0 means that the person experienced pain during a test and is advised to see a physician for diagnosis.

"The purpose of the screen is to find the weakest link," explains Cook. "Once the prescribed therapy program has been completed, the athlete retakes all seven tests." Why? "Because correcting one problem, such as muscle imbalance, may solve problems identified on the other tests. If not, the next weakness is addressed."

Cook says the average for high school football players is 14–15, but the tests are given to athletes in all sports. "A score of 11 or lower usually reveals a history of sports injuries or a high probability for future injuries. We encourage athletes to be retested twice a year because the physical demands of any sport can cause a migration back to muscle imbalance."

What do the tests and their results have to do with identifying potential for success in athletic performance? "The Screen is the base of a three-tier pyramid that supports overall athleticism in the middle and sport-specific skill at the top," says Cook. "If an athlete, at any age, scores high on the seven tests, the movement foundation for greatness is there."

Functional Movement Screen workshops are accredited by the National Athletic Trainers Association and the National Strength and Conditioning Association. For more information, contact Cook by email at ATS@D-K.com or through the Athletic Training Services Web site at **www.functionalmovement.com**.[2]

SPORT-SPECIFIC TESTS

Specific tests of physical ability and skills are commonly used in some sports, but nonexistent in others. The 40-yard dash has long been used as a tool to measure speed in football players. Whether or not it is valid as an indication of football playing ability is questionable, but the test has been used for decades and will probably be used well into this century.

Don't ask golf pros and coaches about a sport-specific test. They can't give you one. Those who evaluate golf talent want to know what the person scores, period.

The measures (if they exist) used to identify talent or the potential for talent in each sport are discussed in detail in chapters 10 through 22, along with tests of speed, strength, power, agility, and so on, that are used by more than one sport. Instructions for the tests are also given. Although the same tests are given to athletes in different sports, the methods of administering and scoring the tests may be different. Table 8.1 offers a list of the 13 sports covered in this book, the names of sports-related tests, if not sport-specific, and comments about each.

INTERPRETING TEST RESULTS

If you are a parent without coaching experience, don't draw any conclusions based on informal test results. Let coaches, scouts, and recruiters do whatever they want to do with times, lengths, heights, distances, and averages. They are trained to interpret results and to put them into the proper context. An athlete who is deficient in one area may be able to make it up in another. An athlete who is superior on one test may fall short on others. Few, if any, athletes will score high on every physical test they take. For the purpose of comparison, the numbers given in this chapter can be informative, serve as reality checks, and provide goals for talented athletes.

Table 8.1   Sport-Related Tests

Sport	Tests	Comment
Baseball	Pitching speed	90 mph: major-league velocity
		83–88 mph: college average
		77–83 mph: high school average
	Home to first	4.2–4.3 sec: major-league average
	First to third	6.8–6.9 sec: major-league average
	Catch to catch	<2.0 sec from catcher to second: excellent
	60-yard dash	6.7–6.8 sec: major-league average
Basketball	Vertical jump	>30 in: excellent at any level (boys/men)
Football	10-yard dash	1.5 sec: good, skill positions (electronic)
		1.65 sec: acceptable, linemen (electronic)
	20-yard dash	Not available
	40-yard dash	<4.5 sec: college receivers/defensive backs
	20-yard shuttle	<4.0 sec: college skill position players
		<4.6 sec: college linemen
	Vertical jump	27–29 in: college linemen
		>30 in: college skill positions

(continued)

Table 8.1 *(continued)*

Sport	Tests	Comment
Golf	18-hole scores	High 70s: 13- to 14-year-olds Mid-70s: 15 and over
Gymnastics (girls, 10–14)	20-meter sprint Push-ups Pull-ups Leg lifts in 10 sec Splits Shoulder flexibility Vertical jump	80th percentile: 3.04 sec 80th percentile: 14 80th percentile: 7 80th percentile: 7 80th percentile: 13.9 in 80th percentile: 21 in 80th percentile: 19.9 in
Hockey	Not available	
Soccer	Illinois Agility Run Vertical jump Intermittent recovery 7 × 30m recovery	17.34 (U18 men's national team average) 16.68 (U21 women's national team average) 25.98 in (U18 men's national team average) 20.80 in (U21 women's national team average) Not available 10.86% (U18 men's national team average) 7.99% (U21 women's national team average)
Softball	Pitching speed Running home to first Running home to home Throwing home to 2nd	55–57 mph: average for high school 59–61 mph: average for college <3.0 sec considered good <12.0 sec considered good <2.0 sec considered good
Swimming	Event results only	
Tennis	Match results only	
Track	Event results only	
Field	Event results only	
Cross country	Race results only	
Volleyball	Standing jump Approach jump Slide jump	9-11: average, elite boys, 14–16 9-0: average, elite girls, 15–17 6-0: average, elite boys, 14–16 9-10: average, elite girls, 15–17 6-0: average, elite boys, 14–16 8-0: average, elite girls, 15–17
Wrestling	Match results only	

Chapter 9

Recruiting, Scouting, and Trying Out

*T*here are three people inside every college recruiter. The first one is a talent scout. It is not this person's job to find out who the best high school athletes are, but to discover the athletes who can continue to improve and perform at the college level. Great high school players do not necessarily become college athletes. Some are as good as they are ever going to be when they are juniors and seniors in high school.

Predicting how they will do during the four or five years after high school is not an exact science. But if a recruiter is communicating with your child or an athlete you are coaching, he or she is interested in the person's talent. That is one of the steps in a complicated dance that will last for at least two years.

The second person inside the recruiter is an educator. This educator has dedicated his or her life to teaching, coaching, counseling, and even serving as a stand-in parent for student-athletes. In the overwhelming majority of cases, the person is sincere and honest and wants the best for your child. The recruiter/educator has the power to offer financial assistance that can go a long way toward making a college education possible for many athletes whose families couldn't afford it otherwise.

The third person inside a recruiter is a somewhat cold, calculating businessperson. He or she has to negotiate enough contracts (scholarships) with 18-year-olds and their parents or guardians to fill out a roster with players who can compete at a very high level. One side of that businessperson's brain wants to give as much money to each athlete as possible. The other side is telling the recruiter to get as many good athletes as he or she can for the least amount of money or, in the case of two men's and four women's sports, get the best athletes available with the limited number of full scholarships available.

In minor and spring sports, the more money that is left on the table by one athlete, the more that can be used to recruit another one. Don't take this personally. While it appears dispassionate, it is a necessary part of coaching and recruiting survival. Make too many mistakes and your teams lose. Lose too many games and you get fired.

THE RECRUITING PROCESS

The clock starts ticking on the recruiting process on the first day of school in the ninth grade. At that moment, the person becomes a "prospective student-athlete." There can't be any contact between recruiters and athletes for two more years, but the academic record starts to accumulate when the first set of grades is recorded on the transcript. The person who waits until the junior or senior year to get serious about grades is making a huge mistake that could cost him or her thousands of dollars.

As soon as the recruiting process begins, every athlete who is going to attend a National Collegiate Athletic Association Division I or II school has to be certified. Certification costs $25. The rules for core curriculum, grades, test scores, contacts, scholarships, and visits are complicated. Athletes should ask their school counselors, parents, and college recruiters to help them get through the certification process. Counselors can obtain registration materials at no cost by calling the NCAA clearinghouse at 319-337-1492. For detailed information on the recruiting and eligibility, go the to NCAA Web site at **www.ncaa.org/eligibility/cbsa/div1recruiting.html**.[1]

Every college athletic department has a compliance officer. For straight answers about any part of the process, athletes, their parents, or counselors should call a compliance officer. They are there to keep the school out of recruiting and academic trouble.

THE SEARCH

"Many parents either don't understand the process of recruiting or they are too close to a situation to be objective," says Keith Zembower, a former coach and now a Texas-based recruiting columnist and youth sports consultant. "One of the first things they do is to blame coaches for not recognizing talent. They think that because their son hit .400 during his senior year or was second-team all-district in a sport, schools should be knocking their doors down with scholarship offers.

"If a half-dozen colleges are recruiting your child and the one school that he or she is really interested in has not made contact, the parents may have a point. A good athlete is being overlooked. But if an athlete is not being contacted by any schools, a problem exists that the parents or high school coaches don't recognize. It may be size, speed, strength, power, attitude, whatever. But be assured that college recruiters know about and want athletes who can help their programs. They do not deliberately overlook prospects."[2]

THE LETTER

The second mistake high school athletes and their parents make is to get too excited when a letter expressing interest arrives during the junior year. Being contacted at that point means very little. Recruiters use a shotgun approach at the beginning of the process. They send letters to almost every high school athlete who has even a remote chance of being recruited.

Explains Zembower, "Most schools will contact approximately double the number of athletes they plan to eventually bring in for visits. Football recruiters will send 120 letters, even though they can't invite more than 60 to the campus. If a basketball coach has four scholarships available, he or she will probably write to between 12 and 16 prospects. A baseball or softball coach might contact 40 high school athletes for 10 available roster positions. Getting a letter expressing interest is nice, but don't interpret it to tell the world that a certain school is going to offer you a scholarship."

THE QUESTIONNAIRE

Most college coaches will eventually send a questionnaire for high school athletes to complete and return to the athletic department. An increasing number of university athletic departments (UCLA and USC, for examples) include the questionnaire on their official Web sites. The personal and academic information questions will all be about the same. The remainder of the information requested will be sport-specific and will include some of the following items:

Individual wins/losses (tennis, golf, track, field, cross country, swimming)

Scoring average (golf, basketball, gymnastics, hockey, soccer)

Rebounding average (basketball)

Batting average (baseball, softball)

Assist average (basketball, hockey)

Times (swimming, track, cross country, football)

Positions played (football, baseball, basketball, volleyball)

Honors (all sports)

Coaches' names (all sports)

Other schools under consideration (all sports)

THE COLLEGE VISIT

If a student is not invited for an official visit to a campus, it means that recruiters are not very interested. Even if an invitation for a visit is extended, however, it doesn't guarantee anything. Football coaches, for example, may have to bring in 50 players to sign 20. The visit is for both sides to get to know each other, for the student to get a look at the campus, and for coaches to present a high-powered sales pitch. Just like selling vacation time-shares, they know that x number of sales contacts will lead to x number of scholarships. But unlike the time-share offers, recruiters know who they want—primarily in order of talent.

The NCAA allows an athlete one official paid visit per school to a maximum of five schools. The main problem blue chip athletes have is deciding which colleges to visit. Other recruited athletes should give some thought to the kind of schools they choose to visit and the order of visits. Even at the Division I level, there are large, midsize, and relatively small universities. The stronger a student feels about the kind of environment he or she wants to live in for the next four years, the better. Some student-athletes are only going to be happy at a large university with 20,000 or more students. Others are going to adjust and perform better at colleges and universities with an enrollment of between 10,000 and 20,000. And a third group likes the individual attention afforded to students at smaller state and private schools.

If an athlete thinks he or she can be happy at schools of all three sizes, he or she should include all three sizes in the five visits. If four or five big schools seem to be seriously interested, the athlete should narrow that list down to two, then visit a midsize and a small college or university to get the feel for all of them. Athletes should be careful not to make the mistake that some very good athletes have made. One football player visited five of the biggest names in the country, using up all NCAA-approved trips. When none of the schools offered him a scholarship, he ended up walking on at one of them with no scholarship.

If your student is not a blue chipper but is attracting interest, he or she should not begin a series of visits with small schools. The athlete should go to the big ones, find out if they are going to make an offer, and have a backup plan in case the first and second choices don't work out. College recruiters have a system, usually color-coded, of offers and fallbacks. The prospective athlete should do the same.

Athletes should not waste one of the five official visits, which can last no longer than 48 hours and must be taken during the senior year, on a local school. If your child is interested in a college or university that is close by, take him or her with you as many times as you want. The student can even call the athletic department and request two tickets to a home game. Save the five official visits for colleges that are willing to fly your child or the athlete you are coaching to another part of the country.

THE HOME VISIT

At some point, the recruiter and perhaps even the head coach may make a visit to the athlete's home. That is when the student and the parents need to be armed with a list of questions about the school, the program, the coaches, and the role the athlete is expected to play. Here are some sample questions:

Does the school have my major?

Who will be my academic counselor?

How many hours will I be expected to carry?

What is the average class size for required courses?

How much money will I have to pay to supplement the scholarship?

What happens if I don't graduate in four years?

What is the graduation rate for athletes in my sport?

What happens if I get hurt and can't play?

Can I bring a car? Do I have to pay a parking fee?

Where will I live?

Do I get to choose a roommate?

How many roommates will I have?

Are the cafeterias open on weekends?

Are the dorms and cafeterias open during holidays?

Where do I do my laundry?

Are there curfews?

Can someone help me get a summer job?

Can I work on campus if I have an athletic scholarship?

Can I supplement an athletic scholarship with an academic one?

Is there a tutoring program for athletes?

Am I required to attend study halls?

Do walk-ons ever make the team?

What style of offense and defense will we run?

Will I be redshirted?

What position will I play?

How many players are above me on the depth chart?

Are other players being recruited at my position?

Is the person who recruited me the one who is going to be my coach (in the case of sports such as football)?

What will I be expected to do during the off-season?

If everything is equal, coaches want athletes with the most talent. But things are seldom equal. Whether an athlete is offered a scholarship or how much that offer is worth may depend on what happens during the visit between coaches and athletes.

Attitude counts. Coaches like student-athletes who have "a good attitude." That's a pretty vague term, but it includes things like dedication, dependability, courtesy, respect, appearance, vocabulary, and a willingness to do what is asked to contribute to an athletic program. The student-athlete should approach the personal visit with a coach in the same manner that a person seeking a job goes about an interview. In more ways than you think, they are both business deals.

THE OFFER

There are two kinds of scholarship offers. The first is a full ride—room, board, tuition, and fees—and is given in men's football and basketball and women's basketball, gymnastics, tennis, and volleyball. The second is a partial scholarship and could be any combination of the items listed. The partial is the kind of scholarship offered to athletes in all other sports.

Don't be offended if your child is offered less than a full scholarship in sports other than the ones mentioned earlier. A Division I baseball coach, for example, is allowed the equivalent of 11.7 full scholarships. Those scholarships have to be divided among more than twice that many players on a team. In today's market, a half-scholarship is a great deal. See tables 9.1 and 9.2 for the number of scholarships Division I and II colleges and universities can offer athletes. They are not required to offer the maximum in each sport, but they are allowed to by the NCAA.[3]

Great athletes in minor sports occasionally end up at second- and third-tier schools because of the financial package. A big school might offer tuition only, while a midsize institution offers tuition and books, and a small school offers tuition, room, and board. The one that comes closest to paying for the total amount of money that it costs to go to college may get the athlete, although many other factors should be considered.

THE DECISION

After an athlete has received a letter of interest, NCAA certification, a campus visit, a home visit (perhaps), and a scholarship offer, it's time to make

Table 9.1   NCAA Division I Allowable Scholarships

Head count (HC) scholarships cannot be split. Equivalency scholarships can be divided between two or more student athletes. Equivalency scholarships are awarded in all sports except men's basketball, football, women's gymnastics, women's tennis, and women's volleyball.

Sport	Men	Women
Archery		5.0
Badminton		6.0
Baseball	11.7	
Basketball	13.0 (HC)	15.0 (HC)
Bowling		5.0
Cross country/track and field	12.6	18.0
Fencing	4.5	5.0
Field hockey		12
Football	85 (HC)	
Golf	4.5	6.0
Gymnastics	6.3	12 (HC)
Ice hockey	18.0	18.0
Lacrosse	12.6	12.0
Riflery	3.6	
Rowing		20.0
Skiing	6.3	7.0
Soccer	9.9	12.0
Softball		12.0
Squash		12.0
Synchronized swimming		5.0
Swimming	9.9	14.0
Team handball		10.0
Tennis	4.5	8.0 (HC)
Volleyball	4.5	12.0 (HC)
Water polo	4.5	8.0
Wrestling	9.9	

Adapted, with permission of the National Collegiate Athletic Association.

a decision. If the athlete is good and lucky, he or she may have to decide on equal offers from two or more schools. If the athlete is merely good, he or she may have to choose between unequal financial offers.

Parents, don't advise your child to automatically go for the most money unless money is a deal-breaker. For a talented athlete to be successful in college, there has to be a good fit academically, socially, and athletically. Players can practice and play only 20 hours a week. The rest of the time they have to live in a different environment and interact with students, teachers, and members of the community. Even if the athletic program is great, the student-athlete has to be reasonably happy with everything else.

Table 9.2   NCAA Division II Allowable Scholarships

All Division II scholarships can be divided between two or more student athletes.

Sport	Men	Women
Archery		5.0
Badminton		8.0
Baseball	9.0	
Basketball	10.0	10.0
Bowling		5.0
Cross country/track and field	12.6	12.6
Fencing	4.5	4.5
Field hockey		6.3
Football	36.0	
Golf	3.6	5.4
Gymnastics	5.4	6.0
Ice hockey	13.5	18.0
Lacrosse	10.8	9.9
Riflery	3.6	
Rowing		20
Skiing	6.3	6.8
Soccer	9.0	9.9
Softball		7.2
Squash		9.0
Synchronized swimming		5.0
Swimming	8.1	8.1
Team handball		12.0
Tennis	4.5	6.0
Volleyball	4.5	8.0
Water polo	4.5	8.0
Wrestling	9.0	

Adapted, with permission of the National Collegiate Athletic Association.

Provide guidance but let your child make the decision. Make sure he or she understands the financial implications and sacrifices the family must make if a full scholarship has not been offered. It's great to get a half-scholarship from a well-known university, but half of $30,000 a year is a lot of money for most families.

The idea is to provide what is best for your child, not what is best for you. A great program a long way from home may be better than a bad one close enough for you to see all of the games. The chance to play at a midsize university may be better than sitting on the bench of a national power. Getting a degree from a school with a great academic reputation may be better than playing for a school that is only known for winning games. Take the long view. How will this experience affect your child's life after college?

Once your child signs a scholarship offer with a college, both sides are committed to one year. If things don't work out, student-athletes (with some important restrictions) can change their minds about playing or transfer to other schools. The institutions are required to honor scholarships on a year-to-year basis. In most cases, everyone is happy. Sometimes, coaches make recruiting mistakes and athletes make mistakes by accepting offers. It may be awkward for both sides, but correcting those mistakes early is in the long-term interest of both.

PROFESSIONAL SCOUTING

In its purest sense, and that may not be a good choice of words, scouting is primarily conducted by professionals in football, basketball, and baseball.

At the elite level, baseball scouts and college coaches are competing for the same athletes.

Pro football scouts evaluate college talent in preparation for the National Football League draft or to sign players to free agent contracts. Teams in the National Basketball Association also have scouts (although they may be called something else) who monitor the progress of college players before the draft.

The odds of a high school football player making it to the pros for any period of time are about 6,000 to 1. The odds of a high school basketball player playing professional basketball are 10,000 to 1.[4] Given those odds, and given the fact that almost all talented athletes reach the peak of their careers without playing at the professional level, no more attention will be given in this book to football and basketball scouting.

Baseball scouting, however, is another issue. Major-league teams have scouting staffs, which include full- and part-time personnel. These people cover the United States and other countries on a year-round basis. You can see them at tryout camps (see the sidebar) and in the stands at high school, summer team, and fall ball games with notebooks, clipboards, and radar guns. They are looking for the same skills that college coaches are looking for. Those skills are discussed in depth in chapter 10, "Baseball."

What Happens at Baseball Tryout Camps and Showcases

Following is a typical agenda for a tryout camp held by a major-league team or a "showcase," where college coaches and scouts can evaluate potential recruits or signees.

- Run 60 yards, starting from a stealer's stance. Many players are weeded out solely on this time. Infielders and outfielders have to be under 7.0 to get anyone's attention. A time of 7.0–7.2 is average in tryout camps. "If a player is over 7.2," says Al Goetz, "he'd better be able to hit lots of home runs."[5]
- Throw from right field to third and home (outfielders).
- Field ground balls hit straight ahead, then to right and left (infielders), and make the throw to first base. Regardless of position, grounders are usually taken from the shortstop position.
- Take batting practice (all position players). Each player gets 10 to 15 swings with a wooden bat. "Lots of kids make the mistake of not practicing with wood, and the bat feels like a lead pipe when they have to swing it," warns Goetz.
- Pitch off the mound to a catcher, not a live hitter (pitchers).
- Best hitters bat against best pitchers.

Bill Clark, director of international scouting for the San Diego Padres, offers the following suggestions for players who participate in tryout camps:

"The primary thing is to be yourself. Don't try to press and show how cocky you are or how you can dominate a situation. If you are not a take-charge guy, you won't be a take-charge guy by making noise. A scout will pick up on those things immediately and dial that player out.

"Always be available with a glove when the scout needs somebody to fill in at a position," he continues. "If the right fielder has to leave early and you are a second baseman, volunteer to get in there. Always be ready to help out and be prepared physically to work hard all day. Your work ethic will show up in a tryout camp. Scouts look for that.

"Regardless of how you do, don't alibi. If you complain about a sore ankle, he'll wonder why you came to the tryout session. Leave that scout a very good impression of your ability and that intangible of desire, in that order."[6]

What makes baseball scouts different from football and basketball scouts is that they are competing against college recruiters for athletes right out of high school, as well as after the junior year of college and after a player's college eligibility has expired. Baseball scouts are not bound by the same NCAA rules that restrict college recruiters, so parents and youth baseball coaches have to take on more of the responsibility for protecting the athlete's interests.

At the upper end of the talent pool, a high school graduate may have to choose between a college scholarship at a university with a premier baseball program and accepting a contract to make a million or more dollars playing in the minors immediately. The decision is more difficult for players who are drafted in later rounds and have to choose between playing in college on scholarships and receiving far less money to turn pro.

"We start noticing athletes who are playing on a varsity high school team when they are sophomores and juniors," explains Paul Weaver, major-league scout for the Houston Astros. "In rare cases, a potentially great player may make a varsity team when he is in the ninth grade. Chipper Jones, Ken Griffey Jr., and Mike Lieberthal are examples.

"In the free agent market in the states, there are several methods that scouts use to cover their areas. They stay in touch with high school coaches and, in some cases, make them associate scouts in order to have continuing contact with prospects on their teams and others. 'Bird dogs' are part-time scouts who look for talented players. These recommending scouts are more likely to be used in remote areas of the country than in heavily populated cities."[7]

But there are exceptions. Al Goetz, an associate scout for the Atlanta Braves, is located in the middle of one of the largest metropolitan areas of the country. He signed five players during a four-year period in the late 1990s.

Although the process is widespread and more sophisticated than it used to be, scouting in baseball is not a science. Experts estimate that less than six percent of players who sign professional contracts make it to the major leagues. Big-league rosters are packed with free agent signees and players who were drafted in the lower rounds.

Bill Clark, the San Diego scout, has spent a lifetime traveling the world and evaluating talent. Many of the players who became household names as big-leaguers in their 20s were watched by Clark when they were in the their middle teens. Based not on science but on decades of experience, Clark has put together a list of characteristics he uses to assess the talent of baseball prospects. Table 9.3 presents Clark's checklist and what he hopes to see in relationship to each personality feature. Even if you don't agree with Clark's subjective methods of evaluation, the checklist provides a glimpse into how baseball scouts think.

Table 9.3   Baseball Assessment of Talent Checklist

Characteristic	Response sought
Handshake	Firm
Eye contact	Looks scout in the eye during conversation
Facial expression	Relaxed off the field; determined on the field
Voice	Strong; uses inflection; not flat
Aggressiveness	Takes charge; makes plays
Depth of voice; thickness of beard	Still has room to grow, mature
Ease of communication with scout	Shows respect as equal
Relationship to parent	Positive, respectful
Relationship to coaches	Listens, learns, responds to suggestions
Relationship to teammates	Gets along with them; supports them
Medical history	Not injury prone
Dealing with adversity	Doesn't make excuses for performance
Work ethic	Goes beyond minimum practice requirements
Intelligence	Makes good decisions

Adapted, with permission, from Bill Clark, *Assessment of Athletes Guidelines*, Columbia, Missouri, 2000. Unpublished paper.

A WORD TO COACHES AND PARENTS

The attention that an athlete receives when he or she is being recruited or scouted by a college coach or professional scout is seductive. Some of the light that shines on a player also illuminates those family members and coaches who have helped the person achieve recognition.

There is a tendency to be proud of the accomplishment, flattered by the attention, eager to promote, and downright giddy about the prospects of your child playing a college or professional sport. But rather than push, now is the time to back off. Let the recruiting/scouting game take its course. Be close enough to monitor, to advise, and to protect, but not so close that you interfere in the process. Coaches, recruiters, and scouts want you to be supportive, not meddlesome.

Youth Sports Tryouts

At the other end of the recruiting and scouting continuum are tryouts for young children in sports such as baseball, basketball, and soccer. These tryouts can be as traumatic for the kids as they are for their parents, but there are things parents can say, refrain from saying, and do to make the process easier for everyone.

First, no face-to-face, game-day speeches. Most kids respond better to indirect, occasional suggestions than to last-minute pep talks.

Second, spend time getting your kids ready for tryouts. Nobody can just walk onto a field and hit a baseball thrown by a machine without practicing first. Take them to a batting cage. Emphasize short, level swings to make contact with the ball. Play catch with them at home. Work on a smooth, three-quarter (not sidearm, not directly overhand) throwing motion. Let them practice catching regular tosses, pop-ups, and grounders, using both hands.

In basketball, teach them to shoot layups (and to jump off the foot opposite from the shooting hand), free throws (shoulders square to the basket, arm extended on the follow-through, and slight backspin on the ball), passing (hands behind the ball, elbows in), and dribbling (especially crossing over from one hand to the other).

Don't send them off to a tryout with new or oversized equipment. Bats that are too heavy and gloves that are too big are common causes of tryout disasters. More leather does not mean more catches. Kids should be able to feel the fingers of gloves. Outfielders' gloves are bigger than those used by infielders and pitchers—or they should be. Ask what kinds of shoes are acceptable and what most kids will be wearing. Peer acceptance is a big deal.

Don't feel compelled to be present at tryouts. Some kids want you to be there; others feel more pressure with you in the stands. The one thing you don't want is your child watching and worrying about your reaction rather than paying attention to what the coaches are saying. There will be plenty of time to watch once the season starts.

Children have to know that how they do in tryouts has nothing to do with how you love and care for them. Asking, How did you do? is not likely to get a meaningful response. Asking, Are you ready for lunch? or, Any homework tonight? are better questions.

Everybody gets nervous about tryouts. It's normal behavior. Do and say everything you can to keep things around the house as routine as possible. Neither you nor your child need any more stress than you already have.

Part III

Evaluating Talent by Sport

Chapter **10**

Baseball

"The age of 12 for Little League baseball players is like the senior year of high school or college for older players," says Keith Zembower, a youth sports consultant and writer in Dallas. "Most kids start playing T-ball at six and continue playing on a field with 60-foot baselines and a pitcher-to-plate distance of 40 to 43 feet for six years.

"During that last year at those distances, exceptional talent begins to show," he continues. "The good ones simply overmatch the dimensions of the field. They dominate the game. Very seldom have I seen a player with that kind of strength and power not become a talented older player.

"I was sitting in the stands at the Little League World Series in 1992 and watching Sean Burroughs of California take batting practice," recalls Zembower, whose own son also made it to Williamsport. "He was the only 11-year-old in the tournament, but he was the best hitter at that age that I had ever seen. I said to myself that if this guy doesn't play in the major leagues some day, then I can't judge talent."[1]

At 17, Burroughs was the high school player of the year in the United States and was drafted with the seventh pick of the first round by San Diego. Since then, he has been rated as the second best minor-league player in the country by *Baseball America*, hit .360 at Class A, and was expected to play in the majors by the time he reached 20.

EARLY INDICATORS

In addition to showing strength at the plate, some 12-year-old third basemen and shortstops can backhand a ball and throw a bullet to first base. That is another sign that they are ready to break out of the Little League age limit. Less talented players will field the same ball and lob it to first or throw rainbows from the outfield to home plate.

Al Goetz, an associate scout for the Atlanta Braves and owner of a baseball training facility, comments on pitching prospects. "At 12 and 13, we can start to see signs that pitchers can play at the next level. The good ones can throw in the upper 60s and low 70s at a distance of 54 feet."[2]

While determining outstanding potential for success at higher levels is relatively easy at 12, it is much more difficult at 13 and 14. During those two years, there is typically a physical growth spurt and a developmental spurt in baseball skills. Players, particularly pitchers, can blossom as late as 17. There is a danger of missing late bloomers during the early teens because of unpredictable growth patterns. Part of that danger can be minimized by looking at the size of parents or siblings.

Whatever the age, coaches, recruiters, and scouts look for bat speed, leg speed, and arm speed in position. Those three skills might improve along the way, but they basically come with the package that is the player.

Pitchers

Among the players Goetz works with are high school athletes hoping to play at the college level, as well as some who are able to play professional baseball. "We look for pitchers with loose arm action. They don't look like they are trying to muscle the ball. However, there are players who have good, loose arms, but who can't throw hard because of some mechanical problem. Those players have a chance if they can change their technique.

"The Braves don't like high-effort pitchers, either. Some kids are very successful at young ages because they are just big and can throw hard. The Little League stars who fade by the time they get to high school were primarily big kids who were simply stronger than others at that age. I'd rather have a young player with a loose arm throwing in the mid-60s than one who is working very hard to throw in the 70s. Sooner or later, pure talent and athletic ability will overtake the kid who was big and strong at an early age."

Goetz, however, does not downplay the importance of size, particularly among pitchers. "We try to look for ones who we can project as growing bigger and stronger. A 13-year-old who is 6-2, weighs 180, and has a loose arm has a chance to play at a big-time level if he doesn't get hurt."

Paul Weaver, major-league scout for the Houston Astros, looks for pitchers who are over six feet tall. "The success rate for pitchers below six feet is not good. We'd like to have them a little bigger and taller. That will give them a good arm angle, it's better for ball movement, and better for throwing breaking balls."[3]

Left-handers have an advantage because they are scarce. A left-handed high school pitcher who can throw 85 to 87 miles per hour might get a chance to play college or professional baseball. Right-handers, at the same age, are going to have to throw in the 87- to 90-miles-per-hour range. Neither Weaver nor Goetz think that throwing breaking balls at an early age is a good idea

Baseball scouts do not think that the ability to throw breaking balls at an early age is a good idea or a sign of special talent.

or a sign of special talent. Kevin Millwood, the Braves starter, did not throw a curve ball until he was 16 years old.

Weaver agrees that throwing speed is important, but not as important as delivery, arm action, and body control. "The first thing you look for in high school players is projectability. We look at attributes such as size and maturity. Can the person put on more weight?"

But Weaver concedes that evaluating pitching potential is a gray area for scouting. "Greg Maddux threw in the 87 to 91 range in high school, but he could move the ball around. Rudy Seanez, the well-traveled reliever, threw a 95-mph fastball, but didn't know where it was going."

Infielders

Elite youth baseball coaches, college coaches, and scouts like infielders who have "soft hands" and who don't look stiff fielding the ball. At camps, they are timed from catch to release. Less than a second (0.8 seconds) is a good time at any level.

Measuring the arm strength of middle infielders is rather subjective, but talent evaluators want to know if the ball is still carrying when it reaches first base. If it's declining in speed or dying as it gets to the first baseman, that is an indication that the arm isn't as strong as it needs to be at a higher level. Second basemen, third basemen, and shortstops can expect to be put in the hole at short and to make the longest throw (to first) an infielder will ever have to make. First basemen aren't expected to show exceptional arm strength, but it is another tool that is nice to have. More important, they have to field their position and hit with power.

Range is also subjective, but quick feet are very important. How well does a player go to the right or to the left? Most will move better to the left (glove side) than the right.

"Speed is the only tool that can be used on offense and defense, so it is a key to exceptional talent," explains Weaver. "But it is more of a priority up the middle (second, short, and center field) than for corner players. With the first group, I'm including quickness and agility along with outright speed."

Size among middle infielders is not as important as at other positions. Young players who are too big may not move as well as those with smaller body types. A player like Alex Rodriguez is an exception in terms of size at shortstop. Joe Morgan, the hall of fame second baseman, is 5-7.

Catchers

"We want catchers who have athletic, mesomorph body types," says Weaver. "They have to endure a lot of physical wear and tear, so they need a build that can withstand the demands of that position." If a player is 140 to 150 pounds at the ages of 12 to 14, he may be a 200-pounder at 17 or 18.

At any level, arm strength and delivery time from catch to catch (catcher to second base) are critical. A time of 2.0 seconds is good. That same time (2.0) applies to the 12-year-old. He has to throw at the shorter distance of a Little League field, but if he can do it in two seconds or less, he'll have an opportunity to continue.

Outfielders

Sooner or later, outfielders will be timed in a 60-yard dash. It is the longest they will ever have to run in the outfield and anything under 7.0 seconds is good for older players. In the 12 to 14 age group, 7.5 is considered a good speed.

"The average 60-yard time for major-leaguers is 6.9," according to Weaver. "If a player can run in the 6.5 to 6.6 range, it will get someone's attention. When that distance is covered in 6.2 to 6.4, you're talking about players like Dione Sanders, Kenny Lofton, and George Lombard."

Speed is measured not only by times in certain distances, but in running gait, length of stride, and explosiveness. Andruw Jones, for example, is not exceptionally fast out of the box (explosive speed), but is well above average from first to third and second to home.

Weaver warns coaches and parents about the difference between speed and "usable speed." Some players have great speed, but no instinct about how or when to use it. Others, like Jeff Bagwell, are just the opposite. They don't give you great times, but know how to use their base-running skills effectively.

A player's speed from home to first is measured for any position player. A time of less than 4.1 seconds from the left side at any level is exceptional. Home to first in 4.0 to 4.1 from the right side would be considered exceptional. Weaver says that 4.2 is the major-league average from the left side, and 4.3 for right-handed batters is considered big-league speed.

The Astros' Weaver thinks that size can be overlooked in positions other than pitcher and catcher if the player has other tools. The five tools are speed, throwing, fielding, hitting, and hitting with power. "In 20 years, I've only seen a few like Griffey, Rodriguez, and Jeter who have the whole package. Most talented players have some things that they can do better than others, but they also have shortcomings."

Major-League Speed

Gene Coleman, EdD, strength and conditioning coach for the Houston Astros, has recorded the times of several thousand major-league baseball players in various distances. He classified those times into average and exceptional ranges. Use table 10.1 to compare the times of your players with those of big-leaguers who bat right-handed.[4]

Table 10.1   Average and Exceptional Major-League Speed

Distance	Average	Exceptional
60 yards	6.7–6.8 sec	6.3 or less
Home to 1st	4.2–4.3	4.1 or less
1st to 3rd	6.8–6.9	6.7 or less
Home to 3rd	11.4–11.7	11.3 or less
Inside-the-park HRs	15.0–15.5	14.0 or less

Adapted, with permission, from *Georgia Tech Sports Medicine & Performance Newsletter*.

Arm strength for outfielders is usually measured by having them throw from right field to third and from right to home. If a player can make that throw all the way on the fly or on one bounce, he has an above-average arm. Goetz says that, on a rec team, you might have two out of ten or eleven players who can do that. On a travel team, as many as half can make the throw.

Bill Clark, international scouting coordinator for San Diego, has developed standards for measuring arm strength. He is one of the few scouts who use the radar gun for every position. Table 10.2 shows how hard prospects have to throw to get Clark's attention.

Table 10.2   Throwing Velocity

Position	Velocity
Catchers	80+ mph
Infielders	80+ mph
Outfielders	90 mph
Pitchers	90 mph

Clark makes exceptions for center fielders and some pitchers. "A center fielder but may not be able to throw 90 miles an hour," explains Clark, "but if he can throw accurately and get the ball to the cut-off man, who cares? They don't pay center fielders to throw runners out at the plate unless he's Andruw Jones."

Clark, who formerly held the same type of scouting position with the Braves, points to Tom Glavine as an exception among pitchers. "Glavine doesn't throw 90 miles per hour and never did, but he has always had absolute control of his off-speed pitches."

LATE BLOOMERS

How do you know if a player has peaked physically? While science can tell us very little on the subject, scouts have a lot of experience. Weaver looks at the size of parents, the nature of a young man's beard (believe it or not), and the mature or immature appearance of the person. "Maddux," he says, "weighed only 150 in high school. He was 17 or 18 years old, but his face made him look like he was 15. You knew he had some room to grow."

Scouts also look at body structure. Does a player have broad shoulders, big hips, and a thick chest, rather than a small bone structure that probably won't support much more growth? Again, the experience of the person evaluating a prospect seems to be as important as any other factor in projecting size.

"The Braves," says Goetz, "might take a chance on a late bloomer if they see overall athletic ability. You might not see it consistently, but there would be flashes of excellence. A hitter, for example, might drive a couple of balls you almost can't believe, then miss the next five pitches. A pitcher might throw one or two balls at 88, but the rest are 83 or 84 mph."

Skip Bertman, the LSU coach whose teams won the College World Series five times between 1991 and 2000, thinks that predicting success in baseball in more difficult than in other sports. "Only six percent of those who sign professional contracts make it to the big leagues. Albert Belle wasn't even drafted out of high school. Todd Walker was drafted by the Rangers, but they

There is not any single quality that is essential for baseball success other than the willingness to put in lots of time and effort.

didn't offer him any money. Baseball prospects need outstanding physical skills, but you can't identify any single quality that is essential. In that sense, talent is not as important as the willingness to put in the time and effort to prove they can play at the college or professional level."[5]

IF YOU HAVE A PROSPECT

Given the uncertain nature of predicting future success among baseball players, there is no standard pattern of development a player must follow. However, some decisions about the developmental process have to be made along the way.

Camps and Clinics

Zembower, the Dallas consultant who has coached and taught baseball at every youth level, thinks that camps for children at the ages of six, seven, and eight are a waste of time and money.

"There are just too many players," he says. "If there are 150 players at a camp, the instructors may keep them busy, but the kids are not learning very much. The only plus is the opportunity for your child to interact with others and have a good time in a baseball atmosphere."

Zembower believes that your money is better spent working privately with a pitching or hitting coach. An hour a week for five weeks with a professional instructor will produce better results than a four- or five-day live-in camp where there are hundreds of players. For better players, seeking out individual coaches or going to academies has become almost a necessity.

Older players have two kinds of camps to consider. The first is a team camp, in which players from a school or travel team enroll in a four- or five-day camp as a unit. The usual agenda includes working on fundamentals during the mornings and playing games in the afternoons. The advantages are the chance to play a lot of baseball in a short period and the possibility that you might be seen by scouts or college coaches during the games. The disadvantage is cost.

Day camps and clinics have become very popular. A normal fee is $75 for two days for either hitting or pitching sessions. Players show up for several hours a day, then go home at night.

In either live-in baseball camps, day camps, or clinics, players age 13 to 15 get to refine basic baseball techniques. If pitching mechanics, for example, are not corrected by the age of 15, the player is likely to develop arm problems or will fail to develop the power needed to pitch in college or at the professional level.

If a player has hopes of playing college ball, camps are valuable after the sophomore or junior year in high school. College coaches are able to evaluate and sign players because they have seen them in their camps. These camps provide a legal way to talk with, test, and drill potential recruits. Both the player and the coach enjoy the advantage of getting to know each other personally, as opposed to relying on brief encounters, videos, or recommendations from others.

FALL BALL

Another decision that has to be made by the player, parents, and coaches regards fall ball—a second or third season that is played during September and October. The problem with fall ball is that the player is never given a chance to rest and allow his body to recover from a season that probably started in January or February.

Many baseball coaches would just as soon see their players take some time off or even play another sport during the fall. The risk of playing year-round is baseball burnout or, worse, an injury caused by overuse. This is a particular problem for pitchers, whose arms can take just so much work over time. While most schools have rules about maximum numbers of pitches, innings, and games, overly aggressive coaches often find ways to get around the rules and, in the process, risk injuring promising players. Hitters who play fall ball or take private hitting lessens are not necessarily more likely to become injured, but the burnout factor is definitely there.

Goetz says some traveling teams play 60 to 80 games a year. "I know a 10-year-old who played between 70 and 80 games during a season. By the time those kids are 17 or 18, they hate baseball."

Adds Goetz, "At the ages of 12 to 14, players should be playing a maximum of 40 to 45 games during the spring and summer seasons and, at the most, another 10 to 15 games in the fall. Kids need a rest from baseball."

WHAT COLLEGE COACHES LOOK FOR

At the Division I level, college coaches want immediate help. With only 11.7 scholarships spread over 25 or more players, they can't afford to take on many "projects." College coaches might take a pitcher who can throw in the 90s but who can't find the plate, but even with that kind of potential, he is not as likely to get a look by a coach of a top-25 team as he is by a junior college or midlevel program.

"If we offer you a scholarship," says Danny Hall, head coach at Georgia Tech, "we expect you to come in and play as a freshman. We can't wait on you to develop, but rather we want you to contribute right away."[6]

There are exceptions. Jeff Guy, an assistant coach at Tech, says that Tech will occasionally take a chance on a late bloomer. "We've had guys who we thought would help us down the road and they really came on to contribute to our program. Perhaps they didn't get much of a scholarship when they got here, but they were awarded more assistance as they got better.[7]

"We also have walk-on tryouts, and we use recruited walk-ons. These are players we think might be able to help, but we don't have any available scholarship money at that time. At Tech (and many other universities with high academic standards), we have to base our selections on baseball skills and grades. No matter how good some players are, their transcripts and SAT/ACT scores are just not going to qualify them to play at our school."

The second thing that college coaches want are players who don't need full scholarships. While some superstars get them (perhaps 2 out of 25 players), the overwhelming majority of college players do not. In elite programs, it is almost considered a privilege to play because of the exposure to big crowds, television, and big-league scouts. The good news is that a player who does not receive a full scholarship is allowed to work on campus a limited number of hours per week to earn extra money.

The third asset that a player can bring to a college program is versatility. This does not apply to pitchers, but being able to play second and short, first and third, catcher and first, or any combination of infield/outfield positions gives a coach some flexibility with his lineup.

"We tell prospects that the more places you can play, the more playing time you'll get," according to Hall. "We recruit a lot of shortstops who may or may not end up playing at that position. It is a premier athletic position in baseball. It would not be unusual for us to have a second baseman, shortstop, and third baseman who all played shortstop in high school."

Unlike in college football, college baseball offers little time for a learning curve to develop. You don't hear much about redshirting in baseball. A player can either hit or pitch and might emerge as the best player on a team in the first intrasquad game. Teams recruit according to specific needs and will look all over the country, especially at junior colleges, to fill those needs. However, junior college players may be playing at that level because their grades won't get them into universities or because they want to be drafted. Both of those factors pose recruiting risks for the coach at a four-year school.

College coaches look more at performance than at size and speed in all positions except pitching. A pitcher is not likely to be recruited by a top college program unless he is big and strong (nothing under six feet). Each college coach has his own philosophy of how to win, and the players he recruits have to match up with that philosophy. Skip Bertman of LSU has consistently taken teams to the College World Series that were built around power. Other programs build around speed and defense.

The pathway to playing Division I college baseball is seldom straight. Division I programs, junior colleges, and major-league baseball organizations compete with each other for the same high school superstars. A major university that signs five high school players with the potential to play right away or go pro may get two of them. The other three will be drafted early and offered a lot of money. "At Georgia Tech," says Guy, "at least half the players we sign will have already been drafted." The ratio is even higher at some other top programs.

It is difficult to convince great players to stay in school for four years. Most of them sign professional contracts right after high school, while they are in junior college, after their junior year at a four-year school, or when they become 21 years old. The money for potential major-leaguers is too good to turn down.

JUNIOR COLLEGE BASEBALL

College baseball programs, more than any other sport, rely on junior college talent. Many outstanding players will go to junior colleges with good baseball reputations. Two-year schools located in states such as California, Arizona, Texas, Kansas, Mississippi, and Florida are loaded with great prospects. Division I programs recruit players out of junior colleges to fill specific needs. During any one recruiting year, as many as half the players on a roster may be junior college transfers.

There are no restrictions regarding the free agent draft and junior college players. They can sign at any time. Some of these players are drafted, signed, and followed for one year before they sign a professional contract. Others stay for two years, then sign with either a Division I school or a major-league team. Once a player signs with a Division I college, he can be drafted after his junior year or when he turns 21.

An unwritten rule for evaluating junior college offensive talent is to take half of what a player does in terms of numbers to project what he will do at the Division I level. A junior college first baseman, for example, who hits 30 home runs in a season can be expected to hit 15 or 16 at the next level.

Some players bounce among colleges and training grounds. Bobby Howry began his college career at Arizona State, but was not throwing enough strikes or getting enough innings to make it work. He transferred to a junior college and was subsequently drafted, but not offered big money. Next, he went to a midlevel university where he did get innings and exposure. After one year, he was drafted again, this time by the Chicago White Sox, and has gone on to play an important role in the Sox's bullpen.

The players most likely to play for a major or midlevel university for four years are local athletes who can afford to play as walk-ons or with minimal financial assistance. They are not likely to be drafted, but are talented enough to fill a role for some teams. Hall describes a four-year player as one who might not get to the big leagues, but who will probably get a chance to play professional ball, and who will be very close to getting a degree.

A WORD TO COACHES AND PARENTS

Paul Weaver has three pieces of advice to the parents of promising players. The first is to encourage them and let them experience success and failure in the game. "Make the game fun," he urges. "Too many parents put so much pressure on their kids that they burn out."

"Second, expose talented players to better competition. Get them to clinics. Let them learn from a variety of teachers and coaches. Allow them to practice with older kids or to play up occasionally in competitive baseball."

Finally, Weaver thinks that talented players should experience different sports and different activities, especially at younger ages. "Most major-leaguers played more than one sport in high school. We would like to have prospects who are well-rounded persons, not just players. In the 12 to 15 age group, they should be doing more than just playing baseball."

Goetz adds his wisdom to Weaver's advice for parents and youth coaches: "Be realistic. The most important thing is for parents to give their children a chance to continue playing baseball. When kids sign up for our college recruiting program, many of them tell me that they want to play at NCAA Division I top-20 schools. Most of them don't have a chance to do that. They are setting themselves up for failure. I'm not saying that they can't play college baseball, but their skill level and potential might be better suited for competition at other levels of the game."

Every college coach and every baseball scout will tell parents not to push. The burnout rate between the ages of 10 and 17 is very high. "They just don't want to play anymore," concludes Goetz. "There is more desire for a college or professional career among the parents than among their children. Support your children. Be there when they need you, but don't try to live your baseball fantasy through your kids."

Adds Hall, "Let the kid's talent identify himself. Keep baseball in perspective and remind everybody in the family that this is a game and should be fun. Once he gets to the high school level, pick out some schools that are a good match baseball-wise and academically. The rest will take care of itself. There aren't many sleepers out there. Everybody knows about the ones who can play baseball at the college level."

Chapter **11**

Basketball

"I saw Stephon Marbury at a Syracuse camp when he was in the sixth grade and everyone knew he had the potential to be great," recalls Paul Hewitt, head basketball coach at Georgia Tech. "But we also knew he would probably never be any taller than 6-2 or 6-3, so he was not a lock to become a great player. As gifted as he was, he wouldn't have made it if he hadn't continued to work on his game. There are too many things that can happen in a player's life that can prevent him or her from getting better at each level.

"Unless you are talking about an obvious thing such as tremendous height—a player who is 6-8 in the eighth grade, for example—I don't think there is a particular age or age group at which enduring basketball talent begins to show," thinks Hewitt. "It's not like baseball, where you know that a high school left-hander who throws 85 to 90 miles per hour has a good chance of playing in the major leagues someday.

"Basketball is a lot more like golf and tennis. In those sports, you have to constantly work hard honing your skills in order to have a chance to someday play at the next level. There are thousands of 'can't miss' basketball prospects who never make it, and there are just as many 'nice players' who work hard enough and long enough to become stars. Don't forget that Michael Jordan was cut from his high school team when he was a sophomore."[1]

Bonnie Hendrickson, women's basketball coach at Virginia Tech, says she has attended an AAU 12-and-under tournament, but that coaches have to be very careful about evaluating talent at that age. "It is easy to find young women who are literally heads and shoulders above other girls of that age," she observes. "Then there is a span of three to four years during which you have to watch closely to see if they get any better. Talent can be deceptive because some players can be very good in age-division basketball, but they never improve."[2]

EARLY INDICATORS

Whether or not the talent is lasting, basketball appears to be one of those sports in which talent can begin to appear at any age. Former Georgia Tech coach Bobby Cremins says that he knew when he watched Kenny Anderson during the summer after the eighth grade that he would play Division I basketball. "At the other extreme," remembers Cremins, "was Matt Harpring. He had no serious offers going into his senior year in high school, but then he had a fantastic season. We recruited him very late and he ended up being an All-American and a first-round NBA draft pick."[3]

Agility

Morgan Wootten, DeMatha Catholic High School's famous coach, says that you can see a child at seven or eight and tell that he or she is going to be a good athlete. "Even at that age, there are certain players who show great agility and a nose for the ball. They always seem to be around the ball, and you can't coach that. If you want to find out where the ball is, just find that player.[4]

"In other players," adds Wootten, "talent might not show up until later. The late-bloomer effect is present in basketball, but it depends on the individual as to when the talent will show up."

Work Habits

Wootten does think that by the time a player is in the seventh or eighth grade, you can tell that he has a good chance to become a pretty good high school player. "When I saw Adrian Dantley in the eighth grade, I knew that he had a chance to go all the way because his work habits were so incredible. I felt the same way about Danny Ferry when he was in the tenth grade. This talent factor varies from one player to another. I remember one player who was cut from our freshman team, then came back to be captain of our varsity and led us to a city championship. He went on to play college ball at Mt. St. Mary's."

Shooting Ability

In evaluating young talent, shooting ability, innate quickness, and even size (unless it's unusual size) are not reliable predictors of talent. As long as basketball goals are set at 10 feet, kids will use whatever style it takes to get the ball up to the basket. Once horrible shooting habits are established, they are almost impossible to break. Elementary and middle school players who develop their shooting skills on eight- or nine-foot goals have much better shooting technique when they get to high school and beyond than their friends who learned to shoot on goals that were too high for their strength. So, shooting ability, not necessarily scoring ability, is an indicator of talent if it is done correctly. Good shooters are scarce at the youth basketball level.

Hand-eye coordination is as close as you can get to a reliable predictor of long-term success in basketball players.

Quickness

Quickness is not a predictor of future success unless it is controlled. There are plenty of quick, young basketball players who play out of control. Harder to find are those who combine the two skills.

No less an authority than former UCLA coach John Wooden, when asked about the single most important piece of advice he would give to a potentially gifted basketball player, responded, "Work on quickness under control."[5]

Height

Even height at an early age is unreliable as a predictor of future talent. Some athletes in all sports are bigger, stronger, and consequently better than their peers. They often depend on their size to dominate the game instead of developing skills that they will need later. When everyone else catches up in growth and development, the height advantage is lost and the great (or, better stated, big) youth players become average, and probably frustrated, high school players.

Coordination

One early indicator of future success is relatively reliable: hand-eye coordination with the ball. If a player in the fourth, fifth, or sixth grades can pass and catch a ball, shoot right- and left-handed layups, dribble with both hands, and execute a crossover dribble in both directions, that athlete has a legitimate head start on playing high school basketball. How far the player can go beyond that depends on too many factors, but hand-eye coordination is as close as you can get to a reliable predictor of long-term success.

Rick Ruedlinger, vice president of operations for Youth Basketball of America (YBOA), says that early indicators of basketball skill, if not athletic talent, are directly related to coaches who teach fundamentals such as using both hands, moving without the ball, boxing out on rebounds, and setting picks. "Those elements of the game are difficult to teach once an athlete is 16 or 17 years old," says Ruedlinger.

He also thinks the three-point line has become a serious obstacle to teaching shooting technique. "Young players either want to drive to the bucket or step outside and heave it to the basket rather than shooting the ball correctly. The short jump shot is almost a lost art."[6]

IF YOU HAVE A PROSPECT

The path of success for young basketball players has been pretty well established. They begin playing for local school or recreation league teams, then move on to middle school and high school teams. Simultaneously, young players sign up for or are recruited to play with teams associated with Youth Basketball of America, the Amateur Athletic Association (AAU), Basketball Congress International (BCI), or one of several similar organizations around the country or the world. Competition for YBOA and AAU begins at nine and under and continues through the senior high school level. Play progresses from local leagues and tournaments during the winter

John Wooden's advice to basketball players: "Work on quickness under control."

months to travel teams for the better players in the spring, then to tournament schedules that end with national tournaments in July.

Parents and coaches should be careful about the number of games young athletes play. Al Nierwinski, national field director for YBOA, is a firm believer that the more a child plays, the better. However, he has concerns about youth basketball schedules and the demands placed on schoolchildren. "If a coach schedules a team to play a tournament every weekend from September to June, the kids will burn out. One coach told us, before regional and national tournaments had begun, that his team was 63-4. That's ridiculous. When do these children study?"[7]

Ruedlinger says that the problem is even more critical with outstanding 16- and 17-year-old players who are trying to get the attention of college coaches. "It is not uncommon for these athletes to be constantly away from home during the months of June and July. Some of them are in a different city every week."

CAMPS AND CLINICS

Basketball camps and clinics are not hard to find. Practically every college and many high schools sponsor summer camps for basketball players of all ages. The advantages to elementary and middle school players are supervised instruction, competition, and the enjoyment that comes with socializing with other kids with similar interests. For juniors and seniors in high school, camps held at colleges offer the chance to be seen by college coaches and to get a feel for college campuses. The disadvantages of most camps are the cost and the fact that group instruction implies little individual attention.

Wooten tells parents and high school coaches to get their players into camps that have the reputation for teaching fundamentals and working on the individual development of players. "Stay away from camps that devote most of the time to playing games," he warns.

Wooten is particularly concerned about the decline in shooting skills of young players. "I don't think people work enough on shooting. Shooters spend too much time trying to make the spectacular play or trying to dunk the ball. Even kids who can't dunk want to dunk. Bill Bradley used to tell people that if they wanted to be great shooters, they should make 50 shots from each of the five spots around the three-point line every day. But now it's hard to find anyone who wants to shoot 250 shots a day."

Hewitt is very direct about what prospects should do. "They should be able to dribble with both hands, make foul shots, and hit the 15-foot jump shot. At young ages, nobody knows how tall a player is going to be. They should all take the attitude that they are going to be less than 6-5 and develop their games accordingly. If they get taller than 6-5, they'll have the size needed for inside play and the ball-handling and shooting skills of perimeter players."

WHAT COLLEGE COACHES LOOK FOR

"I start making a list of prospective players when they are in the ninth grade," says Georgia Tech's Hewitt. "By then, you start to find out who the top players are, and by the beginning of the tenth grade, you get a much better idea.

"Except for the number five position," says Hewitt, "I look for players who are versatile. The pros can pick and choose players and match them with positions. We don't have that luxury at the college level." (Division I centers average a height of 6-8; forwards, 6-6; and guards, 6-2.)

Physical Skills by Positions

Positions in basketball are becoming less defined. Coaches look for players who can face the basket and play well, for others who can play with their backs to the basket, and for a third group who can do both.

Regardless of position, every coach is looking for quickness. It's not how fast a player can run 100 yards, but how fast he or she can move during the first few steps. Explains DeMatha's Morgan Wootten, "You hope your center is quicker than the other center, that your forwards are quicker than their forwards, and that your perimeter players are quicker than the other team's outside men. If they are, you'll probably win."

Although many coaches agree with Paul Hewitt's "one-size-fits-almost-all" type of player, plays are drawn up with a one-two-three-four-five personnel scheme. Instead of guards, forwards, and centers, coaches refer to ones, twos, threes, fours, and fives.

Ones—point guards—require quickness, ball-handling skills, and great vision. Says Wootten, "The point guard has to be an extension of the coach. He sees the floor and understands the total picture more than other position players. Size is a bonus, not a requirement."

In today's game, the two player is a shooting guard. Qualities such as the ability to run the floor and drive to the hoop are important, but he or she is the one who has to knock down the jump shot when his or her number is called.

The three player is the small forward. He or she has to be the most versatile of the five starters. This player is a swing player, strong enough to rebound, but with the shooting skills of a number two player. The three has to be able to move outside to shoot against a zone and at times against a man-to-man in order to leave room inside for the four and five players.

The four player is the power forward. He or she has to clean the boards, block out, and be able to play with his or her back to the basket. Most of all, the four player is a dominating rebounder.

The five player is the tallest man or woman on the team. He or she jumps at half-court to begin a game, blocks shots, rebounds, plays with his or her back to the boards, and is the primary inside scorer.

"Recruiting is an inexact science," Hewitt continues. "We look at the skill level of a player, regardless of the numbers he puts up. We also consider a player's physical condition or the lack of it. We have to be satisfied that he can improve his physical condition well enough to endure college basketball. A lot of players can do things well when they are fresh, but we want to know what they can do when they are tired."

Bobby Cremins, now a television commentator for college basketball, points out that certain players don't have great athletic ability, but they know how to play the game. "They have a sense of what should be happening on the court. In other cases, there are great athletes, but they just kind of stand around. They don't know how to use their athletic ability. College coaches have to be very careful about which of those players they recruit."

"In a few instances," adds Cremins, "a coach will spot a high school player who might not do anything for 20 minutes. Then, all of a sudden, that player makes an incredible move, and the coach knows that he or she needs to take a closer look. This happens more often with late bloomers than with players who develop early."

Virginia Tech's Hendrickson attends the AAU tournament in July to scout players. "It's difficult during the high school season to see a player more than once or twice. Our window is July 8th through the 31st. We rarely see a player at a high school game for the first time. We don't go to high school games looking for players. If we're there, it's because we already know someone is there we want to see play. We also like to get players on our campus for a camp in July. It gives us access so that we can talk with them."

Hendrickson emphasizes another element of recruiting. "Anybody can identify a great player," she says. "My mother can go with me to the gym and pick out a great player, but the potential for improvement is hard to figure out."

"I pay attention to how hard a kid plays and for upside intangibles. I'm more sensitive to that than I ever have been. Sometimes, as coaches, we think we can cure all of a person's attitude problems once she gets here. Some of those characteristics have been ingrained for 17 or 18 years, and we can't change them. I'm talking about work ethic, respect for teammates, and respect for coaches. It is very important to me how a player interacts with her teammates and with her coaches. There is more to it than just having basketball skills."

Hendrickson has flexible guidelines in terms of how tall her players are. "There is a gray area in which we could have a six-foot post player if she has a 25-inch vertical jump. Some players play bigger than their stature, especially if their wingspan is big. Low post players at the Division I level are about 6-3 or 6-4. Power forwards are 6-1 to 6-2. Swing players (threes) are anywhere from 5-11 to 6-1. Two guards are 5-9 to 5-11, and point guards are about the same height." (Hendrickson's numbers are slightly inflated when compared to the average heights of players who participated in the 2000 NCAA tournament. See tables 11.1 and 11.2.)

Table 11.1   Average Heights of NCAA Tournament Players—2000[8]

Position	Men	Women
Centers	6-8	6-2
Forwards	6-6	6-0
Guards	6-2	5-7

Table 11.2   Team Shooting Percentages of NCAA Tournament Players—2000[8]

Position	Men	Women
Field goals	46.0%	44.5%
Free throws	68.9%	70.2%
Three-pointers	35.9%	32.5%

"Five years ago those numbers would have been different. Tall female athletes are playing basketball now. They are more skilled than they used to be. In the past, players who were 5-10 had to play the post. That's not the case anymore."

What would get John Wooden's attention in a college prospect whose numbers or size do not measure up to those of more physically talented athletes? "Unselfishness, team concept, self-control, and intelligence," he says, characteristically.

A View From Rocky Top

The University of Tennessee's Lady Vols are a near-dynasty in NCAA basketball. One of the reasons for the program's success is the recruiting work of assistant coach Holly Warlick. Here are some of her thoughts about recruiting talented players.

"The AAU basketball program has become a showcase for girls' basketball. We begin to notice those players when they are about 14 years old. A few begin to show Division I talent potential even earlier.

"Although we would like to have all-around players, they are hard to find. I would advise young players to develop at least one skill that separates them from everyone else. It could be shooting, rebounding, playing defense, leadership, whatever. But the ones who make it here have that one outstanding skill and have the athletic ability to improve the other parts of their games.

"We also want to see how players handle pressure situations and how they communicate with those around them. How do they respond when a coach criticizes them? How do they react when a teammate makes a bad pass? How hard are they willing to work? If two players have equal skills, we will always recruit the one with the best work ethic.

"Size is important to us, but we don't say that our front line has to be a certain height. A player can make up for lack of height with other qualities. Overall athleticism is very important. Speed, quickness, strength, and aggressiveness can overcome deficiencies.

"We make mistakes in evaluating talent about 20 percent of the time. A player may be great in high school, but she simply burns out and never

(continued)

A View From Rocky Top *(continued)*

Recruiters for the Tennessee Lady Vols begin to take notice of talented players at about the age of 14.

gets better. This is especially true if a coach works a kid too hard. It is possible for a player to be too consumed with basketball. Sometimes a player who has been overcoached and overworked will get to college and develop other interests, so that basketball and academics become secondary.

"We consider the player's background. Parental support is necessary, but we don't want parents calling us and telling us who should be playing. We tell them that we are going to take care of their child, to trust us, and that they can call us about anything except playing time.

> "Remember that timing is everything. There may be a great guard out there, but we don't need one at that time. I would encourage young players to leave their options open. Just because you don't get a scholarship offer at your favorite school doesn't mean that you aren't good enough to play at the college level."[9]

A WORD TO COACHES AND PARENTS

What would John Wooden tell parents and coaches about basketball players with the potential to play at the college level? "I would tell them that their children should work on balance—physical, mental, and emotional. I would also encourage young players to develop the ability to keep their quickness under control."

Morgan Wootten's advice: "Basketball players have to get better during the off-season. Get them into the hands of someone who can teach fundamentals. They need an organized, intelligent program to work on their games."

Says Hewitt, "Players need to get into a gym or onto a court and work on fundamentals. They can do a lot of work on their own, just shooting, dribbling, and passing against a wall."

Hendrickson, who was an assistant coach at the University of Iowa before moving to Virginia Tech, worries that young players participate in too many games. "Some teams play hundreds of games during the course of a year, including a 50-game schedule during the spring and summer. That's too many. With that many games, kids often just practice bad habits. They also get used to losing, and it doesn't seem to have much of an effect on them.

"I'd like to see more camps that emphasize skill work. I'm not just saying that they should do drills only, but there ought to be a balance. Maybe playing a 25- to 30-game schedule during the off-season would allow time for individual work."

Hendrickson also thinks that recruiters and parents are guilty of telling players how great they are. Then they get to college and coaches start breaking their games down. When these players are told that they are not so great, they have trouble making the adjustment.

"Parents, hold your children responsible for their performance at this level," Hendrickson advises. "Don't blame everybody else if things don't go well. It may not be the high school or college coach's fault. Teach them to objectively evaluate their basketball and personal skills."

Chapter 12

Football

"**I** think the seventh grade is the earliest that a kid should start playing contact football." In Texas, where football is a cradle-to-grave near-religious concept, that statement almost amounts to heresy. But it came from Joe Martin, head football coach of the Garland High School Owls, winners of the Texas 5A state championship in 1999.

"That's the rule at my house," continues Martin, "and I have a sixth-grader who is driving me crazy because he wants to play. I worry about injuries when they start too young, I worry about the quality of coaching and the kind of drills they run, and I also worry about burnout. We see the number of kids in this area who play in something called the Turkey Bowl. It's like the Super Bowl of kids' football. They take it to the extreme with a parade, banquet, the whole thing. I'm talking about children in the second grade. If they go through all of that, there's not much left to do by the time they get to high school."

Martin is not finished. "I'd rather them play soccer or baseball or just ride a bicycle and enjoy being a kid. Any activity in which they can run, play, and develop hand-eye coordination is good training for football."[1]

EARLY INDICATORS

What would project middle school football players into consideration as high school varsity players? Martin thinks that they begin to show talent at the seventh- and eighth-grade levels. The attributes that would get his attention are size, coordination, and movement skills, regardless of position.

Size and Speed

Although players are getting bigger (see table 12.1 on size, weight, and speed), the game is increasingly based on speed and quickness. This table is

Table 12.1   Top 100 NCAA Division I Recruits in Texas—2000

Positions	Average height	Average weight (lb)	40 speed
Quarterbacks	6-3	200	4.7

Comments: The height range was 6-1 to 6-6. Height is not a concern with option quarterbacks, but they must run 4.6 or faster in the forty.

Running backs	5-11	190	4.55

Comments: The height range was 5-8 to 6-2. None were slower than 4.6. The fastest was 4.4.

Wide receivers	6-0	180	4.5

Comments: The height range was 5-8 to 6-5. Receivers must run 4.6 or faster.

Tight ends	6-4	225	4.75

Comments: The height range was 6-2 to 6-6. None were slower than 4.8.

Centers	6-2	240	n/a

Comments: Many high school guards are converted to centers in college.

Guards	6-3	265	n/a

Comments: The height range was 6-2 to 6-5.

Tackles	6-5	290	n/a

Comments: The smallest tackle was 6-4 and 265 pounds. The biggest was 6-8 and 320 pounds. Recruiters look for long arms and quick feet.

Defensive tackles	6-3	275	4.85

Comments: The range in weight was 255–320 pounds. Recruiters look for a combination of strength and size.

Defensive ends	6-4	240	4.7

Comments: The height range was 6-1 to 6-7. Recruiters consider a speed in the forty of greater than 4.9 unacceptable.

Linebackers	6-1	220	4.65

Comments: The forty range was 4.45 to 4.70. Recruiters look for speed, speed, and more speed.

Defensive backs	5-10	180	4.5

Comments: The forty range was 4.3 to 4.6. Cornerbacks are short and quick. Safeties may be as tall as 6-3.

a summary of size and speed numbers for the top 100 recruits in the state of Texas during the 2000 recruiting season. Keith Zembower, who writes an online high school recruiting column, provides information and comments in the table about each position.[2]

Other Characteristics

Martin looks for mental toughness. It is reflected by what players do to prepare during the off-season, whether or not they can play when they are "hurting, but not hurt," and how they handle the pressure of a long season or of being behind in a big ball game.

"There are lots of kids who make big plays. Most of that is mental composure, not luck," according to Martin. "Our quarterback this year played the best game of his life in the state championship game. It was the biggest game in his career and he played the best he had ever played. You always dream about that kind of performance, but some people actually live through it."

Talented football players have confidence. They handle every situation in which they are placed, and their self-confidence shows up in practice as well as in games. "It goes with every player and every position," explains Martin. "We kicked a field goal with one second in the state semifinal game to get us into overtime, then the same kid kicked another field goal in a driving rainstorm to win the game. And it wasn't just the kicker, but the deep snapper, the holder, and the players protecting him."

Like coaches in other sports, Martin sees great work habits in talented players. "They like to be there. They work even when they don't feel good. They are self-driven. It's a big deal for them to be successful, and they do everything they have to do to get there."

What would get Martin's attention from a less-than-gifted player? "He would have to make plays. We had a player who just signed a Division I scholarship. He wasn't that big or strong or fast, but he kept making so many plays in practice that we had to find a spot for him. I had to tell college coaches about him. There wasn't any tape of his junior year because he never got to play. The college people just assumed that he had always been good, but he hadn't had the opportunity to show anybody but us."

IF YOU HAVE A PROSPECT

The good news for parents of talented young athletes (12 and under) is that there is no need to rush them into a formal program of instruction and competition. Sandlot, backyard, and neighborhood football up to a certain age seems to be just as fertile a training ground for talent as organized peewee football. Private lessons that are common in tennis, golf, and baseball are seldom part of the development of a football player.

The middle school years (grades six to eight) appear to be an acceptable (but not essential) time for getting talented athletes onto school-sponsored football teams. Whether it is grade six, seven, or eight does not seem to matter. Tommy Tate, head coach at perennial Division I-AA power McNeese State in Louisiana, doesn't even think that it is necessary to play football in middle school. "They just have to play high school ball and attend at least one summer camp to have a chance to get to the next level," he says. "But if they come out of a strong middle school program, they will usually be far ahead of those who either don't play in middle school or come from a weak program."[3]

To have a chance to play college football, according to Garland's Coach Martin, athletes should be practicing, training, and playing by the time they are in the 10th grade. There are exceptions, of course, and some late bloomers make it at the college level even though they played in their first game as juniors or seniors.

Weight Training

Football coaches are unanimous in their belief that prospective players should participate in strength training programs, although they don't agree about when that training should begin. William Kraemer and Steven Fleck, authors of *Strength Training for Young Athletes*, think that resistance exercises can be designed for children as young as seven, but sport-specific exercises using advanced lifting techniques should not be introduced until the ages of 14 or 15 (see chapter 6, "Speeding Up the Process"). Kraemer and Fleck recommend a general resistance program that includes lifts such as the incline dead lift, bench press, back squat, seated row, lat pull-down, knee curl, knee extension, and overhead press, among others.[4]

Camps

High school and college coaches differ strongly on the issue of summer camps (at colleges) for football players. Many high school coaches, including Garland High School's Martin, think they are a waste of time in terms of developing football skills. There are too many players and not enough individual attention to justify the expense.

College coaches, however, see them as a vital part of the recruiting process because camps give athletes the opportunity to spend time on the campuses of schools they are interested in. More important to the coaches, camps give them a chance to test, evaluate, and get to know athletes, which is not possible during the NCAA-regulated recruiting periods.

Participation in Other Sports

It is difficult to play two sports in the supercharged, specialized atmosphere of high school football in states such as Texas, Ohio, and Pennsylvania. But those who play multiple sports have an advantage in terms of exposure to pressure situations and developing comprehensive physical skills.

"Playing two or three sports in high school is an advantage," says former Nebraska coach Tom Osborne. "Those athletes experience a variety of competition that one-sport players do not. If a person has played in a state high school basketball tournament or competed in important track meets, we know he probably has the confidence that he needs in football. He has been in a lot of competitive situations. This is particularly true for quarterbacks and safeties."[5]

The path from youth football to college or beyond is much clearer and straighter in football than in other sports. For most players, it begins by playing on a middle school or freshman team, then to junior varsity and varsity at the high school level. Along the way, a year-round program of strength and conditioning has become the norm. The only two variables during that four-year period are decisions about summer camps and playing more than one sport.

WHAT COLLEGE COACHES LOOK FOR

Colleges can't actively recruit until the beginning of the senior year, but they start the process during the junior year. Division I schools are allowed 85 scholarships and have a little more margin of error in recruiting players than Division I-AA programs. I-AA recruiters can't afford to make mistakes. They have to get players who can contribute four years instead of giving them two or three years to develop. The more of those players they recruit, the more successful they will be.

Big plays in football are consistently made by players who exhibit mental toughness.

Football has become so specialized that it is impossible to identify general skills and qualities. It is almost like recruiting athletes for several different sports, all with varying demands. Division I and Division I-AA coaches seek players with specific physical and emotional qualities for each position. Following is a summary contributed by coaches around the country of some of those qualities.

Quarterbacks

"Physical attributes are determined by the style of offense," says Greg Davis, offensive coordinator and quarterback coach at the University of Texas. "For the drop-back, pro style offense that we employ at UT, we want a quarterback who is 6-1 to 6-5 and who has an arm strong enough to make the necessary throws. The quick post is a good example for our offense. The quarterback has to be able to take a five-step drop and get the ball 16 yards deep on a line. We would like at least 4.8 to 4.9 speed and the ability to make some plays.

That doesn't mean we wouldn't take a quarterback who is 6-0, but he would have to have some other extraordinary skill like a rocket arm or 4.6 speed.[6]

"Teams that depend more on a running game might look at other qualities, such as speed, strength, and the ability to break tackles," Davis continues. "Height would not be as important.

The Michael Vick Profile

Michael Vick was a near-perfect example of a quarterback who, while not the tallest in his class, had extraordinary physical attributes as a freshman at Virginia Tech. He was 6-1, weighed 212, ran 4.33 in the 40-yard run, benched 320, handled 500 pounds in the squat, and had a 40-inch vertical leap. Maybe that is perfect.[7]

"Quarterbacks have to be pretty smart. You are placing the game in their hands. We look for leadership because the team has to believe in him. He can't hang his head or blame others after a bad play. The way we identify those intangibles is to find out if he played more than one sport in high school, to learn if he was captain of his football team or other teams, and if he participated in school activities other than football."

Running Backs

"We look for something called 'burst' in running backs," explains Bill Conley, recruiting coordinator at Ohio State. "It's the ability to accelerate, to change directions through the line of scrimmage, and to pull away from a tackler at the line of scrimmage. Burst is much more important than flat-out speed. Some guys can run fast, but they can't outrun anybody.

"We put them through an agility shuttle run in which they have to start in the middle, move five yards in one direction, ten yards in the opposite direction, and five yards back to the starting point," Conley says. "A time of 4.0 to 4.2 is good. On the 40-yard run, we want tailbacks to be 4.4 or below, and we want them to be able to break tackles. Size is irrelevant."[8]

Size does matter to other coaches with other offensive philosophies. They like running backs who are 5-9 or taller and who weight at least 180 pounds. A 4.5 in the 40-yard run will get their attention.

Receivers

Wide receivers should be able to fly—4.5 or less in the 40. Many schools also look for two-sport athletes, such as football players who can also run track. If they can run a 10.6 in 100 meters, someone will be interested.

The average height and weight for receivers in the top 100 high school players recruited out of Texas was 6-0, 180 pounds. The range was from 5-8 to 6-5, and the average 40 speed was 4.5.

Offensive Linemen

Ohio State's Conley says that offensive linemen need three things. The first is good flexibility in the knees and hips. "This is very important for pass protection. They can't be stiff-legged."

The second prerequisite is quick feet. It's not how fast they run, according to Conley, but how fast they come off the ball and how agile they are. "We measure their times at 10 and 20 yards more than in the 40. Starting from a three-point stance, a time of 1.75 to 1.80 seconds is very good.

"The third thing we want in an offensive lineman is a player who can finish a play. He maintains his blocks, he gets down the field, and he stays off the ground."

At Ohio State, offensive linemen range in height from 6-3 to 6-8 and are near or above 300 pounds in weight. At Virginia Tech, the offensive line that played against Florida State in the 2000 Sugar Bowl averaged 6-4 and 289.

Tight Ends

Tight ends are part offensive linemen and part wide receiver. They have to be physical enough to be good blockers (especially combination blockers), skilled enough to catch the ball, and fast enough to run downfield. Conley recruits 4.7 to 4.9 speed in tight ends who weigh 245 to 265 pounds. A tight end can't be shorter than 6-3 at the Division I level.

Defensive Linemen

Larry New put together defensive lines at Alabama and Georgia Tech, among other schools where he coached over a 34-year period. "Size is important (6-4 or taller), but height is not always the deciding factor. If you can get a guy who weighs 280 to 290 and has flexibility, speed, and agility, then you have something.

"Defensive linemen have to be great athletes because of the way the game is played now. I've had guys who ran 4.9 and 5.0, which isn't that fast, but who were very good players. If they have all the other qualities and can run a 4.7, that's even better because they can get to places faster. If you ask me what I want, it is a player who is at least 6-4, weighs 290, runs a 4.7 forty, and has great flexibility and strength. But there aren't many of those out there.

"The bench press is an important measure of strength (275 to 300 is pretty strong), but I've had really good linemen who didn't bench as much as other players. The lift I think that's more important than the bench press is the incline bench press. That's the angle they play from. They don't play from the flat position of a bench press. If they do, they are standing straight up and getting knocked down.

"One of the best players I ever coached was Willie Wyatt at Alabama. He had tremendous upper-body strength and he understood leverage. He also had feet that moved liked pistons and he had good balance. He was an all-state wrestler and a great athlete."[9]

Linebackers

Mike Collins is defensive coordinator and linebackers coach at the University of Louisiana, Monroe. "A great linebacker has to have great speed to keep up with running backs, receivers, or the ball. He has to cover some players who can run a 4.5 or 4.6. He might run a 4.7, but he'd better be able to play faster than that.

"We like them to be tall enough to get leverage on an opponent and to see what is going on. They need to be at least in the 6-1 to 6-2 range. They also have to have good upper-body strength—300 to 315 or above. We pay as much attention to what they can do in the power clean and squats as much as the bench press. They have to show us what their legs can do."[10]

Defensive Backs

"At least half of the skilled people in high school end up being defensive backs," says Tate. "Most of the time, they are very skilled players who just don't have good hands, so they are a better fit on the defensive side of the ball.

"Speed, acceleration, and agility are the most important assets of a defensive back," says Tate, who played defensive back in college. "They have to run the forty in 4.4 to 4.6, and they have to be able to run backwards. Size is becoming more of a factor because wide receivers are getting bigger. A back under 5-8 is a liability."

Tate says that defensive backs have to have bad memories. "They can't dwell on bad plays or play with the fear that something bad is going to happen again. Playing this position is about overcoming adversity."

TESTING TO PREDICT SUCCESS

Predicting how good a football player will be based on physical tests is as common as it is unreliable. Although he acknowledges that there is a risk of placing too much emphasis on test scores, Mike Arthur, assistant director of performance at the University of Nebraska, and his colleagues used 10 years of data to correlate results with performance on the field.

Nebraska players took a variety of tests that measured physical attributes such as strength, speed, agility, flexibility, and endurance. Four tests emerged as valid and reliable predictors of football success. They were the 10-yard dash, the 40-yard dash, the vertical jump, and the 20-yard shuttle run.

At the same time, players were placed into categories one, two, and three. Ones were starters, twos were substitutes who got significant playing time, and threes were scout team players and those who got very little playing time.

A composite score for the four tests was developed and statistically compared to playing time categories. Arthur and his colleagues found a strong correlation between a high composite score and players in the one category. The correlation was consistent, regardless of playing positions. Arthur believes that the test results would carry over to sports such as volleyball, soccer, basketball, and other sports that require lower-body power.

The strength and conditioning staff at Nebraska then determined that the best way to improve scores

The 20-Yard Shuttle

The 20-yard shuttle, also called the pro agility test, is widely used to determine the ability to run short distances and change directions. To take the test, draw two lines parallel to and five yards on either side of a center line. The subject begins the test in a three-point stance straddling the center line. A timer starts the clock with the subject's first movement. He or she (1) turns and runs either to the right or left toward an outer line; (2) touches the ground beyond the line; (3) reverses direction, runs, and touches the ground beyond the other outside line; and (4) reverses direction again and finishes, crossing the center line. For a skill-position football player, less than 4.0 seconds is considered fast. For linemen, a time under 4.6 is acceptable.

on those four tests was a lifting program that includes hang cleans, hang snatches, power presses, and jerks. Those exercises now represent an important component of strength training for football players at Nebraska.[11]

A WORD TO PARENTS

Joe Martin recommends support to a degree. "Make sure you don't push a kid over the limit. Lots of parents watch a game on Friday night, tape it, then go home and replay the game, telling their kid what they did wrong on every play. Many parents are so conscious of getting a scholarship for their son, they don't see that this is a game and should be fun. Keep things in perspective and stay positive."

Says Tate, "Be aware of college academic requirements beginning with the freshman year of high school. College is not all about football. Have a plan academically, socially, and athletically that will put your child into a position to play at the college level. Lead them in the right direction."

"I would encourage parents to let their children have a well-rounded background," advises Tom Osborne. "The football players who are successful after their college experience are those who have a sense of balance between athletic, social, academic, and spiritual areas of their lives. It is important that parents don't make a child's worth depend on how well he plays on Friday night."

A Glimpse Into an NFL Combine

For an idea of strength, speed, and jumping ability scores posted by college football players at the National Invitation Camp (NFL scouting combine), table 12.2 shows the best numbers for three tests.[12]

Table 12.2

Event	Position	Score
225-pound bench press	Defensive tackles	45 reps
	Defensive ends	32
	Guards	35
	Tight ends	31
40-yard dash	Running backs	4.41 sec
	Receivers	4.34
	Defensive backs	4.40
Vertical jump	Running backs	41.5 in
	Safeties	41

Chapter 13

Golf

"No matter how much coaching young players get or how much learning has taken place," says Rick Martino, director of instruction for the PGA—America, "they still have to figure things out for themselves on the golf course.

"Very talented players seem to be able to do this," continues Martino. "They take whatever skills they have and make them work. Frequently, their scores are better than their talent. Among professional players, Justin Leonard is a great example. He is not one of the most talented players on the tour, but his scores don't show it. The less talented players are good until they get into a situation with which they are not familiar."[1]

Derek Nelson, vice president of the American Junior Golf Association, agrees with Martino. "The difference between talented and less talented players is their overall competitiveness. Some kids just know how to win. When they are put into a situation where they are on the verge of winning, they can do it. I have seen junior players come back on the final day of a tournament from seven or eight strokes to win. Lesser players, even though they might have better strokes, can't come through in the clutch."[2]

The ability to perform in the clutch is a common denominator for talented players in all sports, but it seems to be more important at relatively young ages in golf. It is a harsh standard that young golfers have to do deal with, but it is one of the prices of participating in an individual sport. In golf there are no teammates to hide weaknesses or cover mistakes. A player, whether 13 or 63, is solely responsible for the outcome of a round or tournament.

EARLY INDICATORS

Competitiveness may be the single most important characteristic of golf talent, but there are others. "Talented players also have a strong desire to earn the rewards of playing at a higher level," thinks Martino. "They are willing to accept where they are in their development, but they want more. They want to keep playing against better players and in bigger events. If they are playing at a country club level, they want to play in the area junior events. If they are playing in the area junior events, they want to play in the national junior events. If they've already done that, they want to qualify for the U.S. Amateur. They want to beat adults. Their drive and ambition are limitless."

While young people who "play up" always run the risk of a loss of confidence, young golfers who do so are less at risk than, say, young tennis players. A tennis player who goes up against better and older competition can lose confidence if he or she gets beaten badly and consistently. In golf you are competing as much against yourself and a golf course as you are against other players. At a higher level, a young player can shoot an 80 and still feel good about it, even if the winner shoots a 68.

"Certainly," adds Martino, "highly talented individuals want to compete against other talented players, but the truth is that they are developing a sense of themselves playing the game and the course."

Size

Although not as important in golf as in other sports, size is becoming a marker of talent, especially among boys. Today, young golfers are bigger, stronger, and more athletic than players in the 1970s or 1980s. Nelson says there are plenty of 13-year-olds who can hit the ball 270 yards off the tee. Ten years ago, 240 yards would have been the standard for distance.

Martino does not think the size factor is as important among girls. "They tend to hit a wall physically between the ages of 13 and 17, so they have to develop skills that don't demand power. Some boys continue to develop physically well into their 20s. Tiger Woods is still developing—a scary thought."

Good size does not necessarily translate into distance among girls, and small frames do not mean they can't hit the ball hard and long. "There are twin 13-year-olds," says Nelson, "who are among the best juniors in the country. They are small, but routinely hit 230 to 240 off the tee. I see a greater difference between long and short hitters among the girls than among boys. If they are always hitting short, they will struggle because they are always farther from the green and are forced to use clubs that are difficult to master."

Martino uses Christie Kerr to illustrate the size factor among young female golfers. "Christie came out of high school and was about as developed as she was going to get. After beating Raymond Floyd's son, a highly rated junior golfer, to win the Florida state high school championship, she went straight to the LPGA."

Maturity

Nelson thinks talented golfers display other, subtler characteristics besides just the ability to put up good scores. "The good ones seem to be mature beyond their years. They can analyze their games. They can carry on an intelligent conversation with adults. They are comfortable around people. They can make a speech at a presentation ceremony." Nelson's observations are very subjective, but ones that parents and coaches should note.

© Anthony Neste

Golfers compete as much against themselves and the course as they do their opponent.

An AJGA Story

"One of the most impressive players I ever encountered," recounts Derek Nelson, vice president of the American Junior Golf Association, "was a young man who had just won a tournament in New Orleans. I asked him about his play, which had been exceptional, and he told me that he really wanted to win this particular tournament. He had played in it the year before and knew the golf course. So before each round, he sat down and visualized every hole—where he wanted to put his first drive, how he wanted to set himself up for each iron, and where he wanted to be on the green before his first putt. Not many 16-year-olds have the maturity and discipline to do that.

"The best part of the story is that he got a full scholarship at a Division I school, played four years of collegiate golf, then quit major competition. He went to medical school instead. He said golf was fun, but what he really wanted to do was to use golf to get through undergraduate school and into medical school. He was totally focused on what he wanted to do with golf and with his life at a very young age."

Judy Roer, a former tour player and now a Class A PGA teaching professional at The Boulders in Arizona, also notices special personality characteristics of young and talented players. "They are very good listeners. They don't mind working hard. They have discipline in their games. With them, it's not just banging balls, as it is sometimes with many juniors."[3]

Scores

Scores are obvious indications of golf talent, but they have to be considered in the right context. Players in the northeast part of the country, for example, are likely to post higher scores because the playing season is shorter and many of the older courses are tougher.

At the 13 to 14 age level, scores consistently in the high 70s will get the attention of those who evaluate talent. A handicap of two or three is good, but Nelson points out that handicaps are always established on home courses, not at away tournament under competitive conditions. "We don't pay a lot of attention to handicaps," he says.

By the ages of 13 to 16, talented golfers are shooting in the mid-70s and occasionally play a round under par. They start to give the appearance that they can put up low numbers—2, 3, or 4 under par. The same applies for the 17 to 18 age group. Tables 13.1 and 13.2 show the top five scores in two separate American Junior Golf Association tournaments.

Table 13.1   American Junior Golf Association Arizona Classic—
2000 Top Five Scores[4]

Boys–Par 72–6,905 yds	Girls–Par 71–5,974 yds
68–69–137	71–69–130
70–68–138	72–70–132
68–70–138	72–72–134
68–72–130	72–73–135
73–68–131	74–72–136

Table 13.2   American Junior Golf Association Golf Texas Junior Classic—
2000 Top Five Scores[4]

Boys–Par 72–6,859 yds	Girls–Par 72–5,922 yds
71–73–134	73–75–138
75–71–136	77–72–139
76–70–136	72–77–139
74–73–137	72–79–131
76–71–137	80–73–133

WHEN DOES TALENT SHOW?

When do emotional qualities such as competitiveness and drive begin to show? "I don't think it can happen until they compete," says Martino. "Once they start competing, it can happen at any time. I know a 10-year-old who shot a 74 on the short course at Doral. There are other great players who didn't even play golf when they were 10."

Nelson confirms that talent can show up at almost any age among juniors. "We have some that come out when they are 13 and are incredible players. Among that group, there are those who keep on getting better and dominate from 13 to 18. Others have had it by the age of 16. A third group is one that we don't hear much about until that final summer before they go to college. At 17 or 18, they start to put it together."

Davis Love III is an example of a player who was in the late-blooming group. He never won and was rarely in the hunt in AJGA events, although his father was a well-known teaching professional and gave his son every opportunity to be an early bloomer. He really didn't find his game until he got to college.

Teaching pros and junior golf officials all keep coming back to the competition factor in identifying talent. Scores don't count as much as the results of tournaments. At the risk of oversimplifying the whole concept of talent among junior golfers, most believe that those who win the most are usually the ones with the most talent. That is not necessarily true in other sports.

IF YOU HAVE A PROSPECT

"We had a call to the American Junior Golf Association from a parent asking about lessons for an 18-month-old child," recalls Nelson. "I was stunned."

Nelson thinks that 18 months is a bit early, but he does not believe the age at which children begin playing matters as long as they are competing by the time they are 12 or 13. The athletes all catch up around 16, anyway. "The most important thing between the ages of 5 and 10 is for them to have fun playing sports. If swinging at a golf ball is part of the fun, that's okay."

Most children who play golf begin to become interested at about the ages of seven or eight, sometimes for questionable reasons (like wanting to drive mom or dad's golf cart). Then, they decide it looks like fun to swing at a ball in the fairway or to try a putt. Finally, that interest develops into an appreciation for the game.

Instruction

The sequence of events in the development of talent begins in the backyard or in going to the course solely for the enjoyment of spending time with parents. The next step should be formal instruction. Most PGA professionals won't take children until they are seven or eight, but instruction with a teacher is generally recognized as a key element of developing talent. Children who are playing at the ages of nine or ten should get help from a qualified teaching professional.

Martino sees two distinct areas in golf—distance and ball control. Young players tend to develop distance relative to body size first. Once they get distance, they start to get body control. "Basically, that's how everyone learns. Once I can hit it as far as I can hit, then how can I control it? We don't have lots of people who are willing to go out and hit straight 100-yard shots all the time.

"Talented players have to be coachable," says Martino. "You can't develop an outstanding game on your own. It's really rare if you do. Some kids become more coachable when they realize that golf is important to them, but I think that most are coachable or not from the beginning. It's either there at birth or they come from an environment that prepares them to accept instruction.

"Finding the right teacher or coach is important," he continues. "Too many of them take whoever is available at the time, and that is not how it should be. Tiger has been through four coaches. He went as far as he could go with each one, then moved on."

This is not everyone's tactic. Some parents and their children keep hopping from coach to coach, always seeking some elusive formula for greatness that doesn't exist. Sooner or later, the player has to assume responsibility for his or her game.

Competition

The next step in the development of talent is to begin competing in tournaments. Most communities have junior golf associations that offer programs of instruction and competition. They are also good environments for learning rules, etiquette, and how to behave. The behavior of golfers is different (and, most would agree, more sportsmanlike) than that of any other sport. It has to be learned.

Nelson advises junior players to increase the volume of competition as they move into the 13-to-14 age groups. He doesn't want them to sacrifice practice time, but warns that there are a lot of good players on the practice range. "If you can't transfer practice skills into an atmosphere of tournament play, you are limited in how far you can progress. The only place to get that kind of experience is in organized tournaments."

Golf teachers and coaches are consistent with coaches in all other sports on one topic. They all like to work with players who have had experience in more than one sport, and they all think that one of the indicators of talent is the ability to play other sports. "I definitely encourage them to play as many sports as they can comfortably fit into their schedules," states Martino.

At some point, probably around the age of 15 or 16, the ones who are serious about continuing to play at the collegiate level make a decision to devote most of their spare time to golf. But many high-school-age golfers take a break from golf during one season of the year and use it to play a second sport.

Martino is adamant in believing that an athlete who wants to play college golf must compete in sectional tournaments as well as in high school events. These tournaments are the place to get playing experience. In terms of competition, more is better if it is within reason. A correlation does exist, although it is not absolute, between juniors who won national championships and their presence on the professional tour.

WHAT COLLEGE COACHES LOOK FOR

"Players begin to make a name for themselves at about the age of 13," says Bruce Heppler, men's golf coach at Georgia Tech. "But college coaches have to be careful not to get caught up too much in players who are good simply because they have developed physically earlier than others. Some of those who dominate their peers early fall back when everybody else catches up with them in size and strength.

"Matt Kuchar is a good example of a high school player who had a slight build and who had, at best, average distance on his shots. But he was always one who chipped and putted well. When he got to college, he added 25 to 30 pounds in weight and 30 to 40 yards in distance. Now, he hits nine irons on shots where he used to hit seven irons. Par five holes are like long par four holes, but he is used to using all of the clubs in his bag because he had to do that before he got stronger and longer."

"Don't get me wrong," adds Heppler. "Length is hard to replace. A guy who hits the ball 270 or 280 yards and may get into the rough occasionally has an advantage over those who hit 230 to 250. Putting is the other special quality of talented players. If a young player is a real bad putter, that is a serious disadvantage. It is hard to improve that part of the game."[5]

Bob Brown, who saw 30 years of college golfers as men's coach at the University of New Orleans, began noticing prospects when they were sophomores in high school, but just made mental notes. "By the time they are juniors, most are in the 160- to 170-pound range and are working with good coaches. Then, you are not surprised to see their names appear frequently in tournament results."

Brown lists four criteria he thinks are necessary for a player to reach the college level. First, they have to have a club or course where they can play almost without restrictions. Second, they have to have been working with a teaching professional. A pro can work them into a swing that will hold up in the long run. The third prerequisite is a willingness to practice, which is something most kids don't want to do, according to Brown. Finally, he reinforces the message of Martino, Nelson, and Roer. "You don't have to play at the national level, but those who want to play college golf better get into as many local, summer, and regional tournaments as possible."

Brown doesn't back away from players who are a bit cocky. "You almost have to be a little cocky to play well. I'll take an edgy attitude because I think I can control that part of a person's behavior. I don't have as much control over their golf skills and their ability to play well under pressure."[6]

College golfers with exceptional talent have to be self-motivated. They can put in only 20 hours a week, including tournaments. The good ones find time on their own to work on their games. If they have been on the golf course all of their lives because somebody made them be there, they probably won't make it at the college level.

Linda Vollstedt: A View From the Desert

The women's golf team at Arizona State University is one of the top-ranked programs in the country every year. Linda Vollstedt is the women's coach at ASU and offers these observations about college-level talent.

Q: *How and where do you look for prospective players?*

A: I look at American Junior Golf Association scores of the top high school players. We want players who score well—those whose names consistently pop up among the top 10 finishers in national tournaments.

Q: *Would you take a chance on a player who does not always finish in the top 10?*

A: Yes. I would base my decision on an intuitive feeling about someone who shows exceptional desire to compete and drive. I can work with a player who has weaknesses in her game, but competitiveness either has or has not already been ingrained by the time I see a player.

Q: *What would scare you off a player who consistently scores well?*

A: A bad attitude that would be reflected in how a player carries herself on and off the golf course. I watch how she treats her peers, parents, volunteers, and tournament staff members. Someone who curses, throws clubs, or whose behavior is not indicative of a champion will have to find another program.

Q: *Is there a physical profile that you look for in golfers?*

A: No. They come in all shapes and sizes, but we are seeing more and more athletes taking up golf. They look like athletes, too. They are strong and physically fit.

Q: *What do you think about high school golfers who play more than one sport?*

A: I think it's terrific. It's something I look for because it means that they are athletically skilled. Their bodies respond to movement, they tend to have good hand-eye coordination, and they understand the team concept. However, elite players are going to have to specialize by the time they are seniors in high school and give it all up for one sport. If not, they will miss out on recruiting opportunities.

Q: *When players reach your level, what tend to be their weaknesses?*

A: Course management and the mental aspects of playing golf. They also have to learn to deal with life experiences—all of the things you are going to learn while in college.

Q: *What goes wrong with the ones that don't make it?*

A: Sometimes they choose college or they are playing golf for the wrong reasons. Or, they don't really want to put in the amount of time it takes to play at this level. Other players just don't fit in and disrupt team unity. Most coaches will give them a second chance, but they are not going to let a player have a negative effect on the whole program.

Q: *What should a promising player do to get noticed by college coaches?*

A: The best thing to do is to contact the coach and let him or her know who they are and what they have done. We know where they are, but most of them sit back and wait for us to contact them. They need to let

(continued)

Linda Vollstedt: A View From the Desert *(continued)*

us know that they are interested in our school. We'll pay more attention to the ones who do.

Q: *What advice would you give young players, their parents, and their teaching pros?*

A: I would tell all of them that the player needs to get a tremendous amount of tournament experience, not just locally, but regionally and nationally. That is what will separate them from other players.[7]

A WORD TO PARENTS AND PLAYERS

"I tell parents that if they don't have enough money to pay for college, they shouldn't send their children all over the country to play in junior golf tournaments in the hope of getting a scholarship," says Heppler. "Send them for the experience and to improve their games, but not to earn scholarships. When parents do this, they are turning their children into professional golfers at an inappropriate age.

"I would tell junior players not to get too focused on playing in the top 25 college golf programs," he adds. "Golf is not like football or basketball where, by just making the team, you get to travel, wear a uniform, and play in at least a few games. We have only four and a half scholarships, and we travel with five players. There are lots of opportunities in Division II and III schools for good golfers who don't play at a Division I university."

"Make the game fun," says Roer. "When it quits being fun, it's all over. Very young children will let you know when they are ready to play golf. Teach them the correct grip, but a split grip is okay at the beginning. Emphasize good posture and balance more than stroke production. When you work with them, change the focus frequently. Their attention spans are short. Go from putting to chipping to hitting in short spells. Keep it creative. Help them build their swings from small to big, but keep it simple. Less is more."

Roer likes the idea of short clubs, but not cut-down clubs. "Adult clubs that have been reduced in length and regripped are too heavy for kids. They need graphite more than anybody."

Nelson thinks that the best thing parents can do is to set an example in the way they swing the club and in the way they behave. Their children will mimic both. "Parents who recognize talent in their children should get them into an organized program where they can compete against others their age," concludes Nelson.

Chapter **14**

Gymnastics

"Our Olympic team is never, never made up of the seven most talented gymnasts in the country," declares Geoff Eaton, director and head coach of Desert Devils Gymnastics in Mesa, Arizona. "It is always the seven hardest-working athletes.

"Even with the 1996 U.S. team that won the gold medal," he continues, "I can think of five people who could have done just as well. Hard work is always going to supercede talent. Talent helps, but the ones who work the hardest are the ones who are most successful. Talent will carry you only so far. On a bad day, the amount of work an athlete has put in will pay off."[1]

The "work is more important than talent" theme is common among coaches in every sport, but it seems to be particularly strong in gymnastics. "Talent and success are not the same thing," says John Spini, women's gymnastics coach at Arizona State University. "Someone who has talent does not always have the most success. The ones who have talent and good work habits and good coaching are the ones who become successful."[2]

Karolyi on Talent Versus Work

Bela Karolyi, perhaps the most successful gymnastics coach ever, confirms what Eaton and Spini have to say about the talent-versus-work issue. "I have seen less physically talented athletes become great athletes through an incredible amount of work, self-discipline, seriousness, and consistency. As a coach, it is much more exciting and rewarding to work with those who are less talented but more dedicated and committed to success than athletes who try to get by with physical talent alone."[3]

EARLY INDICATORS

The physical qualities that serve as the basis for gymnastics talent are speed, strength, quickness, and flexibility. "By the age of 9 or 10 you can recognize if a child has the physical talent to become a top-level gymnast," says Eaton. "But there are so many outside factors between the ages of 9 and 15, you have to be very careful about trying to pick out the perfect package that represents a super talent.

"I have been surprised by young athletes a million times," he exaggerates. "And I have disagreed with my wife, who was an eight-time NCAA champion, a million times on who would have and would not have become great gymnasts. A kid who was not that good at the age of nine can come out of nowhere and blow the doors off with her performance at fourteen. We kept one girl in our program mainly because she was a good person and a hard worker. She was not particularly quick and certainly not as flexible as others in our program, but now she is one of our most talented athletes. In fact, she just won a national championship." Eaton thinks that a lot of coaches accidentally turn away good kids just because they don't see what they want to see at the age of nine.

Leg Strength

Debbie Kaitschuck, an elite coach at Brown's Gymnastics in Houston, sees leg strength as one of the most important indicators of early talent. "Three

Karolyi on Early Indicators

"Ideally, the physical and emotional characteristics of talented gymnasts are equally important. You look for the athletes who are 50-50—the ones who have developed both areas.

"Speed is the physical characteristic that is most important. Speed of movement, explosiveness, and speed of repetition, all combined with agility, separate good gymnasts from great ones. Next in importance to speed is strength. Gymnasts need the strength to handle their own bodies. While speed is a prerequisite, their performance will ultimately depend on how they use the combination and speed and strength.

"But the thing that catches your eye in very young athletes is agility and coordination. You can begin to see that even when a child is four or five years old. Emotional characteristics don't begin to show up until children are seven or eight years old. At about that time, they come out from under the umbrella of timidity and start to show their personalities in public."

events in this sport are leg events, and we don't usually have an idea of how strong a gymnast's legs are going to be until she is at least eight or nine."[4]

Attitude

That perfect package includes more than just the physical assets already mentioned. Gymnastics coaches add aggressiveness and fearlessness to their list of desirable emotional qualities. Casual observers usually associate those features with football players more than with gymnasts, but those inside the gymnastics community know that aggressiveness and fearlessness are essential for a successful gymnast.

Size

The package also includes size, although it is not a popular subject among gymnasts or their coaches. Said one coach, "It's just easier to flip and twist if you are small than if you are bigger. Since scoring is subjective, size can be a factor with judges." Other coaches agree, but say that, as long as a person can carry his or her weight and do good gymnastics, there are really no limitations.

William Sands and J.R. McNeal reported on the size of outstanding young gymnasts who participated in the 1998 national championships in *Technique*, a USA Gymnastics publication. Not surprisingly, gymnasts were found to be smaller and lighter than the average girls of their age. The results, shown in table 14.1, indicate that female gymnasts tend to be shorter than half of all average-sized girls at the age of 9, and that trend becomes more pronounced through the age of 12.[5]

Eaton warns that gymnasts who are very young had better not take competition too seriously. It's okay to be focused and to be disappointed with a loss, but it's not the end of the world. If a Desert Devil cries about a loss or a bad performance, he pulls her out.

Table 14.1 Percentile Rank of TOPs Athlete Stature and Mass Compared to a Sample of American Girls

Age	Stature	Mass
9	25–50th	25th
10	25th	25th
11	25th	25th
12	5–10th	10th

Reprinted, with permission, from *Technique*.

EARLY AND LATE BLOOMERS

Children begin showing up in gymnastics classes as early as two years of age. This doesn't mean that they should, but they do. Eaton says that when parents come to him with an apparently precocious but very young child, he tells them to come back when their child is eight or nine. That doesn't mean they can't be in the program as preschoolers or primary grade students, but he does not believe they are ready to be put on a fast track until later. "We can recognize at 9 or 10 if the child is as interested in becoming a skilled gymnast as the parent wants her to be."

Are there late bloomers in gymnastics? It depends on your definition of the term and the perspective from which you are evaluating talent. Eaton thinks a girl who has been in a program but has not taken it very seriously can get serious as late as 15 and still become good enough to earn a college scholarship. Kristin Smith, associate head coach at Arizona State, says that most gymnasts reach their peak at about the age of 14. Even if both Eaton and Smith allow for a margin of error of a year or two, there is still a relatively small window of opportunity for a gymnast to excel once she reaches her mid-teens.[6]

IF YOU HAVE A PROSPECT

The first step toward success in gymnastics is to find a well-established program. If there are signs that your child or one you are working with has outstanding athletic talent, the program should be one that has proven itself at the Level 10 and Elite categories. The idea is to get the person into a program that allows him or her to go to the top.

Some programs are good at lower levels, but not at the Elite level. Children who stay in a lower-level program until the age of 12 and then try to make the switch to an Elite program often get flattened by the skill level required, the competition, and the number of hours expected of them. By getting into a system early that produces Level 9, 10, and Elite performers, a young child becomes familiar with the practice and competition routine, and progress can be monitored by coaches at upper levels. If the child turns out to have outstanding talent, he or she is in the right place to develop into a champion.

The number of hours required to reach the upper levels of gymnastics competition is intimidating to parents and athletes, and rightly so, considering the time and cost sacrifices that have to be made. In Eaton's Desert Devils program, serious gymnasts commit to 25 hours a week during the school year and 36 hours during the summer. Those athletes who are on the top team (out of approximately 1,000 gymnasts) pay $450 a month just for instruction. The number of hours and the costs vary at various facilities around the country, but the numbers will be close to those of the Arizona program.

Speed, strength, quickness, and flexibility are markers of talent in young gymnasts.

According to Eaton, exceptional gymnasts will have reached Level 9 or 10 by the time they reach the 9 to 12 age group. "They are almost at the top of their game and competing well at that level."

Most gymnasts also get dance training in the gymnastics club. Some, but not many, participate in second or third sports at the high school level. However, because of the huge time commitment required of gymnasts, those aspiring to become Elite or college-level competitors have to concentrate on one sport by the time they are juniors or seniors, if not sooner.

Karolyi on Prospects

"One of the biggest mistakes in gymnastics happens when parents take a promising young athlete to a self-serving coach. The coach tells them that their child is great, a future champion, and perhaps even one who will someday represent his or her country in international competition. I say that this self-serving because that is exactly what the parents want to hear.

"First of all, this is a flat-out lie. At that point, the coach has no idea of the emotional characteristics of the child. And the athlete who has physical talent but not the emotional qualities that are needed to succeed will experience incredible failure.

"Instead, any coach who is presented with a physically gifted athlete should be careful and straightforward with the parents. The coach should compliment the child and the parents on the progress made so far and explain that, if he or she rigorously follows a systematic program, the child may develop into a competitive athlete. To make claims beyond that is a disservice to everyone."

Talent Opportunity Program

USA Gymnastics has one of the most organized talent identification programs of all sports, the Talent Opportunity Program (TOPs) for girls between the ages of 7 and 12. It is certainly a pathway to success that all parents and coaches of gymnasts should consider. The goals and objectives of the program are summarized here:

- To identify talented young gymnasts between the ages of 7 and 12
- To notify parents, guardians, and coaches of talented gymnasts
- To assist coaches in the development of outstanding gymnasts
- To identify and remedy deficiencies in fitness and skill factors
- To enhance the flow of information and educational opportunities
- To place talented gymnasts on a fast track of development

Once athletes enter the TOPs program, they are tracked from year to year to see how they are progressing. Gymnasts in the 9- to 12-year-old age group are invited to participate in regional testing. Those who qualify can advance to a national test that is evaluated by the USA Gymnastics national staff. They are then ranked with other gymnasts their age across the nation. A select group of athletes is invited to attend a training camp at USA Gymnastics' expense. Coaches of TOPs participants are eligible to attend the national testing sessions and the national TOPs training camp.

The athlete must absorb some costs associated with participation in TOPs at the regional and national levels. The first is a physical examination by a physician. The second is a $35 entry fee for regional testing. In addition, the athlete has to pay for transportation, lodging, meals, and other expenses related to both regional and national test sites. The national TOPs training camp is completely funded by USA Gymnastics for qualified athletes, but personal coaches pay their own expenses.

The TOPs test includes specific gymnastics skills on each of the five apparatus: vault, bars, beam, floor, and dance. Several basic tests of strength, speed, and flexibility are given before the skills tests. Among them are the 20-meter run, push-ups, pull-ups, leg lifts, forward splits, and shoulder flexibility. Following are instructions for taking the tests and national norms for each. According to Dr. Sands, director of research and development for USA Gymnastics, those most likely to achieve outstanding success in the sport would probably rank in the 80th percentile or higher in each of the tests.[7,8]

20-Meter Sprint

65.5 feet

1. Gymnast assumes a position with one foot behind the starting line and the other against a wall or immovable object.
2. The administrator stands at the 20-meter finish line.
3. Start the watch when the gymnast's foot first strikes the floor past the starting line.
4. Stop the watch when any part of the body crosses the finish line.
5. Record the better of two attempts to a hundredth of a second.

Girls 10–14 years	Percentile
3.24	20%
3.14	50%
3.08	70%
3.04	80%

Tests adapted, with permission, from William A. Sands, PhD, director, research and development, USA Gymnastics.

Push-Ups

1. Start in an "up" position, arms extended, hands on the floor or mat.
2. Partner or tester places hand under the forehead of the gymnast.
3. Perform push-up in a straight-body position, lowering until forehead touches the hand of the tester.
4. Start a stopwatch when the gymnast makes the first movement downward.
5. Score the total number of successful repetitions completed in a 10-second period.

Girls 10–14 years	Percentile
11	20%
12	50%
13	70%
14	80%

Pull-Ups

1. Begin from a full hang, locked elbow, overgrip position.
2. Bend arms and shoulders to pull yourself upward.
3. Rise to position with chin above the bar.
4. Start the stopwatch when the gymnast makes first upward movement.
5. Record the number of pull-ups completed in 10 seconds.

Girls 10–14 years	Percentile
4	20%
5	50%
6	70%
7	80%

Leg Lifts

1. Begin in a hanging position grasping the upper rail of uneven parallel bars with both hands in an overgrip and body in full hip and shoulder extension.
2. Perform leg lift by bending at the hips to bring feet, ankles, or shins to touch the bar between the hands.
3. Legs remain straight throughout lift.
4. Start the stopwatch when the gymnast makes her first movement upward.
5. Record the number of leg lifts completed in 10 seconds.

Girls 10–14 years	Percentile
5	20%
6	50%
6	70%
7	80%

Splits—Left and Right

1. Assume a forward split position on the floor.
2. After checking posture, an assistant lifts the forward leg off the floor.
3. Movement ceases when the gymnast announces the limit of her range of motion or until the pelvis comes off the mat.
4. Measure the distance in inches from the bottom of the heel to the floor.
5. Repeat the procedure with the other leg.

Girls 10–14 years	Percentile
8.0	20%
10.9	50%
12.8	70%
13.9	80%

Active Shoulder Flexibility

1. Lie in a prone position on the floor with both arms stretched overhead.
2. Grasp a dowel with both hands (separated by touching the tips of the thumbs along the dowel).
3. Chin is in full contact with floor at all times, wrists straight.
4. Lift the dowel (and arms) into hyperflexion off the floor, keeping elbows straight.
5. Record the distance in inches from floor to bottom of dowel. Do not exceed 45 degrees.

Girls 10–14 years	Percentile
14.1	20%
17.6	50%
19.7	70%
21.0	80%

Vertical Jump

1. Begin by placing a generous amount of chalk on the dominant hand.
2. Standing with side pressed against a wall, reach with the dominant hand and touch the wall, leaving a smudge of chalk at the highest point.
3. Stand approximately 12 inches from the wall, arms lowered.
4. Jump by swinging arms, bending then extending legs, and jumping to make a mark on the wall at the height of the jump.
5. Record the distance in inches between the top edges of the two chalk marks.

Girls 10–14 years	Percentile
16.2	20%
18.1	50%
19.2	70%
19.9	80%

Future Stars

The boys' version of TOPs is called Future Stars. The goal of the Future Stars program is to identify talented athletes, their coaches, and clubs, and to provide them with educational and training support. The first year the Future Stars program targeted the 10- to 11-year-old age group; in 1997 a 12-year-old age group was added; and in 1998 an 8- to 9-year-old division was included.

The Future Stars program uses a special competitive routine format to evaluate the skill, strength, and flexibility development of the athlete. These routines are at the same time progressive, developmental, and educational. The intent is to identify talented athletes and to get them started on the right developmental path to national and international success. The Future Stars program and routines are also designed to enhance the regular age group competition program. Test norms are not available.

Future Stars athletes go to a regional evaluation that is also designed to be a learning experience. Qualified athletes progress to the Future Stars national championships held in the fall. The national championships are held in conjunction with a clinic for athletes and parents and include a national workshop for coaches.

Future Stars program and routine information can be found in the National Team Program Manual available through USA Gymnastics Member Services. More information about the specifics of the Future Stars program at the state and regional levels is available to coaches from their state chairman.[9]

WHAT COLLEGE COACHES LOOK FOR

"We start tracking gymnasts when they are freshmen and sophomores in high school," says Spini, "but a coach can't start writing them until they begin their junior year. We look for prospects in gymnastics clubs and at national meets.

"We hope that athletes we recruit can contribute immediately. In gymnastics, the older you get, the harder it is on your joints because of the pounding they take. In terms of aggressiveness, the freshman year can be the best over the course of a season, but at national championships freshmen are more likely to be inconsistent than upper classmen."

Smith, the associate head coach at ASU, coordinates the recruiting program. "We want the ones who are still excited about competing. At Level 10, there is a lot of burnout, so we look for those who still love to compete and who are at the peak of conditioning. They are still learning and progressing."

Arizona State carries from 7 to 14 members on a squad. Spini and Smith would be cautious about recruiting two types of gymnasts—those who have a history of injuries and those who don't compete well. Neither coach is particularly concerned about size. Members of their teams range from 5-0 to 5-9 in height and from 107 to 128 pounds. Says Spini, "I can have a kid who

College coaches prefer recruits who can compete in at least
three events but will take an exceptional one-skill athlete.

weighs 140 if she is strong and can move her body around and do the right
positions. That's fine with me, but judging is subjective and sometimes small
size helps."

Smith adds that the performance level at the college level is "spectacular."
Because the athletes are older, the skill level continues to increase throughout
the college career.

Arizona State and other elite college gymnastics programs prefer a recruit
who can compete in at least three events. But most schools will take a one-
skill athlete if she is really powerful or can score a 9.8 or better in her specialty.
Still, most college coaches want all-around athletes.

A WORD TO COACHES AND PARENTS

Sands says that finding a good coach and staying at home is very important to the development of a young gymnast. "I've seen it both ways (living at home and living at a site in another city or part of the country) and feel strongly that children need the support that a normal family atmosphere provides.

"Parents also need to recognize that anyone who is a high achiever goes through three stages, and that there is usually a different coach for each level," adds Sands. "The first stage is what I call a 'love level.' The coach may not know a heck of a lot, but he or she makes the sport fun and teaches the child to love the sport. The second-stage coach is a strict technician who teaches the nuts and bolts of the sport. This person is more like a dictator than a 'love level' coach. At the third level, the coach brings an artistic quality to the athlete by allowing her personality to show in her performance. This coach takes her to the pinnacle. A few coaches can change roles, but most of them who try get stuck at the dictator level.

"Unfortunately, training gets more expensive at each level. Not only that, but there are only a few upper-level coaches, and the outstanding athletes tend to gravitate toward them. These coaches get a lot of credit that they may not deserve because someone else has laid the groundwork for success."

Kristin Smith advises parents and coaches of talented athletes to keep them involved in the sport without burning them out. This may be easier said than done. She also emphasizes the need for parents to keep gymnasts healthy. The female triad of inadequate calorie intake, amenorrhea (absence of menstrual cycle), and later in life, osteoporosis is a concern of those who supervise and coach young female athletes, especially gymnasts. Finally, Smith tells parents, coaches, and the athletes themselves to get information, including tapes, resumes, and meet results, out to schools that they are interested in. This is especially important if the college or university is in another part of the country.

Whatever the training and coaching environment, parents need to be aware of the developmental process. In doing so they can recognize when a child is outgrowing a situation and find a program that suits his or her needs.

Chapter **15**

Hockey

*I*n a state where college football has a long and rich tradition, it is understandable that Ron Mason, head hockey coach at Michigan State, talks about hockey talent in football terms. "When you have the puck," he explains, "you are the quarterback. When you don't, you're the receiver. When the other team has the puck, you are either a defensive back or a lineman."[1]

Because hockey players have to play so many roles, those who evaluate talent emphasize the importance of reading, processing, and understanding the total game. The individual physical attributes are not valuable unless they can be implemented in the context of the game.

Dan Brennan, coordinator of coach and player skill development for USA Hockey, reinforces the "total game" concept in discussing speed, which is near the top of nearly every coach's talent wish list in his or her players. "There are speed tests for hockey players, but many coaches don't put a whole lot of stock in them. Some athletes can skate extremely fast, but when you put a puck in their hands, they are worthless. Their brains can't keep up with their feet."

Brennan adds that you can tell if a player "has something between the ears" at the peewee level (12 and under), but that doesn't guarantee that the player will blossom into a star later. It may not be until the bantam (14 and under) and midget (17 and under) levels that you get a good idea of whether he or she will continue to improve right through college.

"From a physical perspective," says Brennan, "a young player who is 5-10 and 130 may be kind of average until he is 16 or 17. All of a sudden, he grows to 6-2, 195, and the game is a lot easier than it used to be."[2]

EARLY INDICATORS

"Talent in players six to ten years old," says Tom Rennie, head coach of Canada's Men's Hockey Team, "may or may not manifest itself. But by the age of 13, you seem to be able to tell if a player is going to be something special. You may even see some exceptional skills earlier than that, but those skills are not likely to be predictors of success. Gifted young players still have to go through a maturation phase that can affect the whole developmental process.

"The player who is a great 9-year-old may not be great at 16. It happens all the time," continues Rennie. "On the other hand, a late bloomer may not have the game figured out at 16, but puts it all together at 19 or 20. I think it's fair to say that if some parts of the talent package are there, that is a pretty good indicator of what you might get at the other end of the process."[3]

Other hockey coaches agree with Rennie that enduring talent may emerge much later than in most other sports. "We can identify extraordinary talent at about the age of 15, but most players don't come into their own until they are 17 or 18," according to Bob O'Connor, national coach-in-chief for USA Hockey. "If players don't have good mechanics by the age of 15, they are unlikely to catch up with those who do."[4]

How late in starting is too late to become a talented hockey player? "There are always going to be late-blooming exceptions to the rule," declares Brennan, being very careful to leave that door open, "but I think that the child who isn't playing by the time he is six to eight years old will be behind the eight ball by two or three years from then on."

So, Brennan, Rennie, and O'Connor make the case that getting started early is important, but that gifted hockey players can take 10 years or longer to separate themselves from average players. What, in terms of skills, are they looking for?

Skating Skills

"The early indicators for me," says Rennie, "are (1) skating skills, (2) puck skills, and (3) how they process the game. Speed seems to be what catches your eye initially. You catch yourself thinking that if you could ever get your hands on an athlete with speed, you can fix the rest." Rennie wants the "quiet skater," the one who is light on the skates and who seems to skate with little effort.

Says O'Connor, "The number one skill is the ability to skate. That means moving in a tucked position similar to that of a skier coming down a hill, feet spread to about shoulder width, ankles titled slightly inward on the blades, knees pushed forward, buttocks in almost a sitting position, and hands out in front. Speed is important, but speed without quality technique is a waste of energy."

But O'Connor adds that it is difficult to measure skating skills at young ages. "The way hockey players hold their bodies and move is not natural," he explains. "It has to be taught before exceptional talent begins to show." He also looks for skaters who can shift weight from the inside edge of one skate to the opposite skate. If O'Connor is right, skating skills might be one of those dormant qualities that won't show until later.

Speed and Quickness

Rennie points out that hockey speed is different from hockey quickness. "Speed is something that shows itself over a distance or in a straight line. Quickness is something that you identify in small spaces—short-space hockey, I call it. Players show quickness in close quarters when the first two or three strides are explosive. Quickness doesn't always go with speed."

Puck Skills

Hockey coaches are looking for players who have the ability to control the puck as they skate in and out of traffic. They want to see how a player distributes and shoots the puck. O'Connor watches for young players who can handle the stick with their eyes up. They have good peripheral vision and the can make creative moves to get open as pass receivers.

In the United States and Canada, hockey has become a power game. "Even the way today's players hold the stick has changed (power hand lower on the stick)," says Brennan. "Players can shoot the puck a heck of a lot harder than they could 20 years ago. You see more power but less finesse."

Hockey coaches look first for skating skills and puck skills.

Rennie acknowledges that players in Europe seem to be more complete players than those in North America. "Canadians are criticized for being up-and-down players who lack a certain degree of imagination and creativity. Here, we identify with the emotion of playing hockey. In Europe, they identify with the artistry of playing hockey."

Brennan concurs that puck skills are missing in many of today's young players. "We have spent too much time involving kids in systems when they are very young. Now they think they have to play a certain position or certain style to succeed when they get older. That's a shame. They should be working on skating and puck skills, playing different positions, and getting an overall grasp of the game."

Processing the Game

Brennan's comment about getting a grasp of the game reflects the third of Rennie's criteria for hockey talent. Says Rennie, "Talented players process the game. They are able to take an inventory of what is happening and make wise decisions based on what they see."

O'Connor says that talented players continually read and react. "Too many kids are being taught to play hockey without having any idea why they are asked to do something on the ice. All great hockey players have spent time practicing by themselves. They never get enough ice time by just going to practices and games. In addition to structured time, they spend hours handling the puck, creating situations, and imagining themselves playing the game."

Size

"Size is becoming a huge factor," comments Brennan, "and, in some ways, that is detrimental to the sport. Everyone goes by the standard set by the National Hockey League, where the trend is toward bigger, taller players. The 6-2, 210-pound player will get a much better look than the one who is 5-10, 185. The smaller player may be faster and carry the puck better, but the pros are looking down the road. They will evaluate a player as being okay for a developmental level of the game, but they would rather have the bigger guy because he will be able to handle the rough going. This is not a fair judgment because the smaller player can be good, tough, durable, and can make the adjustment."

Rennie looks for strength as being an absolutely essential requirement in hockey players. Size does not necessarily correlate to strength, but many people interpret it that way. What is Rennie's ideal player in terms of size? "Between 6-0 and 6-2 in height and between 200 and 215 pounds, with all of the other athletic skills."

While the size factor may prohibit the pros from giving a player serious consideration, it does not apply at other levels. Says Michigan State's

Kramer, "I can take a kid who is 5-7, 5-9, or 5-11. It really doesn't matter as long as he is physically tough. Sometimes you have to surround a kid who is shorter with those who are bigger, but toughness and competitiveness are as important as size."

Toughness

Almost inherent in the talent package among hockey players is the quality of toughness. Mason describes tough players as the ones who are not shy, who drive to the net, and who "are willing to put their noses in there."

Goaltenders

One of the biggest changes in the game has come at the goaltending position. Goalies used to be the ones who didn't skate well or who didn't like going up and down the ice. Those days are over. The quality of play is better than ever because kids grow up wanting to be goalies and they are coached at early ages to play that position. Among the skills that talent evaluators now look for are skating skills, quickness, flexibility, and the ability to get up and down in a hurry. An elite goalie will have to demonstrate superior hand-eye and foot-eye coordination.

Quickness, competitiveness, and coordination are among the most important skills for goaltenders.

Mason thinks that quickness is the most important skill of goaltenders, but competitiveness is a close second. "The goalie had better be someone who is tough because there is going to be a lot of traffic around the front of the net."

O'Connor says that goaltenders have to be very good skaters in specific ways that relate to defending the goal—lots of up-and-back, side-to-side, and stop-start skills. Quick hands are imperative. As much as anything, he looks for goaltenders who have great courage.

USA HOCKEY NATIONAL TEAM TEST RESULTS

The data in table 15.1 provide an inside look at how the United States' best young hockey players measure up in tests of strength, power, and lean muscle tissue. The measurements include vertical jump, pull-ups, bench presses, cleans, squats, and percentage of body fat. The numbers were provided by USA Hockey and represent test results recorded by 16- and 17-year-old members of the USA Hockey National Team before the 1999 season.[5] Note that the 25-inch average vertical jump used to test lower-body power isn't particularly high, and that the 9.77 percent average of body fat is significantly lower than the average of nonathletes.

IF YOU HAVE A PROSPECT

Most of the hockey in the United States is club based. Players register for instruction in a USA Hockey initiation program and in competition that includes at least five age divisions. Coaches identify players who will be "in-house" or "travel team" in ability. Once players begin to develop their skills, people keep their eyes on them. Those at the local level feed information to officials and coaches at the national level.

Players in each of the 11 geographical districts administered by USA Hockey who are identified with the potential for being exceptional are invited to evaluation camps. From there, even fewer are selected for national junior teams. At some point during the developmental process, outstanding players are scouted at showcase and exposure camps by college coaches. Most of those camps are conducted during the summer months, and a few are held during school holiday breaks.

Although Brennan says that players should get into organized hockey instruction, if not play, by the time they are six to eight years old, he admits that burnout is a concern at USA Hockey. "Hockey used to be an eight- or nine-month sport. After that, you played another sport such as baseball, soccer, or lacrosse for a couple of months. Now, a kid can play hockey 11 months a year.

"I think you are going to start seeing burnout in hockey. Players are getting better because of increased opportunities, but we are worried that they will

Table 15.1   USA Hockey National Team Preseason Test Results—1999

Player	Vertical jump	Pull-ups	Bench	Cleans	Squats	Percent body fat
1	28.0	10	165	185	235	6.4
2	27.3	15	245	220	295	9.2
3	31.3	14	300	230	330	7.1
4	23.1	13	205	195	245	6.9
5	26.8	6	210	—	—	5.4
6	23.8	11	225	—	260	16.6
7	28.8	—	250	225	315	6.9
8	23.4	—	225	220	265	13.6
9	25.7	—	225	230	250	4.1
10	24.0	20	225	255	295	8.5
11	24.0	10	200	210	235	15.6
12	26.4	12	185	195	—	6.3
13	23.6	—	—	—	—	12.2
14	25.9	—	225	235	315	8.8
15	25.4	—	205	—	—	7.0
16	26.2	13	275	235	295	12.0
17	23.6	15	230	270	260	8.3
18	24.5	10	245	—	—	7.3
19	26.7	9	195	185	275	8.1
20	23.8	11	205	235	295	11.7
21	24.3	10	195	200	200	10.9
22	—	10	260	—	—	14.7
23	23.0	4	190	—	—	16.4
24	28.4	10	160	185	225	6.1
25	21.4	11	210	195	225	14.1
Average	25.39	10.74	218.96	216.94	267.50	9.77

start dropping out at a time when they are just beginning to refine their skills. I would rather see them go back to playing a nine-month season, then playing another sport or just being a kid for a couple of months."

Throughout the developmental years, Brennan encourages players to work on skating skills and to play at different positions. "Don't get cornered into specialty situations," he warns. "This is especially true for goaltenders. USA Hockey encourages coaches at the younger levels to give every player a chance to be a goalie. It also wants leagues to keep a supply of goaltending equipment that can be passed around rather than having parents spend hundreds of dollars, only to learn later that their child doesn't like it back there."

Mason tells parents to get their children on a team that gets ice time every day and that has a coach who teaches the fundamentals skills of the game and knows how to run a good practice. "Young players need to play enough games—and it doesn't have to be 100 games a year like some teams play—to test their skills at a level that will challenge them."

WHAT COLLEGE COACHES LOOK FOR

Most college coaches get interested in players as potential recruits at about 15 or 16. They find those players mostly in club hockey leagues and tournaments. Minnesota, Michigan, and a few other northern and northeastern states have high school hockey competition in which players can develop their skills and be seen by recruiters.

College coaches also look for players in other countries. On the 1999–2000 men's roster of the University of Massachusetts, 13 of the 30 players came from outside the United States. On Michigan State's roster, 12 of 24 were Canadian, and on the University of Denver team, 15 of 28 were foreign players. Other universities have different recruiting philosophies or rules. Every player on the University of Minnesota roster in 1999–2000 was a resident of that state. Notre Dame had only 2 foreign players of 26 on its team during the same season.

The qualities that college coaches seek are the same that coaches at other levels are looking for. Says Mason, "We want athleticism, someone who skates extremely well, and someone who handles the puck. Even by the time they get to college, they haven't fully developed an understanding of the game, so you have to rely a lot on physical talents and potential."

George Gwozdecky, head hockey coach at the University of Denver, says that some things catch your eye in a player who may not be the fastest or the best shooter. "He does things that turn your head, like making a pass that no one else on the rink could make, or he goes in against two players and comes out with the puck. A goaltender might make an unbelievable save on a rebound when he was completely out of position."[6]

Do college hockey coaches take chances on players? "We have to take a chance on talent," says Mason. "There is a great deal of development from the time they get here at 17 or 18 until the time they leave at 21 or 22. There is a lot we can do with them during that four- to five-year period. How far they go depends on how hard they are willing to work."

Gwozdecky tells the story of a player who was competing at what he describes as perhaps the worst level in junior hockey history. "He was almost lost in the recruiting process because no one ever went to see him play. We signed him because he had pretty good hockey skills. He went on to become an All-American and now plays in the National Hockey League."

Two things will scare recruiters off of seemingly good players. Mason looks carefully at a player's history of injuries, but Gwozdecky does not. He shies away from players who don't display intensity. Asks Gwozdecky, "Does he go on the ice and try to win every shift or does he kind of float around?"

Although college hockey players vary widely in height and weight, compelling evidence suggests that they are big and getting bigger. The roster information on six NCAA Division I universities in table 15.2 shows that 67 percent of players (107 of 160) were six feet or taller and 82 percent (131 of 160) weighed at least 180 pounds.[7]

One thing that is encouraging for prospective college players is that the squads are relatively large. Division I schools can give up to 18 scholarships that can be divided among up to 30 players on a roster. Michigan State carries 26 players—3 goaltenders, 8 defensemen, and 15 forwards. Mason dresses 20 players for games, including 2 goaltenders. At Denver, usually up to 10 players are either walk-ons or play on partial scholarships.

Table 15.2   Height and Weight of Male College Hockey Players—1999-2000

University	Height range	>6-0	Weight range	>180 lbs
Denver	5-9 to 6-5	19/28	165 to 215	23/28
UMass	5-8 to 6-4	18/30	170 to 220	25/30
Michigan	5-8 to 6-3	17/26	172 to 220	18/26
Michigan State	5-7 to 6-3	14/24	154 to 219	19/24
Minnesota	5-8 to 6-3	19/26	160 to 213	21/26
Notre Dame	5-10 to 6-4	20/26	170 to 230	25/26

Women's Hockey: A View From New Hampshire

Probably because of the television exposure that the National Hockey League gets and because of the success of North American national women's teams at the international level, hockey is becoming the sport of choice for many talented female athletes in the United States and Canada.

Karen Kay, women's hockey coach at the University of New Hampshire, gets more than her share of talented players. Here are some of Kay's thoughts on women's hockey at the college level.

Q: *How large is the pool of talent in women's hockey?*

A: The number of gifted players is gradually increasing. Ten years ago, college recruiting was mostly done at the regional level. In most parts of the country, there weren't opportunities for girls to play. At New Hampshire, we have had players from places like Alaska, California, and Texas. One of our goalies is from Miami. We didn't used to see that.

(continued)

Women's Hockey: A View From New Hampshire *(continued)*

Q: *How many college programs offer women's hockey?*

A: In 2000 there were 26 Division I programs. If you count Division II and III programs, there were more than 60 women's teams, and we expect those numbers to increase.

Q: *When do you start getting interested in players as potential recruits?*

A: We begin to track their progress from the time they are in the ninth grade, but we can't talk to them until July 1st before their junior year.

Q: *What are you looking for in off-the-ice characteristics?*

A: We place an emphasis on the academic part of being a student-athlete. Because there is no professional hockey, the highest you can go is the Olympics. We want to make sure they can handle things in the classroom, that they choose the right major, that they have character, and that they are well-rounded individuals.

Q: *What are you looking for athletically?*

A: The women's game is changing. We are looking for athletes who have spent a little more time in the weight room or who are willing to spend time there once they get here. We also recruit from quality scholastic and club programs. That way, we know that they have had a fundamentally sound training program and that they have probably been in the sport longer.

Q: *Does size matter?*

A: Some coaches don't think it's important because there is no full checking in women's hockey. I think, because of the way the sport is developing, size is a factor. The higher you go, the more important it is. If you play on a small rink, size is really important. If you play on a large rink like we do, speed is as important as size. I consider 5-6 or taller to be a good height, but we have players who are 5-2 and very athletic. Given the choice between two players of equal ability, I would probably take the one who is bigger.

Q: *What would make you take a chance on a player?*

A: If our coaches think a player has potential, we'll recruit her. If they are deficient in skills but have a good conceptual understanding of the game, we'll take a chance. And we would take a player who is a great athlete, but who didn't start playing hockey until she was 14 or 15.

Q: *What would scare you off a player?*

A: There are two or three red flags. One is a person who is not comfortable with the players we already have. She can be the greatest player in the world, but if she is going to be disruptive, she won't help the program. We might also pass on a player who has a history of serious injuries or one who stood out on a team that never was successful.

Q: *Are there any particular weaknesses in the players that reach your level?*

A: The lack of upper-body strength is the most common physical weakness. The ability to manage time and adjust to the college routine are major weaknesses that have to be addressed off the ice.

Q: *What advice would you give to parents of promising players?*

A: Parents have to make some difficult decisions about sending their daughters off to cities or prep schools that will give them the opportunity to develop their skills. I'm not saying that they have to do this to be successful, but they should consider the possibility if geography is an obstacle to success. Otherwise, I would tell parents to encourage their children to get to regional camps so they have a chance to be selected for the 16- and 17-year-old national junior camps.[8]

A WORD TO PARENTS

Brennan gives this advice to parents of talented players: "Don't overload your child with false expectations. I am against telling a 12- or 13-year-old that he or she has a real future in the game. They are too young to accept that kind of compliment. Keep doing what you are doing. See to it that they have the opportunity to work hard and enjoy the game at the same time. As they move up in the ranks, you and your children will get a better understanding of where they are and where they can go in hockey."

Gwozdecky advises parents to see that their kids get to play a lot of hockey, including going to camps that don't emphasize scrimmaging more than time spent working on fundamental skills. He also warns that by the time they are juniors in high school, families may have to consider allowing talented players to move to an area of the country where the level of hockey is high enough to allow them to develop.

O'Connor gets the last word. "Regardless of physical ability," he says, "long-term success will depend on a player's motivation to succeed and the amount of emotional control he or she possesses. My advice for parents of exceptional players is to let coaches coach, let players play, and focus your efforts on being a good parent."

Chapter **16**

Soccer

*T*he skills and characteristics that make up a successful soccer player are not as easy to pin down as those in other sports. Those attempting to identify and evaluate soccer talent generally run up against three problems. First, talent in this sport is not a fixed asset; it is dynamic and elusive. Ability that is apparent today may be gone tomorrow. A player of average talent at the age of 12 may end up on a national team at 18.

"Not only do things change during that five-year span, they can change from year to year and even from game to game," says Tom Hart, director of coaching education for United States Youth Soccer. "Chronological age does not necessarily match up with motor skill development or cognitive ability."[1]

"The second problem," thinks Dave Simeone, women's national team staff coach for the United States Soccer Federation, "is that a big part of evaluating talent is the genius (or lack of it) of the coach doing the evaluating. The person who evaluates soccer talent has to have a vision of what a player will be in the future. This is especially important for college coaches, who get players when they are much closer to the finished product."[2]

What Simeone implies, but does not say, is that parents and others who are either not objective or not trained in evaluating soccer talent make mistakes. Parents tend to look at what their kids do in a static environment. A player may be able to dribble through a line of cones, but where do you do that in a game? Even an untrained eye can see that some players don't have all of the physical skills, but the experienced coach or scout looks at the way they solve problems, how they sort things out on the field.

Parents can easily get caught up in the success or failure of a young player and make bad decisions regarding present or future ability. Evaluation of talent starts at the grassroots level of soccer competition and training and continues upward all the way to national coaches, scouts, and teams. Good players get noticed. Soccer has a well-constructed system that does not let talented players slip through the cracks.

The third problem with evaluating soccer talent is that players almost have to be evaluated in the context of competition. While this is true to a certain extent in any sport, it seems to be extremely important in soccer.

"You can't qualify talent by how players perform on a 1–5 checklist of skills," says Simeone. "You can get two players, tell them to move the ball back and forth, and it looks good. But when you put those same two players in a game during which the picture is constantly changing, you get an entirely different perspective on the athletes. Every skill in soccer has an application factor. Players have to figure out how a skill applies to a game situation. The litmus test is the game itself. The game is the teacher and the indicator of talent."

Simeone sees competitiveness as a talent and worries that the present generation of soccer players is not very competitive. "The source of free play in all sports has dried up. Neighborhood sandlot games used to be the breeding ground for competitive athletes. Six-year-olds could watch and play and learn from ten-year-olds. They not only learned soccer skills, but also social skills. And they learned how to compete. Now, everything is planned and supervised. To a great extent, soccer lacks the competitiveness that the street game can offer. As a result, one of the characteristics of talented players is getting harder to find."

EARLY INDICATORS

Given all of these warnings from experts about the difficulties in identifying talent, it is still possible to do so. The first indicators, at any age, are the physical ones. How fast can a player run? How high can she jump? How quick is he? How strong? Athleticism is important, especially when it shows up in dribbling, passing, or collecting the ball.

Physical Assessment Tests

Physical skills have been observed and measured in age-group players and on the U.S. Soccer Federation's national teams. The instructions for two of these tests and the norms that have been established are presented on pages 198–199. Both of them can be administered without sophisticated equipment. Two additional tests (the yo-yo intermittent recovery and 7 × 30-meter recovery) require equipment that is not readily available. The test results shown here are for the purpose of comparison. They are not to be used improperly by parents or others who are not trained to interpret test results.[3]

The average vertical jump by members of the men's national under-18 team was 25.98 inches. The average vertical jump for women under 21 was

Experienced soccer coaches and scouts observe the ways players solve problems in the context of games.

20.80 inches. The highest jump for a member of the men's national team was 36 inches. The highest jump by a member of the women's national team was 30 inches.

The average time on the Illinois Agility Run of the men's national under-18 team was 17.34 seconds. The average time for women under 21 was 16.68. The best performance on the test by a member of the men's national team was 13.47. The fastest time recorded by a player on the women's national B team was 14.79.

Vertical Jump

U.S. national team players

1. Stand sideways to a Vertec (measuring device) or to a wall marked with tape and reach straight up with the arm closest to the Vertec.
2. Measure the distance from the ground to the wands of a Vertec or to taped markers on a wall. Place markers every inch between 10 feet and 10 feet, six inches.
3. Using a one-step approach, jump off both feet and reach as high as possible at the top of the jump.
4. Subtract the highest jump measurement from the standing reach.
5. Record the best of three trials.

Girls/Women	Vertical jump (in)
Elite University	20.17
U21	20.80
National Team	22.19

Boys/Men	Vertical jump (in)
U16	24.03
U17	25.81
U18	25.98
U20	27.74
U23	27.90
National Team	26.38

Illinois Agility Run

1. Starting position on stomach; hands and feet off the ground at flag 1.
2. Clock starts on first movement.
3. Run and circle flag 2, then around flag 3 at the bottom of the 10-foot by 10-foot box, zigzig through 4, 5, around 6, and zigzag back through 5, 4, and around 3, up and around 7, and down to finish at 8 (see figure).
4. Allow two trials.
5. Record better of two times.

Girls/Women	Illinois Agility Run times (sec)
U13	18.71
U14	19.11
U15	17.79
U16	18.62
U18	18.77
National Team	16.20

Boys/Men	Illinois Agility Run times (sec)
U12	18.62
U13	17.93
U14	17.62
U15	17.34
U16	17.68
National Team	15.33

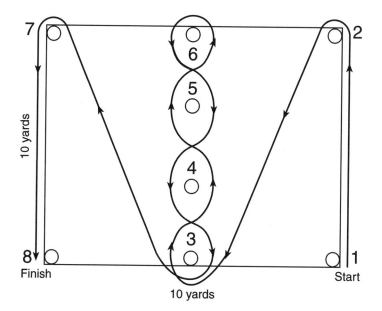

Thanks to the many players who underwent these tests over the past four years and especially to Carolina United SC and all of the national team coaches who allowed access to their players. Tony DiCicco, U.S. women's national coach (1995–2000), deserves special thanks for his help in initiating this testing program. This project is funded by the U.S. Soccer Federation and grants from NIKE, Inc., and the United States Olympic Committee Sports Science and Technology program.

Size

"Everybody is the same height when the ball is on the ground," Hart reassures those who worry about size in soccer players. "Being bigger and stronger is an advantage, but a small, fast player may be more valuable than a taller but slower player. Height is only an advantage when the ball is up in the air. If players realize that they are not going to get control of many balls that are in the air, they have to find a way to work around it."

"At the professional level," says Hart, "a goalkeeper is seldom shorter than 5-10 because it would be pretty difficult to play balls in the air. It's also unusual to see one taller than 6-3 because he would be more likely to give up some quickness and agility." Hart adds that because of rules changes, goalkeepers now have to develop skills as field players. They have to use their feet, demonstrate lateral movement, and catch the ball cleanly.

April Kater, head women's soccer coach at Syracuse, points out that goalies in the women's game have to be great athletes. "It's harder for the female goalkeeper than for the male because she is defending against the same size ball on the same size field in the same size goal. If she is not tall, she'd better have great footwork and be smart about communication and cutting down angles."[4]

GORMAN'S KEYS TO TALENT

Barry Gorman, head men's soccer coach at Penn State, watches for the five pillars of the game reflected in the following elements of talented players:

- Technical (passing, dribbling, receiving, shooting)
- Tactical (using technical skills in game situations)
- Physical (speed, strength, endurance, coordination, balance)
- Psychological (maintaining emotional control under stressful conditions)
- Lifestyle (work habits, nutrition, rest, balance between soccer and other activities)[5]

In the Netherlands, this TIPS formula is used to identify talent: technique, intelligence (soccer), personality, and speed. Speed keeps coming up as the essential quality that separates great players from good players. If a player is lacking in speed, he or she had better have exceptional technique in passing, receiving, and dribbling the ball.

IF YOU HAVE A PROSPECT

Soccer experts agree that at the ages of 12 and under, the emphasis should be on simply playing the game. United States Youth Soccer doesn't even test fitness of players under the age of 12. "Eight- and nine-year-olds don't want to run laps," says Hart. "They just want to come out and play. Unfortunately, not enough coaches let them play. They try to orchestrate everything. We spend a lot of time trying to get coaches to facilitate progress rather than inhibiting it with too much structure."

The developmental process starts with kids who want to play, and most of them start in a recreation league. Everybody gets to play, regardless of ability. As players get older and better, there are opportunities to participate on school, club, travel, or elite teams. High school soccer is an important part of the development process, but few college coaches recruit solely on the basis of high school competition. Making club and elite teams usually involves at least one, and sometimes two or three, tryout sessions.

What Happens at a *Tryout Session*

"The tryout process is a little like a cattle call," warns Simeone, "but we do everything possible to be selective about who attends. Still, there could be 60 players at a Sunday afternoon tryout session that lasts two hours.

"The first part of the session usually includes some warm-up activities and a few drills designed to demonstrate technical skills," he continues. "Then we organize 'small-sided' games with three, four, or five players on a team. With small sides, small fields, and goals that are close, the decision-making

A goalkeeper needs good hands, quick feet, and the ability to move laterally.

process is more frequent. We get to see lots of moments that tell us how players react. The session usually ends with bigger games that may involve the entire field and 11 players on each side. At some camps, players are notified on the spot about who makes the team. Other places send letters to those who have been chosen. I think the first method is better."

Simeone explains that it is not uncommon at tryouts for as many as 70 percent of the participants to be central players. They are usually the best ones on a team, which is the reason they are trying out for a higher level of competition. But those same players may have the skills to play other positions and may be selected because of those skills. He advises players to be as relaxed as possible, not to worry on a minute-by-minute basis about how they are doing, and to be open to playing positions that they might not be accustomed to playing.

"Even if they don't make the cut," Hart adds, "tryout experiences are incredibly valuable. It is important just to go through the process and to get the exposure. I've known players who've been cut off the Olympic team three times who made it in the end. Sometimes it takes the scouts and coaches that long to figure out what each player possesses to make a contribution at the next level."

Olympic Development Program

More than 20 years ago, United States Youth Soccer established an Olympic Development Program to identify outstanding players in each of five age groups on a continuing basis. From the players who are identified, a national team is selected.

In most states, players are selected on the basis of open tryouts. The tryouts are conducted by state association coaches who are recognized for their ability to identify and train players with superior skills. Players are evaluated on the following four components:

• Technique
• Tactics
• Fitness and athletic ability
• Psychological component

U.S. Soccer is divided into four regions—East, South, Midwest, and West—each of which offers a regional camp for state association Olympic Development teams in each eligible age group. The camps are designed to provide high-level competition and training for participating players. During the training and competition, players who are capable of performing at a higher level of play are identified for possible national team camp, pool, or team participation.

National camps and interregional events are held throughout the year at various locations in the United States. The national team coach or a national staff coach is present at these events to observe, train, and identify players for placement in the national pool or on a national team. Players receive the following benefits from participating in the Olympic Development Program:[6]

• The opportunity to train and play with the best players
• Quality competition
• Exposure to regional and national team coaches
• The opportunity to represent one's state, region, or country
• Exposure to college coaches

WHAT COLLEGE COACHES LOOK FOR

"We tell soccer players that they have to have a strong suit—something they can do better than others," says Penn State's Gorman. "Very few will have the whole package, but we look for one part of their games that sets them apart. It could be passing, dribbling, heading, finding the goal, or any other skill. However, 'first touch' ability is critical. Can he cushion the ball, stay with it, and do it at full speed?

"We don't pay much attention to players on high school teams. Instead, we find them on good club teams and in the Olympic Development Program. A lot of our evaluation is subjective, but we want to see how players compete with and against other players of equal talent. We can observe competitive skills among the players on select travel teams that compete in regional and national tournaments."[7]

Kater says that the recruiting process has become more aggressive and that the talent identification process has started earlier. "There are many more opportunities for kids to play and get exposure—probably five times as many club team tournaments now as there were 10 years ago. I make mental notes when I see a prospect at the sophomore level. I also watch for great young athletes who are not great soccer players. We kind of keep our eyes on players with potential to see how they grow and progress over a two- or three-year period."

Kater is not afraid to take a chance on a player. "I love players who may be missing some part of the game, even when they get to the college level. This is especially true at schools that are building programs. Those schools are not going to get blue chip superstars. They have to rely on athletes who are

After the age of 17 or 18, it is very hard to change bad habits.

lacking in technical areas, but who are good enough by their senior years to beat those who were better soccer players earlier."

Ron Quinn, EdD, head women's soccer coach at Xavier University in Cincinnati, agrees with Kater that the kind of player that is being recruited depends on the strength of the program. "We are far enough along at Xavier that our top two or three recruits should be able to step right in and contribute immediately. But a program like the one at the University of North Carolina, which is laden with talent, is different. They can graduate a great player and move an underclassman up who is just as good."[8]

Gorman starts tracking prospects when they are in their freshman year of high school, but waits until the sophomore year before following them closely. "By that time," he explains, "the ones who may have been smaller are starting to catch up physically. Soccer lends itself to players of all shapes and sizes, but players are getting bigger and stronger. Exceptional soccer players have separated themselves from others by the time they are 17 or 18. After that, it is very hard to change bad habits."

Beswick on Soccer Talent

"Signs of developing players must include physical, technical, tactical, mental, emotional, and lifestyle attributes. The positives must exceed negatives so that the profile is one of great strengths that can be developed and weaknesses that can be managed. Key emotional characteristics include a desire to achieve, a capacity to learn, an attitude to practice, dogged self-confidence, and game-playing intelligence. Talented players must also exhibit composure under pressure, mistake management, and the ability to accept criticism and responsibility. I agree with John Wooden that talent opens the door, but character keeps you in."[9]

—Bill Beswick, Consultant,
Manchester United Football Club

Warning Signs

What would scare a college coach off a high school player? "There are a few things that would scare us off good players," explains Gorman. "One is when we get bad reports concerning attitude or behavior. Another is the player who has peaked too early. We also try to find players who are competing for the right reasons. We want a kid who enjoys playing, not one who is playing just to get a scholarship."

Quinn, who is also an associate professor in the Department of Sports Studies at Xavier, would also be cautious about recruiting any player with an attitude problem. "She might be talented, but not very motivated. I'd rather have players with a great deal of desire than ones who try to get by on talent alone. A coach can improve technique, but if players don't have that inner drive, you can only go so far with them."

Weaknesses

At the risk of making unfair generalizations, Quinn observes three technical weaknesses in women soccer players as a group. "Heading is one area that is not as strong in women as in men. The second possible deficiency is strength, but high schools are getting better at developing strength in women athletes. The third weakness is related to the strength factor. It is a deficiency in playing long balls. Men can serve the ball long distances. We need to extend the women's game, for example, so that they can send the ball from one side of the field to the other."

A WORD TO PLAYERS AND PARENTS

"We advise players to learn to work on their own," says Gorman. "Too many of today's players think they can get it all done in practice. Don't leave anything to chance. Touch the ball every day. Every outstanding player I have met spent a lot of time practicing by himself. To be a real player, you have to see the game in your mind's eye, then invent games and situations by yourself."

"Ideal soccer parents let their children make it on their own," he adds. "They can't play for their children. I've never met a parent who had four years of eligibility. I tell them to be a facilitator by encouraging their children to practice, providing the bare essentials, then getting out of the way."

"Let the child dictate the pace of development," says Hart. "If she wants to do two days of soccer and two days of another sport, let her do it. There are benefits of basketball, volleyball, and baseball skills that will pay off in soccer at 16."

"Parents have to understand the difference between being supportive and being pushy," states Hart. "Anybody under the age of 13 is still playing for the fun of the game. They may fantasize about playing college or professional soccer, but they are simply playing a game. The minute they perceive that soccer is work, they are headed toward burnout. I can't tell you how many kids I thought were going to be great but didn't make it," he concludes. "Keep the whole thing in perspective."

Simeone adds his final word for parents who are tempted to become too involved: "If you don't know a whole lot about soccer, thank your lucky stars. The more some parents think they know, the more likely they are to try to orchestrate their children's soccer careers. If your children are still playing by the time they get to be teenagers, take a step back. Sooner or later, they have to be able to stand alone and figure things out for themselves."

Kater gets the last word for parents on recruiting, and it is a strong message: "Don't dictate the process, don't manipulate the process, and don't facilitate the process. If I have a parent who is contacting me more than the player, that is a turnoff. The student-athlete has to take responsibility into her own hands."

Chapter **17**

Softball

"The best player at 8 years old will be the best at 12, at 16, and at 20," declares Larry Mays, the Southern California coach whose Gold teams have won 11 national championships. Mays's position is radically different from that of most coaches in other sports. Predicting future performance on the basis of current performance levels is risky, but Mays doesn't waiver from his position. He has 20 years of national and international experience to back up his views.

"Word gets out pretty quickly on talented players when they are as young as 7 or 8," Mays says. "Some children have innate ability that shows up in games and in offensive and defensive drills. We'll hear about a 9-year-old pitcher who is throwing 53 or 54 miles per hour or an 11-year-old who can throw in the upper 50s."[1]

Cheri Kempf, who operates Club K & Co., a softball training facility near Nashville, Tennessee, disagrees with Mays regarding talent, particularly as it applies to pitchers. "The super talent at 10 who can blow pitches past hitters often becomes a victim of her own success. She gets so much positive feedback, there is a temptation to neglect developing pitching technique and other pitches. At 13, 50 mph pitches are coming back at her at the same speed and she is devastated. When we see talent at a young age, we spend a lot of time with parents to work with their children on developing their ability."[2]

EARLY INDICATORS

Because fast-pitch softball is dominated by pitchers, coaches don't wait very long to look for good ones. And most of them are encouraged to use the windmill motion from the start. The thinking is, Why let them use the sling motion when they are young and have to learn a completely different style later?

How hard do they throw? Table 17.1 provides some guidelines for evaluating pitching velocity among girls from 8 to 18. The numbers are based on speeds recorded by more than 350 athletes and were supplied by Cheri Kempf, owner of Club K & Co.[3]

"In California," says Mays, "we might have three high school girls who can throw 65 miles per hour. Then there will be a dozen who can throw at 63 to 64 and a large group that can pitch in the 59 to 61 range. In the whole country there might be three women who get into the upper 60s.

"I don't even want to see anyone whose parents tell me that their child has more than three pitches. If a pitcher has 12 pitches, that means she has 12 pitches with slightly different spins, none of which are good. You can't get good throwing that many pitches."

Mays has more to say about pitchers. "They should have a drop, a rise, and a change-up. That's it. Curves are not even in our playbook. We have lost more national championships on curves than any other pitch. Our pitchers might throw a curve every 30 or 40 pitches. Some talented athletes may develop a drop screw that goes into the knees of a right-handed batter or a drop curve that goes away, but that would happen later rather than earlier."

The pitcher can be either the best athlete on the team or the worst. If she is the worst, she is usually big and not that coordinated, but has worked extremely hard to become a good pitcher. The bigger the player, the longer the arm, which is good for generating speed. If the pitcher is the best player on the team, she can play any position but is most valuable as a pitcher.

Apart from pitchers, who may or may not be great athletes, outstanding talent finds its way to the shortstop position. Because shortstops require

Table 17.1 Pitching Velocities (mph)

Age	High	Average
8	31	29
9	43	32
10	48	38
11	56	42
12	53	46
13	58	48
14	59	50
15	65	51
16	63	53
17	64	53
18	65	54

Adapted, with permission, from Cheri Kempf.

Great softball pitchers need a drop, a rise, and a change-up, but not necessarily a curve.

a greater variety of skills and touch the ball as much or more than any other player, it makes sense to put the best player in the middle of the action.

The other early indicators of softball talent are not that different from other sports. In this game of speed and especially quickness, the child who exhibits those two qualities plus good hand-eye coordination has a future. As in baseball, if a player doesn't have quick feet and quick hands, she had better be able to produce power at the plate.

The psychological qualities that set great young softball talent apart from others are aggressiveness, competitiveness, and resilience. Talented young players don't mind getting dirty. They want to beat you in everything, not just softball. And if they lose or play poorly, they can't wait to get back out there. Those that don't exhibit these qualities fall into a lower talent pool.

Kempf thinks that confidence is one of the intangibles that sets great talent apart from lesser talent. "When you are talented and athletic ability comes naturally, that builds unbelievable confidence. It starts to happen without everyone else realizing what is going on, whether it's in practice, games, or gym classes. Eventually, the talented one goes into a situation confident in her ability. Nine girls are not sure whether or not they can perform; that tenth one knows she can do it."

Tests of Softball Ability

Softball generally uses only three measurable tests of ability. One is pitching velocity, which has already been discussed. The second is the time that it takes for a catcher to receive the ball, get it out of her mitt, and get it to the second baseman or shortstop covering the bag. Anything under 2.0 seconds is great. Table 17.2 shows average and fastest times from catcher to second (throw-downs) recorded by girls in five age groups at a Club K & Co. camp.[4]

The third measure of talent is speed, which some coaches measure by recording the time it takes to run from home to first base. Under three seconds, from either the left or right side of the plate, is quality speed. The range will be from 2.9 to 3.5. Many coaches don't place an emphasis on home-to-first time because of the margin of error in timing. With a range of 0.6 seconds, there is too much chance of timer error. Technique in handling a stopwatch could make the difference between average and great speed. Speed is also measured by the time it takes to run completely around the bases—home to home.

Table 17.3 gives home-to-first times of players enrolled in Club K & Co. lessons and camps. Table 17.4 shows home-to-home times. In both tests, players can hit off a tee or they can hit tossed balls. The clock starts with the first step toward first base and stops when the player touches the bag (or the plate) with either foot.[5]

Table 17.2   Throw-Down Times, Girls, Ages U10–U18

Age	Average	Fastest
10 and under	3.24	2.50
12 and under	2.21	2.12
14 and under	2.18	1.98
16 and under	2.18	1.95
18 and under	1.94	1.77

Adapted, with permission, from Cheri Kempf.

Table 17.3   Home-to-First Times of Players, Ages 9–16

Age	Average	Fastest
9	3.86	3.48
10	3.78	3.35
11	3.43	2.90
12	3.39	3.01
13	3.41	3.11
14	3.32	2.90
15	3.15	3.03
16	3.46	3.40

Adapted, with permission, from Cheri Kempf.

Table 17.4   Home-to-Home Times of Players, Ages 9–16

Age	Average	Fastest
9	16.29	14.47
10	16.41	15.47
11	15.00	13.05
12	14.67	12.91
13	14.77	13.38
14	14.00	12.18
15	13.31	13.13
16	14.06	13.50

Adapted, with permission, from Cheri Kempf.

IF YOU HAVE A PROSPECT

The developmental path for young softball players is fairly predictable. "They should start playing on recreation teams at the local level," says Mays. "At the second level, good players should start thinking about playing up. If they are 7, they might play with 8-year-olds, for example. At the age of 9 or 10, they can think about playing for club teams. During the first couple of years of club ball, they should try to make a team for which they will get to play. Don't go for the best team out there and sit on the bench. That's not the way to be seen."

Timing is critical in trying to make the rosters of travel teams. Some parents call in May to get a player on a summer team, which is far too late. In fact, even January of that year is probably too late. The recruiting process for club teams starts as early as the fall of the previous year. Get in touch with coaches and teams who are looking for players during August and September to get lined up for fall ball, winter ball, and summer softball for the next year.

At 12 or 13, find the best team and the best coach available, even if your child won't be one of the team's best players. If a player is good, they will find her. The players who make the top five travel teams in their areas are on their way. College coaches will follow those teams. Club softball dominates the sport, but playing high school softball is a must. Even if you are on a bad team or have a coach who is not the best, it's important to get that two hours of practice every day.

Most talented players participate on high school teams during the academic year and play an intensive schedule of summer softball. Summer programs offer a higher level of competition and more games in a shorter period. As much or more college recruiting goes on during the summer as during the school year, when college coaches are busy with their own teams.

The Amateur Softball Association and the National Softball Association are two of the largest organizations that provide competition and training for promising players. They also provide a showcase for especially talented athletes to make national and international teams. The ASA sponsors the Junior Olympic program. In 1999, 83,000 teams and more than one million players participated in ASA/JO events. Competition begins at the 10-and-under level and continues through a 23-and-under fast-pitch championship for women. Local organizations sponsor events for younger ages. There are slow-pitch and fast-pitch tournaments for boys and girls, but the emphasis has clearly been placed on fast-pitch competition for girls and women.[6]

While summer tournaments and travel teams provide opportunities for development as a player, they also draw parents, coaches, and players into a training and competition cycle that can be counterproductive. "It's crazy," warns Tallahassee Community College head softball coach Maria Mendoza. "Some of these girls play 60 games during a summer from the time they are 10 or 11 years old. There is no time for being a kid. By the time they get to college, they are burned out."[7]

Find a team and a program for your child that offers a balanced approach. The emphasis should be on making the experience enjoyable; on developing fundamental hitting, fielding, and throwing skills; and on offering a sensible, manageable schedule of games. Build in some down time during the year. Plenty of great athletes get away from their primary sport at regular intervals. They either take a complete break or play another sport.

Realistically, a majority of girls who play softball have about a six- to eight-year window of serious involvement. If they start too early, are pushed too hard, or have bad coaches that make the experience a negative one, they will use up their six to eight years by the time they are teenagers. It's called burnout. If they start later and gradually develop their skills and interest, they are likely to play the sport longer. Two other obstacles that take potential stars out of the game are cars and boys, not necessarily in that order.

WHAT COLLEGE COACHES LOOK FOR

"With the possible exception of pitchers and catchers, we want well-rounded athletes who can play more than one position," says Carie Dever-Boaz, head women's softball coach at the University of Arkansas. "Positions are not as set as you would think, even at the Division I level. A coach might think that every position is taken care of, but injuries, dropouts, and academic problems can result in needs that you don't anticipate. It's nice to have players who can fill in or even become starters at several positions."[8]

DePaul coach Eugene Lenti agrees. "Players don't stay at the same position before they get to college, and they move around while they are here. Versatility is an advantage."[9]

Catchers are leaders and communicators, but they need quick feet and a quick release.

Dever-Boaz and Lenti both start to identify college prospects early—Dever-Boaz between the sophomore and junior years, Lenti while they are freshmen (he actually starts a file on each player he is interested in during her first year of high school play). At Arkansas, the coaches make out their "dream list" of players during the summer before the junior year. No coach at the NCAA Division I level can have verbal contact with players (in terms of recruiting) before July of the summer before the senior year.

Position-by-Position Tools

What skills do college coaches want at each position? Table 17.5 gives a summary of position-by-position requirements suggested by coaches Mendoza, Dever-Boaz, and Lenti.

No college coach expects to get the five-tool player (hit, hit with power, speed, arm, defense) very often, if ever. There just aren't many of them out there. Lenti tries for the three-tool player. Mendoza says that every player

Table 17.5   Skills Required at Each Position

Position	Skills
Catchers	Good footwork
	Ability to frame pitches, block the ball
	Quick release (glove-to-glove <2.0 sec)
	Leadership and communication skills
	Interact well with pitchers
Pitchers	59–61 mph velocity as high school senior
	Ability to change speed
	Two or more pitches
	Control
Middle infielders	Foot speed; lateral movement
	Quickness
	Good hands; get ball out of glove
	Quick release
	Shortstop may be best athlete
1st–3rd basemen	Good glove
	1st baseman has to know position
	Power hitters
	Lateral movement in one direction only
Outfielders	Speed
	Strong arm
	Power or slap hitting ability
	Ability to read ball

has something to work on and that almost all players have difficulty making the transition from high school to college ball. "All of them are good, but they are put into situations where they play against bigger and stronger athletes. All of a sudden, something is hard that has always been easy."

"Beyond physical skills," says Dever-Boaz, "we want a good attitude, intensity, and knowledge of the game. We listen to high school coaches. They can make or break a player in terms of whether that athlete gets recruited. We also listen to conversations in the stands. It's amazing what you can learn by listening to or participating in discussions among fans, parents, and other players. For example, we would not have known that one potential recruit had five knee surgeries if it had not been talked about in the stands during a game."

The Community College Option

Many college prospects take the community college option. "Talented players attend two-year schools for various reasons," explains Mendoza. "Those players who don't qualify academically may have to go to community colleges to become eligible for Division I or Division II universities later.

"The second type that attends a community college is the pure athlete who can't afford Division I schools even if they offer a scholarship. A half scholarship at an expensive school still requires the player's family to pay more money than they can afford. At a junior college, that player may get more money and position herself to get a lucrative scholarship offer when she transfers.

"The third kind of community college player is the one who could have played at a Division I or II school, but would have had to play behind an established starter for a year or two. By going to the community college, she can play 50 or 60 games a year."

Where Coaches Look

If a high school or community college player is good, the college coach will usually, but not always, know about her. They look for players on high school teams, on summer travel teams, and at regional and national tournaments.

"I can't know everybody," says Mendoza. "There are probably players out there that I would have loved to have had in our program if I had known about them. Kids need to contact coaches when they are interested in playing for them."

Two huge tournaments in Colorado, both held during the July 4th holiday period, attract 100 teams combined. Almost every college coach will be there or send someone there to observe and evaluate high school players. If a player is not going to that tournament, she should make some other arrangement to be seen by coaches.

Sam Ivey: A Parent's View

Sam Ivey was a college baseball player, a girls' softball coach, and a parent whose daughter Ashley played at almost every level of the game. She began in 10-and-under competition, then played age-division, league, club, high school, community college, and NCAA Division I softball. Looking back, here are some of Ivey's thoughts that parents of young players may find helpful.

Q: *What would do with your children to help them get ready to play softball before they are old enough for formal instruction or competition?*

A: I would find some good instructional video tapes that are short, informative, and that demonstrate basic fundamental softball skills. If they see how things are done early, you don't have to break down bad habits later. The second thing I would do is spend plenty of time in the yard playing catch or throwing pitches for them to hit. It's never too early to do those things.

Q: *At what age are they ready for organized competition?*

A: I don't think that very young children should be put into organized sports. I can't see getting them started at less than eight years old. My daughter didn't start playing until she was ten and didn't start pitching until she was eleven, and she did okay.

Q: *Is playing too many games during a year a problem?*

A: It can be a problem if you don't control it. There is more to life than softball, and you have to be careful about letting your child play so many games that it disrupts the life of the family. But I do think it's possible to play on a league team during the week and a travel team on weekends without overloading a child with softball. Don't let softball consume your lives.

Q: *How expensive is it to finance a player's softball practice, travel, and competition for a year?*

A: It depends on how good she is and how involved she becomes in club, summer, and travel ball, but I probably spent $3,000 to $4,000 a year during Ashley's last two or three years of high school. Just one four-day camp (exposure camp) during the summer costs about $400.

Q: *When you have a choice, is there a particular kind of coach that you would recommend?*

A: A coach who wants to give something back to the community, who enjoys it, who knows how to teach, and who doesn't have one of his or her children on the team is a special person. Much of the time, parents don't have a choice. Their children are drafted out of tryouts by coaches whom you may or may not know. It's okay to do your homework and try to get your kid on a team that has a coach you respect, but don't get too pushy.

Q: *How do you feel about players getting locked into positions at an early age?*

A: There is a time when you have to lock into a position, but when they are 10 or 12 and under, they should play everywhere. Even if you have a pitcher who is dominant, don't let her pitch every game. Give her the experience of playing other positions and developing other skills.

Q: *What would you tell parents about letting their children play more than one sport and about weight training?*

A: I'm all for playing more than one sport because of the skills that a well-rounded athlete needs. But keep in mind that a lot of good softball players have seen their careers jeopardized because of knee injuries suffered in basketball and volleyball. If girls are going to play softball or any other sport, they need to get some weight training to strengthen the joints.

Q: *What is the physical attribute that seems to separate talented players from others?*

A: Speed. Softball is a very fast game. One or two girls who can fly can win a game.

Q: *Is there anything you would have done differently in your daughter's development as a player?*

A: I would get a qualified person like a college or elite team coach or player to give me an objective evaluation of the talent level of my child. Some parents think their kids are great when they are average, while others have extremely talented children and don't even recognize it. If you have talent on your hands and know it, you might be able to help your child be more successful.[10]

A WORD TO PARENTS AND PLAYERS

"The message for parents of exceptional players is to demand excellence," advises Dever-Boaz, "but keep softball in perspective. I love parents who require their children to be responsible in every area of their lives. When the game is over, parents should just be parents, not fans or coaches. I am cautious about parents who brag about their kids. If your daughter is exceptional, you don't have to brag. We'll know about her."

Mendoza tells parents to make sure that their children continue to have fun playing softball. "Don't lose sight of the fact that she is a child and there are a lot of good things in life. Being an athlete is a very small part of being a total person. Sometimes parents forget that. They get consumed with the sport and forget that there are other sides to the individual. Let those sides develop. Overall character and personality are more important than what kind of softball player she is."

The message to potential scholarship players from all college coaches is to look for more than softball when they begin considering colleges. They should ask themselves: If softball ends tomorrow, can I be happy at a particular school? Athletes should start the search as early as their freshman year in high school. In doing so, they can rule out the places that are not a good fit and concentrate on a few schools and programs that are right for them.

Chapter 18

Swimming

Swimming is another of those sports made for late bloomers. Ed Moses, a 100- and 200-meter NCAA champion and once a world record holder in the 100-meter breaststroke, didn't start swimming competitively until he was 14. Matt Biondi and John Naber, both Olympic champions, were in high school before they began serious competition.

"The public perception," says Larry Herr, sport development coordinator for USA Swimming, is that swimmers peak early. "But it is a very event-specific process. For younger athletes who swim in distance events, careers often peak at about the ages of 18 to 20. For sprinters, it is much later. They may not reach their full potential until they are 26 to 28 years old. For most competitive swimmers, it is better to be a late maturer and stay in the sport longer than to start early and get out by the time they are 13 or 14."[1]

Still, the average ages of swimmers on the USA Swimming national teams in 1999 were 19 for women and 22 for men. That is young when compared to sports such as track and field, where the average age of Olympic athletes is almost 28 years. The youngest female swimmer was 14; the oldest, 26. The youngest male swimmer was 15; the oldest, 32.[2]

How late is too late for swimmers to have a chance to go to college on a swimming scholarship? Later than most people think. Herr says that girls, because they mature earlier than boys, may be able to wait until they are 13 or 14. For boys, 16 would probably be too late to become a competitive college swimmer. Another coach says that he's had lots of boys who started swimming as freshmen in high school and did very well. Still, compared to other sports, swimming allows plenty of time for athletes to experiment before specializing.

EARLY INDICATORS

Body type is a big thing with swim coaches at the upper range of talent. It is less important at the club and school levels, where coaches really don't have a choice about who participates in their programs. There are enough exceptions to encourage athletes of all sizes and shapes, but as they get older, outstanding swimmers tend to be taller—6-0 to 6-2 in men; 5-8 to 5-10 in women—and leaner than athletes in other sports. At the Olympic level, they are tall, lean, and have long arm spans. When Ian Thorpe, Australia's great 400-meter champion, was 17 years old, he was 6-1, 200 pounds, and wore size 17 shoes. Among swimmers, big feet and big hands are considered assets.

Tables 18.1 and 18.2 give the average physical characteristics of elite swimmers in the United States. Keep in mind that the numbers present a composite picture and do not reflect the wide range of characteristics possessed by individuals in each category.

Table 18.1   Physical Characteristics of U.S. Female Elite Swimmers—1999–2000

Level	Age	Weight (lb)	Height	Sitting height (in)	Arm length (in)
Bronze	13.0	123.5	5-4 1/2	33 1/2	27 1/2
Silver	13.44	125.56	5-5	34	27 1/2
Gold	14.27	126.43	5-5 3/4	34	28
Eagle	15.54	142.31	5-7	35	28 1/2
Junior	14.46	130.64	5-6 1/2	34 1/2	28 1/2
National	19.05	146.02	5-8 1/2	35 1/2	29 1/2

Note: Sitting height measures the distance from the seated surface to the top of the head. Arm length measures the length of the right arm straight out from the end of the shoulder blade to the tip of the longest finger, palm down.

Adapted, by permission, from USA Swimming, 2000.

Table 18.2   Physical Characteristics of U.S. Male Elite Swimmers—1999–2000

Level	Age	Weight (lb)	Height	Sitting height (in)	Arm length (in)
Bronze	14.05	142.25	5-9	35 1/2	30
Silver	14.72	152.68	5-11	36 1/2	30 1/2
Gold	15.62	153.52	5-10 1/2	36 1/2	30 1/2
Eagle	16.50	161.75	5-11 1/2	37	31
Junior	16.84	165.63	5-9	37	31 1/2
National	21.86	177.24	6-1 1/2	38	32

Adapted, by permission, from USA Swimming, 2000.

Technique

Ken Stopkotte, head coach of the Clearwater Aquatic Team, looks for technique first. "Although we are still teaching skills such as body position, kicking skills, and pull patterns to young swimmers, those things come very naturally to exceptionally talented athletes.

"Indicators of early talent are not necessarily predictors of later success," he continues. "We don't know how girls are going to develop physically. Some mature early and others stop growing at around 13 or 14. Many of those just drop out of swimming altogether. In the past, when girls got to college, they stopped improving. Now, because of improved conditioning and training techniques, the peak performance ages are becoming much higher. Women in their late 20s and early 30s are breaking world records. With boys, it's a little easier to at least predict size by looking at their parents."[3]

Times

Swimming is a time-driven sport. One of the first things that many coaches teach their young swimmers is how to read a pace clock. Watch every swimmer at the end of a race and he or she will look at the clock before anything else.

But while the swimmers and their parents look at that clock, many developmental coaches do not pay much attention to times posted by young swimmers. Instead, they look at skills that might indicate greatness later on. "I had a girl in Cincinnati," remembers Stopkotte, "who broke age-group records when she was nine and ten, but she did it because she was so much bigger and stronger than the other kids. She always seemed to be 20 yards ahead of everyone else. But she never learned how to handle failure or the pressure of racing against tough competition. When the competition caught up with her physically, she would crumble at the end of a tight race."

Goals

Jim Sheridan, swim coach at Columbus (Indiana) North High School and at Donner Swim Club, equates talent with the ability to set goals. "The ones who have talent are the ones who can set and reset their own goals and stick with them." What kind of goals? "At the beginning level, we ask them to attend 60 percent of practice and participate in one meet every two months. When they go from the developmental program to an age-group team, the goal becomes 80 percent attendance at practice, one meet a month, and participation in one other sport.

"At the senior level," continues Sheridan, "we consider making nine out of ten practices the equivalent of 100 percent. That gives every athlete the option to choose when he or she will miss a practice. There are times when even a coach doesn't want to see a swimmer show up for a workout, like the morning after a big concert."[4]

Making Adjustments

Tony Young, head coach at Carmel High School and at the Carmel Swim Club in Indiana, thinks that the determining factor in predicting future success is not age-group race results, but how the swimmer adjusts mentally from one age level to the next. "The boy who dominated early because of size and strength finds out that he's just like everybody else when he ages up. In my mind, his talent will show if he is able to make the mental adjustment necessary to compete as he gets older."[5]

Feel for the Water

Brad Burnham, head swim coach at Bowdoin College in Maine, points out that swimming is the only sport where you have gravity and buoyancy fighting each other. "It takes practice to manage that environment. The good ones have a feel for the water because they have done more than just swim laps. They grew up around water and had all kinds of experiences in it to help their brains develop a sense for the water. Once they get to the surface for competitive swimming, learning how to propel themselves is a lot easier."[6]

Jill Sterkel, women's swim coach at the University of Texas, describes this "feel for the water" more eloquently than others. "You can put people in the water and immediately tell which ones are comfortable. They don't try to overpower the water; they just flow with it. They can be swimming and it looks like a symphony. It's pretty to watch. With others, no matter how hard they try, it still looks like they are trying hard."[7]

At the very highest levels of swimming competition, Herr and others admit that talent will win out over hard work. "If you take the athletes who reach the finals of the 100-meter freestyle at the Olympics, everyone has put in the work required to get there. As much as I hate to say it, the athletes who are genetically programmed for certain events are the ones who will probably win. But at the collegiate and club levels, where the pool of talent is larger, factors such as training methods, technical skills, work habits, desire, and access to programs open the door to success."

IF YOU HAVE A PROSPECT

The developmental path varies with coaches and training programs around the country, but Stopkotte suggests these guidelines for developmental age-group swimmers:

• At six and seven, practice twice a week and compete once a month or once every two months. Training sessions should not last longer than

A natural feel for the water is an important quality in young swimmers.

45 minutes and consist of 90 percent time spent on technique and 10 percent on other areas.

• At seven and eight, the technique-to-aerobic exercise ratio should be 85 percent to 15 percent. Training sessions can be increased to three times a week, with a one-hour maximum in the water, and competition once a month.

• For nine and ten-year-olds, Stopkotte recommends four practice sessions a week, depending on the ability and interest level of the athlete, and one or two meets per month. At this stage, 50 to 60 percent of training time should be devoted to technique and 40 to 50 percent to aerobic conditioning.

• Practice periods for 11- and 12-year-olds are held four or five times a week for 60 to 90 minutes. Some programs work their swimmers two hours or more, but Stopkotte says those kids tend to burn out. Any advantages gained by training are offset by a loss of technique.

DEVELOPMENTAL TRACKS

Swimmers can develop their talent on two different tracks. The most prominent path is through USA Swimming member clubs. Competition begins at early ages, and success is determined by times. By the time athletes reach their teens, they are well aware of the times that will place them in the top state or national groups. Getting scholarships is directly related to the times posted at USA Swimming events.

The second path is to participate in high school swimming. Some swimmers do most of their competing in the interscholastic setting, but the majority of them are associated with club teams. Many do both. The advantage of concentrating on school competition is that it allows the athlete to participate in two or more sports at different times of the year. An Olympic silver medallist at the University of Michigan swam and ran cross country while he was in high school.

USA Swimming is one of the few sports organizations that is trying to develop partnerships with other organizations to increase its membership base. The idea is for athletes to play one sport two or three days a week and go to swim practice the remaining days. Herr thinks that sports governing bodies that do not think along those lines are going to get left behind.

What are the obstacles that can interfere with the developmental path? "Friends, family, and lack of commitment," warns Sheridan, who is also dean of students at Columbus North. "Friends will either support athletes in what they are doing or they will try to talk them out of it. Our sport takes a huge amount of family involvement. To be part of our program, for example, a swimmer may have to stay at home and train instead of taking a family trip. And the family has to be comfortable with that. Finally, the athlete has to be willing to give up some other things in life to make the commitment to swimming—not everything, but it may mean going to one concert a month instead of three."

WHAT COLLEGE COACHES LOOK FOR

"You can begin to identify college swimming talent during the mid-teens," says Peter Brown, men's swim coach at Penn State. "We look for a swimmer's body position in the water and distance per stroke. Great swimmers look bigger in the water than they do on land. They seem to have a natural feel for the water and are able to find the right path to move their bodies. They also carry less air into the water with each stroke. In other words, they put their hands in the water properly and move them in a very efficient manner."[8]

At the University of Michigan, John Urbanchek directs the men's swimming program and coached in the 1992, 1996, and 2000 Olympics. He is very cautious about getting interested in male swimmers before the age of 16. He stays away from those who have physically matured by the time they are in their early teens. "If they mature early, they may not have any growth potential," explains Urbanchek. "We like the late bloomers who will catch up later in their teens. They make college coaches look good."[9]

Both Brown and Urbanchek have definite ideas about the body types of swimmers that they recruit. They say that exceptional swimmers tend to be tall and rather lean with big shoulders, long arms, slender hips, and long

Olympic medalist Matt Biondi didn't begin serious competition until he was in high school.

upper bodies. Big hands and big feet are a plus. Tables 18.3 and 18.4 provide data on the heights of college swimmers in men's and women's programs at five Division I universities in the year 2000.[10]

Burnham, formerly an assistant coach at UCLA, is even more discriminating in body types. He looks at the length of the forearm. "I try to get a visual idea of forearm and hand length compared to the length of the upper arm." How does he do that? "You can observe a group of kids who are all about the same height standing next to each other and notice that one girl's elbow is two inches higher up than the others." Why is it important? "Because if the surface area of the hand and arm is larger and the lever of the upper arm is shorter, they can use the arm more efficiently."

Brown also considers the psychological makeup of potential recruits. He likes swimmers who are not too emotional. They don't get discouraged at

Table 18.3 Heights of College Women Swimmers—2000

University	Shortest	Tallest	Average	5-8 or taller
Texas	5-5	6-1	5-8	18/26
Washington	5-4	5-10	5-8	12/22
UCLA	5-3	5-11	5-7	16/36
Arizona	5-3	6-1	5-8	12/21
Tennessee	5-3	6-0	5-8	13/20

Table 18.4　Heights of College Men Swimmers—2000

University	Shortest	Tallest	Average	6-0 or taller
Washington	5-9	6-4	6-1	15/22
Ohio State	5-7	6-6	6-2	26/29
Texas	5-10	6-8	6-3	28/36
Iowa State	5-9	6-5	6-1	21/26
Stanford	5-11	6-8	6-2	20/21

setbacks and they don't let outside events control their emotions. Burnham backs off high school swimmers who are stroke-rate driven. They swim at too high a tempo. Explains Burnham, "Their engines have been modified by hard training so that all they can do is spin their arms as fast as possible. They can use cycling rate when they are 10 or 11 to go fast. As they grow, they can go a little faster, but most of them have burned their engines out by the time they get to college. They have absolutely no awareness of how to carry speed. They keep pounding on the rate side and don't have any distance per cycle."

At the top college programs in the United States, coaches pay attention to national qualifying times. Some recruiters won't even consider a swimmer unless he or she has made established time cuts in the respective events. But Penn State's Brown says that he cannot evaluate swimmers solely by the times they have posted before they get to college. "If we recruited only by the numbers, we would make a lot of bad decisions. We try to get to know the recruits to make sure they will fit into our program."

A VIEW FROM TEXAS

And then there is Eddie Reese, head men's swimming coach at the University of Texas, whose teams are always a threat to win the NCAA title. Reese is near-obsessive about strokes. What would get his attention other than times? "Stroke efficiency, distance per stroke, smoothness of stroke, the ability to fly kick, and improvement curve in relation to the length of time an athlete has been swimming," he explains. "Most of all, I look for somebody who swims easily.

"Let me tell you a story," he says, to illustrate the point. "Two guys came out of high school and both had been amazingly fast. One did a 44.2 and the other a 44.4 in the 100-meter free. I did not like their strokes and I did not recruit them. The first one went 44.7 in his freshman year and slower the next year. The other never broke 44.0. I've had a swimmer who was 47.2 out of high school and he went to 42.4 here. I know what technique can do."

What would make Reese take a chance on a swimmer that doesn't have great times? "Stroke technique," he answers.

As a group, do college swimmers have a weakness? "People are getting lazy on technique," Reese says, not surprisingly. "It used to take recruits two years to get used to my emphasis on strokes. Now it takes them three. We have 600 to 700 kids come through our camps during a five-week period. The under-12 swimmers have good strokes; the 13-and-over group, bad strokes. Some of these swimmers come here every year and they seem to get worse as they get older."

Reese's counterpart at Texas, Jill Sterkel, says that nobody has it all. "You can always find something to work on. It may be improving stroke technique or perfecting a start or turn. But most of all, it's how to swim smarter. Even at this level, many swimmers have to be taught how to compete. There is a lot of fear out there, and you have to reprogram their thinking about race pace swimming."

Here is Reese's final word on, you guessed it, strokes: "Stroke work is like yard work. What happens if you don't do it? It gets ugly and it takes more work to fix it."[11]

A WORD TO PARENTS

John Urbanchek, like elite coaches in most other sports, tells parents to let their kids be kids at least until the age of 12. "Don't force swimming on them. Let them participate in lots of other activities. Those who start a program of intense training and competition too early tend to burn out. The age period from 12 to 14 is critical. That is when they have to seriously focus on swimming if they want to reach this level."

Urbanchek makes one other point about burnout and how to avoid it. "Even among very serious young swimmers, it's okay to take time off—as much as six months—to get away from swimming. They are still going to develop physically during that period of rest or involvement in other activities, and they can catch up with their swimming potential when they resume training."

Stopkotte says the best swimmers are the ones who play other sports. "It makes them well-rounded instead of being focused on just one thing. But this is hard for parents to understand. They think it's like tennis, where the way to get better is to play all of the time. In my experience, those who train at swimming year-round are the ones who don't grow physically. They have their biggest growth spurt during the period when they take a break." Not exactly science, but an interesting possibility.

Young warns against parents pushing their children. "Let them mature into good swimmers instead of forcing them to become successful age-group swimmers. You may have to decide how long you want them in the sport. Those who are pushed too fast, too soon probably won't last as long as those who are allowed to pace themselves."

Says Brown, "We want good parental support without overinvolvement. If swimmers have been pushed too hard by their parents, it's almost impossible to sustain enthusiasm for the sport while they are in college. The athletes who are successful are the ones who are self-motivated."

Brown reminds parents and coaches that good fundamentals are important, but high school and club swim coaches who go to extremes tend to produce swimmers who peak too early. "If they have not overdone the sport by the time we get them," he says, "college swimmers can continue to improve well into their 20s."

Herr encourages parents to give their swimmers direction, but to let them make the decisions about how seriously they want to pursue the sport. "If you see signs of potential, make sure that they get exposed to good coaching. Find someone who has the reputation for knowing about training methods, training intensity, and training volume."

Chapter 19

Tennis

"**M**y father recognized that my brother Pete had something really special even when he was two and three years old," says UCLA women's coach, Stella Sampras. "He had great coordination and could do things with his body that the other kids his age just couldn't do. Everything came so easy to him."[1]

Ryan Case was ranked number one in Georgia and sixth in the southern region when he was 12, was 69th in the country in the 14s, and made the top 50 in the South in the 16s and 18s. He was offered scholarships at Division I schools, but accepted a scholarship at a NCAA Division II college.

Ryan's father Rick recalls two things about his son that set him apart from others by the age of six or seven. "He had very good hand-eye coordination, and he had a very long attention span. He was ready to start playing tournaments by the time he was six."[2]

But tennis talent doesn't necessarily emerge that early. Doug MacCurdy, director of the USA Tennis Player Development Program, says that is it not unreasonable to think that someone who picks up the game seriously at 14 or 15 could become a Division I tennis player. "We tend to think that tennis is a game for the very, very young, but getting to that level is certainly possible. The kids who have had lessons since they were six or eight years old may be very good with the racket, but not exceptional in athletic ability on which to build. Sooner or later, the athletes start catching up."[3]

Evidence and expert opinion do seem to indicate that tennis talent can develop as early as preschool and as late as the teens. Pete Sampras never won a national junior title.

EARLY INDICATORS

No formula can predict when or if an exciting prospect will become an outstanding player. But there are characteristics that many experts can identify in young players who go on to reach higher levels of the game. Hand-eye coordination is a common denominator and is particularly important in a sport that requires learned skills. Many of the movements involved in serving, volleying, and even hitting groundstrokes are not natural. Except among rare athletes who seem to swing the racket perfectly with little or no instruction, tennis players have to master a series of complex moves.

Lower-Body Skills

The other physical qualities that exceptional players may show at a fairly early age are quickness and agility. Bobby McKee, tennis coach at Presbyterian College, looks for what he calls "lower-body skills" such as balance and quick reaction with the feet. Children who demonstrate the explosive type of speed in getting to a ball have an advantage over average players. Speed is an asset, but quickness is more important. The ability to take two or three quick steps, change directions frequently, and decelerate before making contact with the ball is an indication of special talent. It might be there from the start, it might be developed with age, and it can be improved with instruction.[4]

Size

Eventually, size and strength will become important, even essential, physical attributes. Tennis players are getting bigger and stronger, and the game has changed to accommodate those players. But in the 12-and-under age groups, size and strength are not necessarily predictors of later success.

Vision

An increasing amount of attention is being given to sports vision, and outstanding tennis players usually have it. Says Greg Patten, national coach for the USA Tennis Junior Development Program, "Great players have great eyes, exceptional vision. They seem to see the ball coming off an opponent's racket better than others. They see the whole court and know where to be and where to hit better than lesser players."[5]

USTA Elite Player Tests Results

The United States Tennis Association has developed a series of physical tests for junior players. While none of these tests can predict future success, they do provide a method of comparing the results of the players to those of elite players of the same age. These tests were given to thousands of juniors invited to area training centers. The following pages provide the instructions for administering nine of those tests and the scores at the 20th, 50th, 70th, and 90th percentile levels.[6]

© iPhotoNews.com/Clark Brooks

Except among rare athletes, tennis players have to work hard to master movements that are not natural.

Sit and Reach

1. Sit on the floor with knees extended and legs flat.
2. Place a yardstick between legs and parallel to them so that the 15-inch mark is even with the bottom of the heels.
3. Have someone hold the knees in place.
4. Lean forward, arms extended, and hands together so that the index fingers are touching. Don't bounce.
5. Record the number of inches past the toes that the hands reach.

Girls 12 and under	Percentile	Boys 12 and under
.9–1.5	20%	-2.0–-1.5
2.6–3.3	50%	1.1–1.5
3.9–4.7	70%	2.1–2.5
6.1–7.4	90%	3.1–3.9

Girls 16 and under	Percentile	Boys 16 and under
2.1–3.0	20%	-1.9–-.5
4.8–5.1	50%	1.6–2.0
6.1–7.0	70%	3.1–4.0
8.2–9.2	90%	5.1–6.0

14 and under	Percentile	14 and under
1.1–2.0	20%	-3.4–-1.5
3.8–4.5	50%	1.3–2.0
5.1–6.0	70%	2.6–3.5
7.1–8.5	90%	4.6–5.0

Sit-Ups

1. Lie on back with knees flexed at 90 degrees, feet flat on floor or mat and slightly separated.
2. Cross hands and place them against the body at the chest.
3. Complete as many sit-ups as possible in one minute.
4. The elbows must touch the thighs, the shoulders must touch the mat, and the hips must stay in contact with the mat.
5. Players with a history of back problems should not perform this test.

Girls 12 and under	Percentile	Boys 12 and under
35–36	20%	34–36
41–42	50%	43
45–47	70%	46–48
51–54	90%	52–56

Girls 16 and under	Percentile	Boys 16 and under
40–42	20%	40–44
47–49	50%	50–52
52–54	70%	55–58
58–60	90%	62–64

Girls 14 and under	Percentile	Boys 14 and under
35–37	20%	39–41
43–44	50%	46–47
47–49	70%	51–53
53–56	90%	58–60

Push-Ups

1. Lie face down, with hands separated at shoulder width and palms touching the floor or mat.
2. Put weight of lower body on toes.
3. Beginning with arms extended and the body fully extended, lower body so that upper arms are at least parallel to the floor.
4. During the upward movement, completely extend arms and keep body straight.
5. Complete as many push-ups as possible in one minute.

Girls 12 and under	Percentile	Boys 12 and under
16–19	20%	22–24
25–28	50%	32–33
31–37	70%	38–41
44–48	90%	47–50

Girls 16 and under	Percentile	Boys 16 and under
20–23	20%	27–30
30–32	50%	38–40
36–39	70%	45–47
44–46	90%	53–55

Girls 14 and under	Percentile	Boys 14 and under
16–19	20%	23–27
26–29	50%	34–38
33–35	70%	42–45
41–44	90%	51–54

Vertical Jump

1. Stand facing a wall, hands together, and index fingers touching.
2. Extend both arms as high as possible and mark the spot.
3. Attach a yardstick to the wall upward from the highest point reached.
4. Bend knees before the jump, but don't take a step.
5. With chalk on fingertips, turn with side to the wall, then jump and touch the yardstick at the highest point possible.
6. Record the number of inches between the standing reach and the highest point of the jump.

Girls 12 and under	Percentile	Boys 12 and under
10.40–11.40	20%	11.6–12.20
12.60–13.30	50%	13.4–14.00
13.90–14.30	70%	15.1–16.00
15.30–16.40	90%	16.6–17.20

Girls 16 and under	Percentile	Boys 16 and under
12.10–13.00	20%	15.60–17.30
14.60–15.00	50%	19.10–20.00
16.10–17.00	70%	20.80–22.00
18.10–18.90	90%	24.10–25.00

Girls 14 and under	Percentile	Boys 14 and under
12.10–12.80	20%	13.60–14.50
14.10–14.50	50%	16.10–16.70
15.10–16.00	70%	17.60–18.00
17.10–18.50	90%	19.60–20.60

20-Yard Dash

1. Mark a distance of 20 yards along the side of a tennis court (baseline to opposite service line).
2. The recorder stands at the finish line, one arm raised.
3. The command, "Ready, Go," is given and the hand drops on "Go."
4. Using a stopwatch, record the fastest of three time trials.

Girls 12 and under	Percentile	Boys 12 and under
3.90	20%	3.80
3.60	50%	3.55
3.40	70%	3.45
3.20	90%	3.30

Girls 16 and under	Percentile	Boys 16 and under
3.65	20%	3.50
3.50	50%	3.25
3.30	70%	3.15
3.10	90%	3.00

Girls 14 and under	Percentile	Boys 14 and under
3.70	20%	3.60
3.55	50%	3.40
3.40	70%	3.20
3.20	90%	3.10

Hexagon Test

1. Use masking tape to mark a hexagon with 24 inches per side at angles of 120 degrees.

2. Stand in the middle of the hexagon facing forward, a position that must be maintained throughout the test.

3. On the "Ready-Go" command, jump over the tape with both feet and quickly return to a position inside the hexagon.

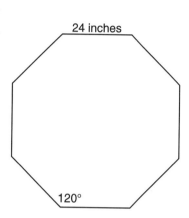

4. Continue jumping in and out of the hexagon in this order: (2) across the line to the right and in front, (3) right and in back, (4) straight back, (5) left back, and (6) left forward.

5. After three full revolutions have been completed, record the time from start to finish—when feet hit the floor after jumping back into the hexagon following jump 6 (left forward).

6. Take one practice trial, then count the better of two actual trials.

7. Add a 0.5-second penalty for each line touch and a 1.0-second penalty for failure to follow the proper sequence.

Girls 12 and under	Percentile	Boys 12 and under
13.80–14.90	20%	15.20–16.30
12.70–12.90	50%	13.20–13.60
11.40–11.90	70%	12.20–12.50
10.50–10.80	90%	10.70–11.50

Girls 16 and under	Percentile	Boys 16 and under
12.70–13.20	20%	13.10–14.20
11.70–11.90	50%	11.80–12.00
10.80–11.30	70%	11.10–11.30
10.00–10.40	90%	10.10–10.40

Girls 14 and under	Percentile	Boys 14 and under
13.50–13.90	20%	13.80–14.60
12.00–12.40	50%	12.50–12.80
11.20–11.50	70%	11.60–11.90
10.10–10.60	90%	10.40–11.00

Side Shuffle

1. Start on the centerline of a tennis court at the T, facing the net, with one foot on either side of the center service line.
2. At the command of "Ready-Go," shuffle along the service line, touch the court with hand on the doubles sideline, then shuffle to the opposite doubles sideline, touch it, and return to the starting position.
3. Do not use a crossover step.
4. Record the better of two trials.

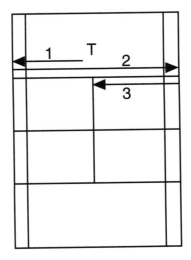

Girls 12 and under	Percentile	Boys 12 and under
7.80–7.90	20%	15.20–16.30
7.40	50%	13.20–13.60
7.00–7.10	70%	12.20–12.50
6.50–6.80	90%	10.70–11.50

Girls 16 and under	Percentile	Boys 16 and under
7.30–7.40	20%	13.10–14.20
6.90	50%	11.80–12.00
6.50–6.60	70%	11.10–11.30
6.10–6.20	90%	10.10–10.40

Girls 14 and under	Percentile	Boys 14 and under
7.60–7.70	20%	13.80–14.60
7.10	50%	12.50–12.80
6.80–6.90	70%	11.60–11.90
6.30–6.50	90%	10.40–11.00

Spider Test

1. Mark a 12- by 18-inch rectangle behind the middle of the baseline, using the baseline as one of the long sides.
2. Place tennis balls in the following five intersections: (1) left singles sideline at baseline, (2) left singles sideline at service line, (3) service line at center service line (the T), (4) right singles sideline at service line, (5) right singles sideline at baseline.
3. Starting at the middle of the baseline on the "Ready-Go" command, retrieve one ball at a time and return to place it in the rectangle, moving in a counter-clockwise direction.
4. Have someone remove each ball to avoid stepping on it.
5. Stop the clock when the last ball is placed in the rectangle.
6. Record the best of three trials.

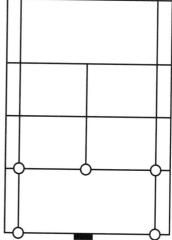

Girls 12 and under	Percentile	Boys 12 and under
19.90–20.20	20%	19.20–19.80
18.90–20.10	50%	18.20–18.30
18.20–18.50	70%	17.80–17.90
17.30–17.80	90%	17.10–17.30

Girls 14 and under	Percentile	Boys 14 and under
19.00–19.50	20%	18.30–18.60
18.00–18.20	50%	17.40–17.50
17.50–17.70	70%	16.90–17.00
16.80–17.00	90%	15.90–16.40

Girls 16 and under	Percentile	Boys 16 and under
18.70–18.90	20%	17.40–17.90
17.80–17.90	50%	16.50–16.60
17.30–17.50	70%	15.80–16.10
16.70–16.90	90%	15.10–15.50

Emotional Characteristics

Emotional characteristics can also begin to surface relatively early, although they don't always. Patten says the first thing he looks for is a childlike sense of play. "Great players abandon themselves to playing the sport. Even if they don't have great physical talent, they have an intangible ability to compete that sets them apart from other players."

Nick Saviano, USA Tennis director of coaching education, says that one thing stands out far and above everything else in predicting success. "The best indicator of future success is a love of the sport. The player who loves the sport will have something to hold them in good stead when things are not going well. When given the opportunity, he or she will go after what they love."[7]

An indication that you have a child or coach a player who does not love the game is one who only plays or practices when he or she has to. You can't keep the really talented ones off the court. Win or lose, they want to get back out there. The carpooled, lessons-only player may have some talent, but is unlikely to have the drive to develop it.

MacCurdy thinks this has become a serious problem over the past 15 years. "Young players have gotten more and more into junior development programs. The kid comes in five days a week and hits balls in an organized fashion. This concept has taken away a lot of practice matches and from the experience of patterns in tennis matches. It seems that there is a lot of ducking of competition. The good ones thrive on competition and seek challenging competitive opportunities."

Dick Gould, the legendary coach at Stanford, adds this insight to the competitiveness and drive among gifted players: "They hate to lose. They are very dedicated, they work hard, they use their time well, and they are resilient. They don't dwell on losses too long, but instead are able to bounce back pretty quickly. Win or lose, they want to play again."[8]

IF YOU HAVE A PROSPECT

Don't be in a hurry to rush children into formal instruction or competition. No relationship has been known to exist between taking lessons or playing matches at the ages of six or seven and later success. Developing coordination through a variety of sports and activities is more important than trying to place a child on a fast and early track to tennis stardom. If fundamental movement activities happen on a tennis court, fine, but throwing, catching, hitting, and racket handling are just as easily taught on the playground or in the backyard. Almost every college tennis coach will tell you that he or she likes an athlete who has participated in more than one sport during the developmental years.

If a player does compete at an early age, don't overreact to great results. The problem with the very young is that the style of game that makes them successful is dramatically different from the style they'll need to win later on. There is not an absolute progression from being number one in the 12s, then in the 14s, 16s, and 18s.

Even among highly ranked players in the 10- to 12-year age groups, predicting success at the sectional, national, college, or professional levels is difficult. Explains the USTA's MacCurdy, "There are a lot of good strikers of the ball at 11 and 12, but you really have to wait and see what happens later, especially with boys, because of the physical nature of the game. By 16 or 17 with boys, and 13 or 14 among girls, they should be making significant progress."

Success at Each Level

Even given the unpredictability of player development, tennis is a sport in which proving oneself at each level is an indication of special talent. "The rule of thumb," thinks MacCurdy, "is to be successful at each level before moving to the next. Venus and Serena Williams are exceptions. There is nothing wrong with a 14-year-old who is ranked number 20 in the country playing an occasional 18-and-under tournament or even a satellite-type event. But there is no reason to get your brains beaten on a regular basis."

Look for rate of improvement. Talent has a way of exploding at some point in many players. One top-10 American junior player went through a five-month period during which his game probably improved by as much as 50 percent. Those sorts of jumps are impressive. Boris Becker was that way. He was not a very good junior player in Germany. Then he became the best junior in Europe. Next, he won the men's singles title at Wimbledon. All of this happened in a period of about two years.

The tennis community lives by rankings and tournament results. For players 10 to 14, rankings are used to determine who is invited to USA Player Development Training Centers. A few players who are identified as having exceptional potential are also invited. Approximately 120 centers are located throughout the country. Training sessions are held several times a year and are used to further develop the skills of those selected. At the next talent level, 12 regional coaches scout and work with the top 15 players (under the ages of 14 and 15) in each section. If you think your child or the one you coach has exceptional talent, contact the USTA office in your state or section for qualifying standards.

Camps

Talented players experience tremendous pressure to participate in boarding tennis camps. The reaction to camps from teaching professionals and college coaches is mixed. Nick Bollettieri, perhaps the world's most famous tennis camp founder, when asked if it is necessary for talented players to enroll at boarding tennis camps, says, "Absolutely not." But he does think that camps are a proving ground for young players and places where they can fight it out with top players every day.[9]

Sampras and others are not so sure. "If you grow up in a place like California, where there are so many good players, there is no need to send a player off to camp for an extended period. I would never send my kids off because I think they need the support of their family. It's a tough enough time for them anyway, and they need all the help they can get."

Bobby McKee, the Presbyterian College (South Carolina) coach, observes that high-profile camps may benefit the elite players because they get to compete against each other daily. "The talented, but not elite, players spend more time doing drills than anything else. I've had players whose parents spent a lot of time and money on camps. But their children get to the college level and are good drillers, not necessarily good players."

Talbert on Talent

Henry Talbert is the executive director of the United States Tennis Association's Southern California section and one of the most experienced judges of talent in the country. He and the coaches he works with have identified the following three characteristics in young players who exhibit special tennis talent:[10]

1. The number and variety of competitive programs they participate in. "There are some players who literally enroll in every program we offer. They have a hunger for competition and play."
2. How well they can understand and master certain nuances in strokes. "In their second or third try, they can execute certain strokes that might take other children several weeks. Like the Williams sisters, they just jump on everything. They even attack volleys."
3. How well they react to their parents and other handlers around them. "Generally speaking, they are not moody and they get along with people. They seem to thrive under those who push them. Whatever is dished up, they want to eat it."

WHAT COLLEGE COACHES LOOK FOR

"What I look for is achievement," says Stanford coach Gould. "I rarely look at video because anybody can look good on tape. The problem is that you can't measure heart. Even in the National Football League, teams are going a lot less on combine results and more on what a player has accomplished.

"I've had guys who didn't necessarily play the kind of game I teach or promote, who walked a little funny, didn't run very fast, or weren't very big, but there is something inside of them that makes them play. I'll miss a late bloomer, but I've never gone wrong with a kid who has won all the way up through each age division. For $35,000 a year (the value of a scholarship at Stanford), I will not take a player on potential. I would take him or her on what he's done."

Both Gould and Stella Sampras, UCLA's women's coach, get interested in players when they are about 14 or 15. Sampras says she starts watching rankings and tournament results when players are sophomores in high school. "You can tell which players are going to get better," she says, "either because of natural talent, stroke production, or competitiveness. Competitiveness is very important to us. They have to be great competitors to win at the Division I level. Talent will take them only so far." Gould adds that if players don't have that competitive fire by the time they are 14 or 15, they probably won't get it.

Mark Philippoussis was a great prospect at 15 but still not a sure thing.

Have They Peaked?

"We love players who haven't peaked," adds Sampras. "They may not have the whole package now, but they can get better. The coach has to go with her instincts and by talking with recruits, getting to know their goals, and determining if they will be a good fit. There are lots of ranked juniors who don't make it in college. Others who were not very good just blossom. We've had late bloomers, but not a lot of them."

In all of his years of coaching and winning national championships, Gould says he's had only three or four players who came to Stanford with the aggressive serve-and-volley game that he preaches. Even John McEnroe and Tim Mayotte were not strong serve-and-volley players. "The single biggest job I have is to teach that style," Gould says, "which is where the game is going at this level. At the least, college players should have those skills as a complement to what they are already doing."

Attitude

One common theme that makes coaches cautious about otherwise talented players is a bad attitude. Negative attitudes toward teammates, coaches, opponents, parents, and others will drop a player's stock quickly. Cheating, whining, and acting out on the court aren't tolerated by many college coaches or tournament officials. Tennis players have been known to be very self-centered, totally unfamiliar with the team concept. A player who can't adjust to a program that is tailored for the team rather than for the individual might be passed over in the recruiting process.

Closely related to the attitude problem is an unwillingness to work hard. Many people are really well coordinated and hit the ball well, but don't want to work very hard. At UCLA, for example, Sampras requires her players to occasionally run at 6:30 in the morning. They always have to participate in very structured practice sessions. Those who are not comfortable with that kind of tennis environment won't make it there or at many other colleges with similar programs.

Importance of Doubles

College coaches want athletes who can play singles and doubles. The format for competition requires both. Says Sampras, "We would like to have players who can play the whole court. We want them to be aggressive and to like to play the net. We wouldn't take a retriever who just stays on the baseline." The point she makes is even more important in the men's game because of the emphasis on strength, power, and aggressive play.

Finally, college coaches don't want players who are satisfied with their games to the point of not wanting to improve. They want to see indications that a player can get better and is willing to take some risks to improve.

Making the Pros

"If you are talking about making it at the professional level, there is absolutely no guarantee," says Michael Wallace, director of promotions at Wilson Racquet Sports. "Pete Sampras was no guarantee. Mark Philippoussis was a pretty good bet at 15 or 16, but still not a sure thing. There was a player in Latin America, number one in the International Tennis Federation junior rankings, who won eleven international ITF tournaments in a row. That had never been done before. He never cracked the top 200 on the pro tour. He just didn't have the physical presence to succeed in the men's game. It's a whole different ball game on the pro tour. Size comes with everything else. You not only have to have the size and strength of a Mark Philippoussis, you have to be able to move like Marcelo Rios."[11]

A WORD TO COACHES, PARENTS, TEACHING PROFESSIONALS, AND PLAYERS

Teach the all-court game, even if a player is too young to develop powerful serves, volleys, and smashes, or too inconsistent to always play well from the baseline. Sooner or later, a player's growth will catch up to his or her skills.

Develop a second serve. Says Dick Gould, "The biggest difference between a pro and a college player is the effectiveness of the second serve." That difference filters down to lower levels of the game.

Allow the player to enjoy the game. Have fun with it. In the end, tennis players have to do it on their terms, not those of parents, coaches, or pros. If someone is not enjoying the game, he or she should stop playing and take a break, even if the break lasts a long time.

Chapter **20**

Track, Field, and Cross Country

*H*arry Groves got into trouble with a school principal for something he said to a group of elementary students. Groves, the longtime head track coach at Penn State, had just returned from a coaching assignment at the Olympics. One of the students asked what it takes to get to the Olympics. In reply, Groves asked the group how many of them walked to school every day. Only four children raised their hands. "Okay," said Groves, with tongue only partially in cheek, "You four have a chance to make it. The rest of you don't."[1]

The principal was concerned about issues such as safety and liability, but Groves had a larger message for future track and field athletes and their parents. His message was that lifestyle has as much to do with talent as genetics, coaching, or training.

Grover Hinsdale, head track and field coach at Georgia Tech, offers this example to illustrate Groves' thinking: "A kid in some part of east Africa grows up running, not walking, five miles to school and back. At home, he does his chores, and if he has any free time, he may, as one former Olympic marathoner did, spend it chasing prairie chickens. Then he eats a very low-fat meal, does his homework, goes to sleep, and gets up the next morning to repeat the routine. Compare that to most American kids who ride to school, may or may not have a physical education period, ride home, watch television, play video games, or work on the computer, and eat a fast-food, high-fat diet. Which child has a lifestyle that is likely to make him a champion athlete?"[2]

In assessing track and field talent, the environment-versus-genes issue surfaces frequently. Some say that the top 10 qualifiers for the finals in the men's and women's 100 meters were determined at birth. Yes, they had opportunity, access to coaching and training facilities, and the drive to succeed, but they were also genetically programmed to run short distances very fast.

If that premise is true, what about the remaining billions of people who don't make it to the Olympics? Everyone is born within a range of physical capabilities. Those who have the opportunity and the desire to develop those capabilities can achieve great things in track, field, and cross country even if they don't become world-class athletes. "But you can't develop something you don't have," cautions Hinsdale. "The work ethic is important, but that certain gift for running, jumping, or throwing has to be there to reach elite status." Hinsdale's observation emphasizes the importance of matching athletes and events. As mentioned in chapter 7, world-class sprinters are not going to make good distance runners, and champion distance runners will never have world-class sprint speed.

EARLY INDICATORS

"The average age of an Olympic track and field athlete is 27.8 years," notes Cathy Sellers, development programs manager for USA Track and Field. "Most elite athletes have been working at their events between 10 and 12 years."[3] Given that information, the concept of early indicators is relative. "Early" in track and field means something that begins to show during the early or mid-teens.

Groves does not have a high opinion of talent as defined by success at national championships for athletes 12 and under. "There are too many things that can turn around their lives. To be labeled as having great talent at a very young age means that the child has to live a long time with the 'great ability' tag. When I see great talent at the preteen level, I think maybe we should take their shoes, wrap them in cellophane, and not let them run for a while. Youth track at the 12-and-under level is okay if success is measured by having fun instead of by winning."

Groves' opinion regarding national 12-and-under competition is not shared by Mike Barber, coach of the Jenks America Track Club in Tulsa. He has coached 20 national champs and more than 300 national medalists at the youth level. "The ones who run fast when they are young will always run fast if they are in a program that makes the sport fun and helps the child to move up his or her own physical potential ladder. Girls are more likely to be the exceptions to the rule because of physical changes as they mature. If their hips stay narrow and their feet point straight ahead, they will stay good."[4]

Sprinters

Because track and field athletes do so many different things (sprinting, running intermediate and long distances, hurdling, jumping, vaulting, and throwing), indications of talent vary for each type of event. Groves says that sprinters can come in all shapes, sizes, and colors, but those who make the finals of a major sprint event tend to be less than six feet tall, powerfully built, and for reasons that are as controversial as they are unexplained, black. The other early indicator of sprint talent is, not surprisingly, lower-body power that allows explosive speed. At its simplest, the early indicator of speed is the gift of speed.

Pat Henry, Louisiana State University's head track coach whose teams have won 20 NCAA championships, has this to say about talented women sprinters: "Body proportionality is very important in sprinters. We look at body weight in relationship to height. History has shown us that relatively slim hips seem to be an indicator that they can continue to improve. A young woman can run an 11.6 in the 100 meters in high school and show good talent, but that may be as good as she is going to get. We also pay attention to what they have done on and off the track. How much work have they already put in? What has been the intensity level of their training? How much time have they spent in the weight room?" Finally, Henry looks for sprinters who can "get their knees up in the air" and run comfortably with that style.[5]

Barber uses several screening tests when young athletes attend their first practice sessions. The vertical jump is one of those tests. Says Barber, "If a female in her teens can jump 17 inches or higher, she has a great chance to become an elite sprinter, long jumper, or high jumper. My standard for measuring sprinting and jumping potential in boys, which is based on seven years of collecting data, is 24 inches."

> ## Mind-Sets: Sprinters Versus Distance Runners
>
> "The mind-set of young sprinters is all or nothing—all out all the time," observes LSU's Pat Henry. "Distance runners think that more is better—all the time. As a result, if distance runners miss a practice or two because of an injury, they think the world has come to an end. Mentally, they're shot. Hopelessly out of shape. But if sprinters can get out of a practice or two, they think they will be better off and able to compete at a higher level. There is room for a middle ground for both mind-sets if the coach and the athlete develop a training plan."

Distance Runners

Among distance runners, the most important early indicator may be work habits rather than physical talent. At Penn State, 15 runners were given a battery of tests, including $\dot{V}O_2max$, and then ranked from 1 to 15. The rank did not change significantly over the course of four years. Recalls Groves, "The athlete with the highest (best) $\dot{V}O_2max$ made the finals of the NCAA national meet. The runner who was in the middle of the pack physiologically broke the American 10K record. The worst performer's $\dot{V}O_2$max was so bad that the other guys made fun of him and said he would never run a mile under 4:10. He got so mad, he broke the treadmill running on it and he later won the NCAA 10K. Application in distance runners makes a difference."

"The only size marker of distance running talent is a slender build," according to Mike Dilley, coach of the Greater Boise Running Club. "Coming out of high school, most women are about 5-5 and in the 110 to 115 range. A typical male distance runner is 5-10, 140 pounds."

Dilley, who coached 108 All-Americans at Central Oregon Community College and at Boise State, also observes form and balance. "The great distance runners don't waste effort. They are smooth and efficient, with everything headed forward. I pay attention to the way they put their feet on the ground. As a group, women tend to pronate. If they have run that way for four years, fixing it can be hard to do. But if they put their feet straight on the ground and if they have the horses under the hood, they are going to be good."[6]

Hurdlers

Most hurdlers don't have a chance to display talent until the freshman year of high school. A typical scenario would be for an athlete to try out for a team and find that there are two or three sprinters who are faster. But this boy or girl is tall and "high cut" in relation to height, so the coach thinks a better use of talent would be the hurdles. In addition to having long legs, hurdlers show basic speed, explosion, and great hip flexibility. A 5-10 boy who is cut like he is 6-2 has a chance to be successful in the hurdles. A 5-9 athlete with poor hip flexibility is not going to have great success. The ideal body type for a male would be 6-2, 170 pounds, with long legs.

Henry, the only coach in NCAA history to win a men's and women's NCAA championship in the same year, thinks women hurdlers can be a little bulkier than sprinters and perhaps have slightly bigger hips. "Short hurdles require muscle mass for explosion, and it is a different kind of explosion than sprinters have. Talented hurdlers can explode off the floor, but they may not have the degree of forward drive possessed by sprinters. Ideally, you want those legs to be nice and long, but height is not a determining talent factor. We have had women at LSU who were 5-3, but cut like taller athletes, who were great hurdlers."

Jumpers

In the high jump, tall is good, but there are enough exceptions to prove that it is not an absolute necessity at the college level. There have been Big-Ten high jumpers who were in the 5-8 to 5-9 range who went 7-4 to 7-6. Hinsdale explains that the Fosbury Flop changed everything for high jumpers. "It allows shorter athletes to be successful because the further over the bar you

Speed, explosion, and hip flexibility are crucial for hurdlers, regardless of their height.

are, the lower your center of gravity. You are actually jumping over a bar at a certain height, but your center of gravity can be lower. Still, most male world-class high jumpers are in the 6-2 to 6-4 height range."

Height seems to be more important among women than men. Few short women are successful at the high jump. Most of the good ones are 5-10 or 5-11.

"Long jumpers and triple jumpers, whether they are men or women, are sprinters," says Henry. "If they don't have speed, they can't jump."

Throwers

Javelin throwers are a different kind of athlete from shot-putters and discus throwers. "They have to be agile, quick, and flexible, but not necessarily as powerful as the other throwers." says Dilley. "Javelin throwers have to be athletic enough to have rhythm on the runway, then stop that rhythm and transfer it up through the legs, shoulders, and arms. Ideally, they will be built like gymnasts, but taller. The ideal size for men would be in the 6-0 to 6-2

Height of the athlete isn't the most important factor for the high jump, but it does seem to be more of a factor for women than for men.

range and about 180 pounds, but they may not be that size coming out of high school."

Of all track and field athletes, shot-putters and discus throwers are the ones most likely to be big and strong at very early ages and to continue to have those advantages throughout their careers. But being big in itself is not enough. Explosive speed, even in a restricted area, and power are the marks of great throwers. All great male throwers are big. At the world-class level, the women are big, but there just aren't many of them at lower levels of competition.

IF YOU HAVE A PROSPECT

Most track and field athletes take one of two primary developmental paths. The first is either the Amateur Athletic Union or the United States Amateur Track and Field programs, both of which revolve more around competition than development. The training component comes through local track clubs that are affiliated with one or both of the organizations. Competitors first have to advance through local and regional championships. The top four finishers in each event at the AAU regionals qualify for the Junior Olympic Games.

The other method by which track and field athletes are developed is through an extensive state scholastic program. Student-athletes who make their high school teams often participate in summer track competition also. "The high school season is too short to develop fully in our sport. To have the optimum chance to develop," advises Hinsdale, "you have to combine high school and summer youth track programs."

Cathy Sellers explains that outstanding athletes select themselves to get the attention of USA Track and Field during the 14- to 19-year age period. "By meeting qualifying standards, they will be in the top 35 athletes per event in the country. At that level, they start competing to make World Youth Championships, World Junior Championships, or the Junior Pan American Games. Elite athletes also get to attend training camps that are held throughout the country. There are separate camps for boys and girls." Sellers adds that her organization doesn't encourage specialization until the age of 12 and perhaps as late as 14. "If they don't play other sports, we get a huge reduction in numbers as they get older."

Sellers says that about 50 percent of the athletes picked up by USA Track and Field come from high school competition; the other 50 percent come through the club system. Occasionally a conflict of interest arises between schools and clubs. "We let schools do most of the developmental work first, then we pick them up from 14 to 19. After that, most of them compete for colleges and universities, and we get the elite athletes again after college. Because world-class track and field performers don't reach their peaks until their late 20s, we have to rely on others. Our organization can't support them for the entire 10 years that it takes to make our national teams."

AN INTERNATIONAL VIEW

Owen van Niekerk has been developing South African champions for half a century. He is now coaching with the Rentmeester Athletic Club after having been the head coach of Rand Afrikaans University for 18 years.

Niekerk has developed a series of coaching books that outline the stages of development for athletes in each event. Table 20.1 illustrates what he thinks are appropriate training goals for each age level. Note that he recommends sprint training to begin by the ages of seven to eight. He says that stride frequency comes to a virtual stop by the ages of 12 or 13, but it is a point that is not shared by everyone. Niekerk's approach also involves repeating some training goals at each level. For some events, he does not break goals down into age groups, but simply describes tasks at different stages. Other specialties are omitted because they are usually developed by athletes beyond the ages addressed in this book.[7]

Table 20.1 Training Phases

Event	Age	Training goals
Sprints	7–8	General physical development
		Interest in track and field
		Basic speed
	13–15	Specialization for specific events
		General physical development
		Track and field experience
	16–17	Specific specialization
		Strength and power
Middle distances	12–15	Running technique
		Basic techniques of other events
		Endurance
		Speed
	15–16	General endurance
		Specific endurance
		Running technique
		Speed
		Power
	17–18	General endurance
		Specific endurance
		Speed
		Technique
Hurdles		Task 1: Rhythmic sprinting over low hurdles
		Task 2: Lead leg movement
		Task 3: Trail leg movement
		Task 4: Total movement
Throws		Mental skills: Concentration, relaxation
		General ability: General conditioning, general coordination
		Strength: General muscular strength
		Throwing ability: Explosiveness, specific technique
High jump	11–14	Technique
	15–18	Improved approach speed
		Specific strength
		Technique
Long jump and triple jump	13–15	Speed, power
		Flexibility, coordination
		Technique
		Jump, sprint, hurdle technique

WHAT COLLEGE COACHES LOOK FOR

Because track and field athletes begin to mature during their high school years, college coaches are looking for the characteristics already described. Groves, Hinsdale, and Henry all share common concerns about recruiting high school and club athletes. "There is a certain amount of guesswork that goes on," admits Henry. "All of us have to look at what the athlete is achieving now, but we also have to project what will happen during the next few years."

The first of those concerns is early maturation. Young athletes who have physically matured may have already reached a performance peak.

A second worry is the athletes who have been in the sport a long time and are just about tapped out on energy and drive. Laments USA Track and Field's Sellers, "If you win a national championship at the age of 10, what is there left to do in the sport?"

Along with the first two problems is the athlete who has been overtrained. High school coaches who train their talented athletes to have their best years in college are as rare as they are noble.

The fourth concern is overlooking the late bloomer. Big-time coaches have to recruit athletes who can produce right away. But when they do, they run the risk of missing out on great talent. "Because of the numbers game at the college level," says Groves, "I worry all of the time that we will kick out a kid who would have been great." The athlete who persists in his or her search for a track and field scholarship may find a program that will allow time for development, but those schools are more likely to be second-tier Division I institutions or Division II and III colleges.

What would scare a coach off a talented athlete? "When the athlete and the parents begin to act like agents," says Groves. "They want things that are not going to make the team any better. I'll stay away from a performer who is pursuing a scholarship because of an ego trip instead of a love for the sport."

Dilley thinks emotional makeup and family background are as important as physical ability to the college coach. "Athletes don't have to be perfect, but I made mistakes trying to fix problems that had existed for 18 years before I got them. If you have to choose between a runner who has a slightly better time but who is going to be a project in terms of behavior and grades and a slower-time, low-maintenance performer, I'll take the second person every time."

Weaknesses

Henry says that distance runners have seldom been educated about the benefits of the weight room. "For the most part, they have no idea regarding a strength program. Male sprinters and jumpers have been in the weight room because many of them were football players. Because of the lack of supervision, they are not likely to spend the time needed to get stronger.

"The second weakness that high school track and field athletes have as a group when they get to college is a lack of technique," Henry continues. "Developing technique during the short high school track season is difficult for the athlete and the coach. Technique development requires a motivated athlete and a coach who has the time to spend with the individual. This is why we see more and more high school athletes who think of the summer coach as their primary coach."

Walk-Ons

Walk-ons are allowed in most college track programs, but the bigger the school, the more difficult it is for nonscholarship athletes to make the team. NCAA rules limit the number of athletes on rosters. Some Division I universities establish minimum standards that walk-ons must meet. An example of those standards is shown in table 20.2.

Table 20.2 Minimum Standards for Track and Field Tryouts

Event	Standard	Event	Standard
100m	10.7	Pole vault	14-0
200m	21.8	High jump	6-6
400m	49.5	Long jump	22-0
800m	1:56	Triple jump	44-0
1600	4:25	Shot put	54-0 (HS)
Mile	4:26	Discus	158-0 (HS)
3200	9:49	Javelin	190-0 (HS)
2 mile	9:51	Hammer	150-0 (HS)
110HH	14.6		
300IH	38.5		
400IH	54.4		

A WORD TO PARENTS

Grover Hinsdale advises parents to find a solid youth program to complement the best high school program available. "Find coaches who are doing it the right way and who will look out for the long-term best interests of your child."

Harry Groves tells parents and coaches to closely monitor growth, development, and attitude. "The less skill an athlete has, the more these factors influence the eventual success or lack of it."

Pat Henry supports youth track programs, but thinks that playing a couple of sports during the school year and running in a couple of summer track meets is just fine. "Those who get into rigid training programs early in life have a difficult time staying motivated."

He also stresses that parents need to drive the point home to their children that high school and college sports consume a very short period of their lives. It is not an end, but a means to an end and a learning process that will carry over into the real world.

"Parents and their children should be aware of and honest about academic strengths and weaknesses," he concludes. "Get help from a counselor and find the right match between interests, skills, and college majors. Remember that the average college student changes his or her mind four times during the first two years of college. In this sense, try not to be the average college student."

Mike Barber lets parents know that if they have an elite child athlete, they are very fortunate. "But having elite talent does not mean their children will be good. To pull out that potential takes a day-to-day commitment that spans seven or eight years. It takes three years before I even get interested in a child's times. Maintaining a balance of interests in addition to running over such a long period requires a commitment of the parents and their children."

College coaches recruit quality parents as well as quality athletes. Says Mike Dilley, "I got calls twice a week from parents who were questioning my training methods. I told them that I would handle the running part if they would take care of the parenting part. If it's a close recruiting call, coaches will avoid those parents and their children. The other kind of parent is supportive and attends some meets. Whatever happens is okay. They seem to enjoy the whole experience and are not so tied up with results."[8]

Chapter 21

Volleyball

*F*or better or worse, there is no T-ball version of volleyball, no Pop Warner volleyball, no preschool lessons at the club. Volleyball is an acquired interest and skill, not even available to those who would carpool their children for volleyball training if they could. The sport is too complex and too demanding to be played by very young children.

The good news about the lack of organized instruction and competition until a relatively advanced age is that those who discover and play are still enjoying it well into their teen and adult years. "We don't face the burnout problems that other sports deal with," observes Tom Pingel, director of high performance junior programs for USA Volleyball. "Even those who have been playing indoors for several years seem to migrate to the beach game during warm-weather months."[1]

The bad news is that athletes enter the world of competitive volleyball without the five or six years of training that they might have gotten in other sports. It is a great sport for late bloomers and a great sport for those who developed their athletic skills in other sports. "Many volleyball players don't reach their potential until their late 20s," adds Pingel. When you ask a college coach if he or she would prefer an athlete who has played other sports, they unanimously agree that multisport athletes are about the only kind they get, and they are happy to get them.

EARLY INDICATORS

"I look for kids who can play a sport where they are participating in a contained area—where they can't run someplace at full speed," says Mark Pavlik, the highly successful men's coach at Penn State. "They have to show efficient movement and a body that is under control. The good ones can execute a skill, have a sense of kinesthetic awareness, and, at young ages, move in athletic ways."[2]

How do they attain those qualities? "By putting themselves in different athletic environments," answers Pavlik, whose teams have reached the NCAA Final Four 14 times. "I don't think you can teach a football receiver to juggle the ball, keep his feet in bounds, and fight off a defender to make a catch. But the more a kid is in a position where he or she has to use body control and kinesthetic sense, the more he or she figures out what has to be done. The player who has only participated in volleyball has seldom had enough athletic experience to be good."

Court Awareness

"When I watch the 12 and unders at the Junior Olympics," continues Pavlik, "I see kids who show great court awareness. My thought is that they are just having fun playing. They have not fallen into a rigid structure that has been coached into them. They go after balls and put their bodies into position."

Bob Gambardella, director of national team programs for USA Volleyball, says that the ability to process information and act on it is a predictor of future success. "The young athlete who can get a picture in his or her mind of what has to happen has a great advantage over those who cannot. Then they have to have a body that allows them to follow through with that image on the court."[3]

Other Markers

The other markers of potential excellence include the kinds of physical attributes athletes need in several other sports. "Look for a lean body, good quickness, explosive jumping ability, and good hand-eye coordination," advises Pingel. "Once they get a little older, they will begin to show touch on the ball." Those qualities would also describe the prerequisites for success in sports such as basketball, tennis, and baseball.

Size

Size matters in volleyball just as it does in most other sports. There is still a place for shorter players, but everything is relative. Listen to Pavlik's answer to the size question: "We'll take a player who is 6-3 if he can do great things such as passing, defending, or jumping." Pavlik's willingness to "take a player" who is only 6-3 tells you where the game is going. His players range in height from 6-3 to 6-7 or taller.

The measurements might be different in women's volleyball, but the direction is still up. The average height of the top seven players on the University of Southern California's women's team in 1999 was 5-10. The shortest player was 5-9; the tallest, 6-1. Some colleges will recruit outside hitters who are 5-8 to 6-0, while others want players at the same position to be 6-0 to 6-2.[4]

Good hand-eye coordination is a given for volleyball players, but the ability to process information is a predictor of future success.

When do these volleyball skills begin to show? Later, but not that much later, than in other sports. Russ Rose, head women's coach at Penn State, whose team won its second NCAA championship in 1999, thinks that exceptional talent begins to show around the ages of 14 and 15. "Up to that point," he says, "a player may be getting by with just size and strength."[5] Pingel agrees, and suggests that any success in volleyball below the age of 12 is misleading.

Pavlik starts noticing players who have good physical and emotional skills when they are 12 to 14. "You put up a flag in your mind that says let's see how this kid develops. Has he picked his parents well? Is he going to grow bigger, stronger, and faster? Will his body increase in its ability to become athletic?"

USA Volleyball Elite Player Test Results

Future success cannot be predicted by putting young players through a battery of tests and calculating a score. But elite junior players are being tested by USA Volleyball, and you can test your players to see how they compare with the best in the country. The following pages give the results of several tests and are preceded by test instructions. The tests were conducted at USA Volleyball training, development, and recruiting events.[6]

The low, high, and average scores for three groups tested are shown. The ages of the elite boys taking the tests ranged from 14.6 to 16.6 (years, months). The girls who took the same tests were ages 13.6 to 15.6. Women, ages 15.6 to 17.6, are also presented.

Height

1. Ensuring that both of participant's heels are secured on the floor, take the measurement with a straight instrument horizontally bridged to the calibrated wall marking or similar.
2. Measure to the nearest half-inch.

	Boys (14.6–16.6)	Girls (13.6–15.6)	Women (15.6–17.6)
Low	5-11	5-9	5-9
High	6-7	6-4	6-5
Average	6-5	6-0	6-1

Reach

Option 1

1. With both heels on the floor, reach with one hand and touch for height on a Vertec.
2. Then reach with both hands to touch for height.
3. Place one hand on top of the other with fingertips interlocked to the first knuckle.
4. Measure to the nearest half-inch.

Option 2

1. With both heels on the floor, reach with one hand and touch for height on a calibrated wall marking.
2. In this case, turn with your reaching side closest to the wall.

	Boys (14.6–16.6)	Girls (13.6–15.6)	Women (15.6–17.6)
Low	7-7	7-3	7-3
High	8-7	8-1	8-1
Average	8-3	7-7	7-8

Tests adapted, with permission, from USA Volleyball.

Standing Jump

1. While standing with both feet stationed directly under a Vertec (or similar measuring device), jump (without the use of any approach or rocker step) for height and touch with two hands as high as possible on the Vertec.

2. Hands should be interlocked as in the two-hand reach.

3. Record the better of two attempts. Measure to the nearest half-inch.

4. Must touch the highest mark with both hands for the measurement to be counted.

	Boys (14.6–16.6)	Girls (13.6–15.6)	Women (15.6–17.6)
Low	9-2	8-5	8-11
High	10-3	9-5	10-0
Average	9-11	9-0	9-5

Approach Jump Off Two Feet

1. Using a normal spike approach, jump (using a two-foot takeoff) for height and touch with one hand as high as possible on the Vertec.

2. Time permitting, the athlete should jump until failing to improve.

3. If time is short, record the better of two attempts. Measure to the nearest half-inch.

	Boys (14.6–16.6)	Girls (13.6–15.6)	Women (15.6–17.6)
Low	9-8	9-0	9-4
High	10-10	10-5	10-3
Average	10-6	9-10	9-6

Approach Jump Off One Foot

1. Using a one-foot or "slide" spike approach, jump (using a one-foot takeoff) for height and touch with one hand as high as possible on the Vertec.

2. Time permitting, the athlete should jump until failing to improve.

3. If time is short, record the best of two attempts. Measure to the nearest half-inch.

	Boys (14.6–16.6)	Girls (13.6–15.6)	Women (15.6–17.6)
Low	9-8	9-0	9-3
High	10-10	10-0	10-6
Average	10-6	9-6	9-11

18-Meter Sprint

1. When participant reaches one end line of a volleyball court, the timer starts the clock and stops when participant reaches the other end line.
2. Allow ample runway room for participant to be at full speed when hitting the start line, as well as ample room for participant to slow down after crossing the finish line.
3. To assist the timer with judging start and stop times, position a cone or some visual aid on the start and stop positions. Record the best of two attempts.
4. Measure to the nearest hundredth of a second.

	Boys (14.6–16.6)	Girls (13.6–15.6)	Women (15.6–17.6)
Low	2.97	2.99	2.82
High	2.30	2.29	2.50
Average	2.61	2.59	2.66

Shuttle Run

1. Beginning at one volleyball court sideline (or end line), the athlete (from a standing start) sprints and touches the opposite sideline (or center line) with a hand and returns to the original line and touches it with a hand. This constitutes one trip. A run is made up of three round trips.
2. Athlete running through the finish line without touching the line by hand completes the run.
3. Record the best of two attempts. Measure to the nearest hundredth of a second.
4. The timer should begin the watch when the athlete begins the run rather than a setting up a "marks/set/go" start.

	Boys (14.6–16.6)	Girls (13.6–15.6)	Women (15.6–17.6)
Low	14.69	15.94	14.33
High	11.90	13.06	12.89
Average	13.04	13.77	13.69

Standing Broad Jump

1. With toes behind the start line and feet stationary, athlete broad jumps for distance.
2. Jump is recorded from the back of the heel that lands closest to the beginning line.

3. If the athlete loses balance and falls back onto the hands or must step back, the jump is redone.

4. Record the best of two attempts. Measure to the nearest inch.

	Boys (14.6–16.6)	Girls (13.6–15.6)	Women (15.6–17.6)
Low	7-10	5-7	7-0
High	10-0	8-5	8-2
Average	8-2	7-3	7-5

IF YOU HAVE A PROSPECT

Volleyball is promoted through a loosely organized system of clubs. It is similar to, but not nearly as comprehensive or controlling as, AAU basketball. There are nationally sanctioned age-group tournaments for every age group, beginning at 12 and extending through 18. Most of these clubs and tournaments are held in heavily populated areas, making it costly and time consuming for good players who live in rural areas to advance to higher levels of the game.

A second avenue for training and competition is at the scholastic level. The popularity of high school volleyball is growing, although there are more girls' teams than boys' teams. Nevertheless, college coaches rarely look to high schools for prospects. Instead, they find them in club volleyball. Says one volleyball official, "The club avenue is the best way to get seen and to start the personal marketing process, if that's what you want to do."

At the national level, USA Volleyball has a variety of training and competitive programs for outstanding players. They find you; you don't find them. Knowledgeable high school and club coaches can direct potentially outstanding players into these programs. Information is also available at USA Volleyball's Web site. These programs include the following:

Junior national teams

Youth national teams

National high performance camps

USA development camps

USA recruiting combine

Regional development camps

CAMPS AND CLINICS

Camps give prospective student-athletes a chance to be on campus at a school that they are interested in. They spend a week with a coach and staff and explore the campus while playing a sport. Not a bad way to spend a week. Camps also give coaches the opportunity to see what kind of person the athlete is. Says Pavlik, "You can be the greatest athlete in the world, but if you are not a good person, you will hurt our program."

Don't overdo the camp routine. The idea is for players to still be excited by the sport when they reach their late teens or early adulthood. Camps are good, but so is playing other sports and playing pickup, unsupervised games with friends.

WHAT COLLEGE COACHES LOOK FOR

College coaches begin taking serious looks at high-school-age players when they are sophomores, juniors, and seniors. Says Penn State's Pavlik, "The first year a young player goes up against varsity competition is sort of the starting signal. That is when the young ones begin to play against athletes who are older, bigger, stronger, and more experienced. Fifteen- and sixteen-year-old club players are matched against opponents who may be 17 or 18. Ninth- and tenth-graders in high school have to play against juniors and seniors. That's when I start looking."

Pavlik and Rose, although coaching at the same university, represent two different approaches to recruiting volleyball players. Pavlik, the men's coach, looks for the best player available. Size, relatively speaking, is not as important as overall athleticism and skill. "If we can get a player who is 6-7 but who has deficiencies, we'll take him. We'll also take shorter players if they have other athletic attributes."

Rose, the women's coach, on the other hand, looks at positions. "I think the success of our program is partly because we look at our specific needs at a given time. We may need the best passer in a graduating class. Or, if we need a middle blocker or outside hitter, we'll go in that direction. Every team is unique. In one year, we may graduate our best right-side player who can pass. The bottom line is that we recruit players who fit our needs at that point in time."

Pavlik adds that whoever the player and whatever the position, the top priority once on campus is to increase the strength of that player. "Almost all of them," he says, "need to get stronger."

As mentioned earlier, college coaches want size, but they are willing to compromise a bit with players who bring other assets to the program. Rose's outside hitters have been as short as 5-8 and as tall as 6-0. Some college programs want their outside hitters to be taller than 6-0. Here are some other physical and emotional qualities Rose seeks in the women he recruits to play at Penn State:

- 5-11 to 6-2 in height
- Good muscular development

- Flexibility
- Explosive power
- Willingness to listen
- Competitiveness

A Profile of the Ideal College Volleyball Player

Patti Snyder-Park, women's volleyball coach at Arizona State University, says that she gets a good idea of what kind of body types women volleyball players will have at about the age of 14 (9th or 10th grade). Her profile of the ideal player who can play at the NCAA Division I level includes the following characteristics:

- Six feet tall
- Broad shoulders
- Narrow hips
- Good vertical jump ability
- Good foot speed
- Can get low on defense
- Can execute a skill while off balance
- Can adjust body position while in the air
- Spirited in play and attitude
- Does not dwell on mistakes
- Can focus on what the coach says
- Does not require high maintenance
- Has played at least one other sport[7]

All college coaches are interested not in the kind of vertical jump associated with basketball, but in how high a player can touch. "It's not how high you jump," explains Rose, "but how high you are touching. If you are 6-1 and touch 9-3, your vertical touch is about 18 inches. But there are some players who are 5-8 and can touch 9-9. We look for ballistic power."

Pavlik agrees. "We don't care how far their feet are off the floor, but how high they touch and at what height they can do something with the ball. For high school players, if they can touch between 11-2 and 11-6, they can play at the same altitude as NCAA players who have been at it three or four years. If a player touches between 10-9 and 11-2, he should be able to increase his touch height as he gets faster and stronger.

"College coaches are always torn between recruiting talent and recruiting potential. Some players peak early, although this is not as common in volleyball as in other sports. Rose points out that you may be getting a player who is just about as good as she is going to get. That's a variable every coach has to consider. We try to find players who play more than one sport. We conclude that she will get better when she concentrates just on volleyball."

Other players bloom late. According to Pavlik, "They may be a little klutzy, like a puppy. Their feet are big or their limbs are long, but they don't have a fluidness of motion. You hope that it develops later. As they get older, they develop better coordination. Unfortunately for us, some players never really bloom, or they do so after college."

A small third group of players just burn out early. They go to college and say to themselves, "I just don't want to work that hard," or, "I want to be good, but I don't want to be that good."

AT THE NATIONAL LEVEL

Doug Beal is the men's national team coach for USA Volleyball. In an article written for *Performance Volleyball Conditioning*, he outlined some very specific qualities required to be considered for the national team. All of these attributes can be projected downward to lower levels of the game. The more of these physical and mental skills a player has, the more likely he or she is to be an outstanding performer.[8]

"The first thing we look for is players who are successful," says Beal. "We want players who are on teams that are winning. This is particularly important if they have shown the ability to win over a period of time. I think you learn a lot more and grow a lot more by being successful."

Next, Beal looks for general athletic ability. Like all of the other coaches interviewed for this book, he sees experience playing other sports as a plus. "I find it very positive when we identify an athlete who has been successful in baseball, basketball, tennis, anything. It doesn't happen as much as I as wish it did, but it is a very positive thing."

Size and other physical components are next on Beal's list. Among those components are the ability to jump well and quickness. He likes tall players with long arms, qualities that are probably overrated, but not discounted. "Volleyball is a big person's game and it's getting to be a bigger person's game as time goes by," predicts Beal. He adds that standing height is not as critical as standing reach. A player who is shorter but who has long arms can play bigger than someone who is a couple of inches taller.

Beal also emphasizes quickness. "It is not a game of size, but a game of quickness. As defensive players or attackers, you have to get to the ball and execute skills quickly, so we are very concerned about quickness."

The next quality on the Beal checklist is competitiveness. He is impressed when he sees a player perform well when his team is behind or when the score is tied late in a match. He also notices the player who has the ability to carry a team at the most stressful moment of a match.

In many cases, how high a player can touch is more important than how high their feet can get off the ground.

In putting together a national team, Beal wants players who are excellent at something. "We are not really concerned about all-around athletic ability—someone who is good in all aspects of the game but not exceptional in anything. I think it is much easier to put a team together with players who are really outstanding in one or two parts of the game. It would be great, of course, if they were exceptional in more than one, but that is unusual." (This is contrary to the philosophy of most club, high school, and college coaches, who don't have the luxury of being so selective.)

Terminal skills—the ability to score points—are important. The serve, the block, and the hit are skills that dominate the game. So good servers, blockers, and hitters are usually more important than good passers, diggers, and setters. All are important, but the first three are more important.

The last thing that Beal looks for is a player who makes significant progress during the time he is being evaluated. "If we see a player as a freshman in college who is in the middle of the pack, but who jumps up to a much higher level by the time he is a sophomore, that sends up a flag for us that we are going to keep an eye on that player. We look for kids who probably haven't completely matured physically, but who have made substantial improvements between their freshman and senior years in college."

A WORD TO PARENTS AND PLAYERS

"I tell parents of potentially exceptional players at the ages of 12 and 13 to get them involved in an instructional camp," advises Rose. "You hope that they learn the skills properly, as opposed to getting into competitive league play with peers or adults where there is no instruction. I don't think you can learn the skills through playing the game. Some would argue that they can learn to compete, but I believe there has to be a base of fundamental skills in place before serious competition is beneficial."

"Athletes should be patient. When you are 13 or 14, it's still early and you haven't quit growing," he concludes. "If you learn the skills before your body develops, you're going to have a head start on the game. And learn all of the skills. Don't be position specific. Don't just be a spiker because you like to spike. Be a tall setter and you will be more marketable to colleges. I want people who can play volleyball, not just give us a tall team picture."

Chapter 22

Wrestling

"Attitude will win more matches in wrestling than anything else," says Dan Gable. He should know. He has been an Olympic champion, Olympic coach, and he led the University of Iowa to 20 Big-Ten and 15 NCAA titles. "You can have all of the skills and natural ability in the world, but a winning attitude can get a wrestler all the way to the Olympics."[1]

EARLY INDICATORS

Although Gable thinks attitude is of prime importance, he and other nationally recognized wrestling coaches are quick to list the physical qualities that complete the ideal wrestling package.

"From our experience at the national level, we can really tell between the ages of 13 and 15 who is going to be exceptional," according to Mike Duroe, national freestyle development coach for USA Wrestling. "At that age, we spot them in our developmental and regional camps." Following is Duroe's list of the physical qualities that begin to emerge in young wrestlers. (Size is not a factor in wrestling because competition is held for various weight classes.)

- Exceptional balance
- Quick feet
- Explosive movements
- Above-average strength in relation to size
- Mat awareness
- Flexibility

How does the right attitude manifest itself in a wrestler? "Most good wrestlers are self-starters and independent workers," thinks Duroe. "They stay on task whether or not they have a coach watching them. Those who excel are the ones who can run into adversity and not let it get them down. They can deal with defeat and disappointment and with not being as successful as they had planned by being resilient. When they lose, they use the experience as motivation to work harder. Wrestlers have to be tough, hard-nosed athletes who are tenacious and resilient."[2]

"A winning attitude can get a wrestler all the way to the Olympics." —Dan Gable

IF YOU HAVE A PROSPECT

"In some parts of this country, children can start folkstyle wrestling when they are in the first and second grade," says Duroe, who also serves as national women's coach. "But most kids get into wrestling during the fourth or fifth grades. From there, they progress to middle school or junior high school competition and to state high school tournaments. A few states (Ohio, Oklahoma, Pennsylvania, Iowa, and Illinois, for example) conduct junior high school state championships. All 50 states have a state high school tournament."

Why Is Cael Sanderson Beyond Exceptional?

One of the brightest talents in U.S. wrestling is Cael Sanderson. By the end of his sophomore year at Iowa State, he was 79-0 and an NCAA champion. What makes him different?

"I have never seen a performance as dominating as the one I saw by Sanderson during the NCAA's national tournament in 2000," says USA Wrestling's Mike Duroe. "Unless something happens to him emotionally, he will be one of the great talents in wrestling."

"Sanderson is a very intrinsically motivated athlete. He has great discipline. When I first saw him as a cadet (15- to 16-year age division), I wasn't sure about his talent level, but I knew there was something about him that was different. He was not then, or is he now, physically intimidating. But he has unbelievable natural strength, including grip strength. He is strong in positions you don't normally see in wrestlers. He can pull in a leg from any position, even when he is bent over on his knees." Duroe calls it farmer's strength. "Some kids just have it. They can grab a bale of hay and lift it over their head." One observer said that in positions in which other wrestlers are on the defensive and in trouble, Sanderson is thinking about how he can score.

Wrestling legend Dan Gable has this to say about Sanderson: "He can utilize every second of a match. If you let up even for one second to take an extra breath, he'll have you off balance and take you down. He's also very versatile. He can attack from both sides, sort of like a switch hitter in baseball."

"Sanderson has an uncanny ability to do things other wrestlers can't," continues Gable. "It is not his power or strength, but rather his mat awareness that makes him great. His positioning is outstanding, whether he is standing or underneath. He can scramble from the top position. Most wrestlers don't wrestle this way because they are afraid of getting tired. He has a natural feel to turn somebody else's action against them. His ability to keep people off balance is his second best quality."

Sanderson seems to be immune to pressure. He told Iowa State strength coach Jeff Reindardy that he doesn't know what reporters are talking about when they quiz him on the pressure of maintaining a winning streak.

Finally, Gable, Duroe, and the strength coaches at Iowa marvel at Sanderson's cardiorespiratory endurance. Not many wrestlers have his capacity to flow for the entire length of a match like he does. "Others may be too lazy to work that hard," observes Gable. "But his ability to move the way he moves and to maintain such a high level of endurance is superior."

Schedule

Wrestlers who are considered outstanding at the high school level don't just compete from November to February at the scholastic level. They also wrestle during the spring and summer months in freestyle and Greco Roman. And they attend camps and clinics that are sponsored by colleges and universities around the country. These camps offer athletes in every sport a chance to see a campus and wrestling program, as well as to be seen by coaches.

USA Wrestling conducts competition for three age groups. The cadet level is for those between the ages of 13 and 15. Junior national championships are held for the 17- to 20-year-olds, and the university national championships include ages from 17 all the way to 24. Every state has the option to send a team to the cadet and junior national tournaments that are held in July.

Late Bloomers

Are there late bloomers in wrestling? Yes. Most teenagers reach physical maturity between the ages of 16 and 18. But some don't have the advantage of good coaching until they get to college or beyond. Once they are exposed to it, they catch up in a hurry. Gable says that wrestlers who continue their careers as adults don't peak until they are 27.

Do they play other sports? Perhaps not as much as athletes who play team sports, but Duroe thinks there is a huge carryover value among big athletes who play football and wrestle. He has also seen athletes who excel in soccer, lacrosse, and cross country become outstanding wrestlers.

WHAT COLLEGE COACHES LOOK FOR

"I start looking at them when they are in junior high school, just to make mental notes or to remember a name," says Oklahoma State University wrestling coach John Smith. "The ones that are going to be future stars are pretty active at that age."[3]

Wins and Losses

In addition to physical skills already mentioned, Smith pays attention to wins and losses. "Good wrestlers always show up when it's time to wrestle. Even in their worst matches, they find a way to get that hand raised." But he also likes to watch prospects to see how they perform after losses and if they are motivated by them. "In wrestling, you are only as good as your last match, so you have to be able to bounce back."

"Division I coaches are getting less of the total package in high school recruits now than they used to," thinks Smith. "High school coaches have more restrictions in how to deal with athletes than 10 years ago. They have to handle them more gently, and it shows in the products they produce. I'm not saying that is good or bad. It's just the direction we are headed."

Understanding the Commitment

Smith says that high school wrestlers who want to compete at the college level have to understand that the whole experience might be different from what they envisioned. "You assume that young, good wrestlers have a strong work ethic, but some don't have it and never will. Others have that quality when they get here, and a third group works through a difficult time to appreciate what it takes. They grow up and deal with the commitment that is required. The key to success for the coach is to teach that work ethic."

Gable, who has had a tremendous influence on high school and college coaches, does not get excited about young wrestlers as college prospects until the 11th or 12th grade. "There are many factors, physical and mental, that can influence what is going to happen to an athlete during the four or five years before college. I usually waited until some of those factors were resolved."

Ability to Score

While Gable thinks that wins and losses are an important part of the evaluation process, his final decision is based on the ability to score. He also emphasizes movement, how a wrestler performs in different situations, and size. "You look at family history, how big the parents are, and growth patterns of the wrestler. Whether or not a scholarship is offered might depend on how much a person will weigh two years later. You have to predict future size or weight. Otherwise, you end up with too many people in the same weight class.

"I always like the kid who has longevity," adds Gable. "I want him to still be excited about the sport when he gets to college instead of being tired of it. There is a burnout factor, and some athletes can get ahead of themselves. A 12-year-old might be competing well against 14-year-olds, but I am a firm believer in staying at the level where you belong. Do well at each level, then move up. This eliminates the 'why am I competing here' syndrome."

Oklahoma State's Smith would take a chance on a wrestler who might be considered a project if his grades are good. He, like most college coaches, wants low-maintenance athletes.

The one thing that would scare him off an otherwise good prospect is a bad attitude toward teammates, officials, coaches, or others in the sport. "You can find out very quickly in a conversation who you are dealing with. That first visit will probably tell me if someone is spoiled or complains about everything or makes excuses."

Competitiveness

Wrestling coaches want athletes who are extremely competitive. Those who demonstrate leadership along with competitiveness will have an influence on everybody. "That person can actually elevate the level of intensity for every other person on a team," explains Gable.

GIRLS' AND WOMEN'S WRESTLING: EMERGING OPPORTUNITIES

"Young women who have some natural ability and who get good coaching can progress very rapidly," says Mike Duroe, USA Wrestling's national women's coach. "There are plenty of opportunities to advance to the national and international levels."

Most people are not used to the idea of women competing in what has traditionally been considered a male sport, but girls' and women's wrestling is growing and is here to stay. Who are these people and where do they come from? Duroe says that there is no stereotype. "Some of them were exposed to martial arts when they were younger, but just as many come from sports such as soccer and hockey. They like the tough, physical challenge that wrestling offers. Other female wrestlers just do it. We don't ask them why."

Duroe adds that wrestling has a way of perpetuating itself. Typically, a family has been involved with their sons in the sport before a younger sister decides to try it. Weight classes start at 40 pounds and age groups for girls start as young as eight.

The opportunities to train, compete, and move up through wrestling's ranks are limited for girls, but increasing. Two states—Texas and Hawaii—have tournaments sponsored by state high school athletic associations. Several other states, New York, Pennsylvania, and Michigan among them, host unofficial tournaments. In all, there were 2,361 girls wrestling at the high school level in 1999 (see table 22.1) and approximately 1,700 female members of USA Wrestling.[4]

USA Wrestling plans to sponsor folkstyle tournaments in every state that does not have a high school tournament. "The reason we do this is to create more opportunities for girls," says Duroe.

Girls Versus Boys

In terms of displaying talent, young girls develop as fast as or faster than boys. Girls have one advantage—superior flexibility—which allows them to be better at certain techniques than boys are. It is not unusual for them to compete with and beat boys up to a certain age level. At about the sophomore year in high school, the boys begin to surpass girls in size, strength, and other physical attributes.

When USA Wrestling identifies a 15-year-old as an athlete who is going to be good, she is encouraged to get into the USA Wrestling's national development program and later into international competition. Throughout the development program, elite girls and women also wrestle in clubs and on high school teams.

Table 22.1   Women's Wrestling Growth Trends

Year	High school athletes	USA Wrestling female members
1990	112	n/a
1991	132	n/a
1992	219	n/a
1993	404	n/a
1994	783	760
1995	804	1,525
1996	1,164	1,733
1997	1,629	1,725
1998	1,907	1,666
1999	2,361	1,699

Adapted with permission from USA Wrestling.

Duroe says that five years ago, he could have picked an athlete from another sport, trained her for a month, and put her out there against good competition. That is not the case now, but the path to success in wrestling for women is still faster than in most other sports.

Women's College Wrestling

Only three colleges in the United States have wrestling programs for women: They are the University of Minnesota-Morris, Missouri Valley College, and Cumberland College in Kentucky. The National Collegiate Athletic Association does not recognize women's wrestling as an intercollegiate sport, but USA Wrestling is campaigning toward that goal. While college wrestling opportunities are limited for women in the United States, 15 Canadian colleges have varsity teams.

A WORD TO COACHES, PARENTS, AND ATHLETES

"Be educated about the sport," Gable advises parents. "Wrestlers have to manage several things at the same time (nutrition, academics, technical skills, emotional obstacles, for example) and their parents and coaches should help them do that."

To athletes, Gable says, "Wrestlers have to understand the importance of technical development also. The ability to master moves such as escaping or defending in the bottom position is essential and takes just as much time as other aspects of the sport. They should also continue to improve the special qualities that separate them from others. If, for example, an athlete has unusual flexibility, he or she should recognize that range of motion is a special tool. By making the body even more flexible, a wrestler can become even more unique than before."

John Smith, the Oklahoma State coach, tells parents to get involved in their children's wrestling life. "Most great wrestlers have great parents behind them," he observes. "One of the worst things parents can do is to let kids make all of the choices about their lives. At 10 or 12, and sometimes at 17 or 18, they don't know what it takes to become outstanding. Give them direction, then help them develop so they can move up to the next competitive level."

Smith recalls that his father was a good example of how parents should display a balanced attitude toward winning and losing. Losing was never devastating nor was winning that exciting to him. "When I won, he would give me a pat on the back and tell me that I did a good job. Then he would remind me that tomorrow is a new day and that I would have to work just as hard to prepare for the next match. When I lost, it was, 'Well, you made a couple of mistakes. But tomorrow is a new day.'

"Don't just be a seasonal coach," Smith tells high school coaches. "Get more involved with the development of your athletes throughout the year. Give them the time they need to gain knowledge and experience. Open up the gym for them during the summer." He adds that too many wrestlers forget about training and competing out of season. "A lot of them get lost and never come back."

Smith tells parents and athletes that the number one issue is academics. "From middle school on, they have to understand that going to college and wrestling in college is not easy. They need a good educational foundation to prepare them for higher education. If a wrestler is always struggling with grades, it will show in his or her performance."

Smith is not finished with advice for athletes. "Knowledge about wrestling doesn't just come from a high school coach. It also comes from going to camps and clinics, observing others wrestle, watching videotapes. The best wrestlers in the world are students of the sport."

Duroe thinks that it is important to find a level of enjoyment in wrestling. This is the responsibility of the parents, coaches, and athletes. "Put yourself, your children, or your team members in situations where they can practice technical skills. There is no reason to be 'under the gun' all of the time. Look for a variety of experiences—different wrestling styles, training methods, coaches, clubs, competitive events—anything that will promote further development in an atmosphere that is fun and interesting."

Because of its physical and aggressive nature, wrestling will never attract as many athletes—boys, girls, men, or women—as sports such as basketball, softball, volleyball, or tennis. Nevertheless, plenty of exceptional athletes now compete as wrestlers and more are on the way.

Summary: The Future of Sports Talent

*I*n the future, identifying and developing sports talent will be as uncertain as it is challenging. The talent pool will increase among young age groups as opportunities for participation increase. However, the number of talented adolescent athletes is in danger of shrinking because of burnout. Talent identification methods will evolve from random to refined, but that process will be slow and always less than perfect. While testing to identify talent will become more accurate, tests will never replace the trained eyes of experienced coaches, scouts, teachers, and recruiters. Methods of developing talent will be designed for the individual more than for the group. A one-size-fits-all approach is necessary at the grassroots level, but it is ineffective with elite athletes in nonteam sports. Athletes will develop a greater awareness of what their bodies require for peak performance, but they will learn that nutritional and training shortcuts carry health risks.

THE FORMULA FOR SUCCESS

The formula for talented athletes to reach their fullest potential is ability plus opportunity plus drive. Remove one of those three elements from the equation and the result is something less than exceptional achievement. While this formula is simple and straightforward, identifying and developing sports talent is less so. The following statements regarding sports talent are based on interviews with more than 100 elite coaches, scouts, recruiters, teachers, researchers, and athletes, as well as a review of the literature. Keep in mind, of course, that there are exceptions to each statement.

- Talent is difficult, if not impossible, to predict.
- Great physical talent does not ensure great performance.
- Talent displayed at one age level does not ensure that it will be present at subsequent ages.
- Talent can emerge at any time from early childhood to adulthood, depending on the sport and the individual.
- In prepubescent children, size, strength, and early physical development are often mistaken for talent.
- The potential for speed is an inherited trait and a marker for talent in some sports.
- An early and enduring indicator of sports talent is coordination.
- Athletes who are placed in rigid training and competitive environments too early are at risk for dropping out of the sport before reaching their full potential.
- Most talented athletes participate in more than one sport during their developmental years, and most elite coaches encourage that participation.
- Parents should not encourage or push talented athletes to participate in a sport with the primary objective of obtaining a college scholarship or achieving professional or world-class status.
- Parents untrained (and in many cases, trained) in developing sports talent should monitor, encourage, and support the process, but should not interfere in the technical development of their children.
- With the possible exception of achieving world-class status, drive and opportunity can compensate for the lack of exceptional physical skills.

THE FOUR TEMPTATIONS

In the pursuit of sports excellence, parents, coaches, and gifted athletes are confronted with four dangerous temptations. The first temptation is to overevaluate talent. Parents and coaches may be so determined to make sports stars out of their athletes that they can't objectively evaluate their ability. They mistakenly think that good to above-average physical skills are absolute signs of exceptional talent. When their children don't perform to their expectations, everyone involved suffers damage that is hard to repair.

The second temptation is to overrate physical talent and underrate mental and emotional strengths. College and professionals rosters are full of overachievers. These athletes are not the biggest, fastest, or strongest, but they use mental skills, emotional strength, and intangible qualities to achieve greater heights than more physically gifted athletes achieve. Don't give up on athletes who test poorly. Give them time and opportunities to show their talent in other ways.

The third temptation is to misuse talent. The practices of starting too soon, pushing too hard, playing too many games, and using substances to enhance performance are destroying the health and sports careers of talented athletes at alarming rates. For every sports prodigy who survives pushy parents and ambitious coaches, there are thousands of casualties who are never allowed simply to be good kids who enjoy playing sports.

The fourth temptation is to overemphasize sports talent. Nothing is sadder than the wasted life of an athlete who can't adjust to the world beyond sports. When the game is over, athletic talent should be just one dimension of a well-rounded person. Parents, coaches, teachers, and friends share the responsibility of helping talented athletes develop other interests.

A PERSPECTIVE ON TALENT

When you discover true talent, support it, develop it, challenge it, and enjoy the experience, but keep it in perspective. It does not necessarily come with other personal skills such as judgment or maturity. Underneath the fleeting gift of sports talent is a normal child who needs the love, time, attention, and discipline that parents and coaches should give to all children, talented or not.

References

Chapter 1

1 Jim Thorpe. Quoted from: **www.cmgww.com** [July 2000].
2 Mildred "Babe" Didrikson-Zaharias. National Women's Hall of Fame. Available: **www.greatwomen.org/zhrias** [June 2000].
3 "Motor Performance." Michigan State University Department of Kinesiology. Available: **http://ed-web3.educ.msu.edu/kin/activities/mps.htm** [1998].
4 Singer, Robert. Telephone interview. February 2000.

Chapter 2

1 Vickers, Joan. Telephone interview. December 1999.
2 Vickers, Joan N., and Raissa M. Adolphe. 1997. "Gaze Behaviour: A Ball Tracking and Aiming Skill." *International Journal of Sports Vision* 4(1): 18-27.
3 National Center for Chronic Disease Prevention and Health Promotion. 2000. CDC Growth Charts: United States.
4 Kraemer, William J., and S. J. Fleck. 1993. *Strength Training for Young Athletes.* Champaign, IL: Human Kinetics.

Chapter 3

1 Loehr, James. Telephone interview. January 2000.
2 "Identifying Exceptional Talent." 1999. *Georgia Tech Sports Medicine & Performance Newsletter* 7(7): 3.
3 Randall, Jim. Personal interview. January 2000.
4 Patten, Greg. Telephone interview. November 1996.
5 Murphy, Shane. Telephone interview. November 1999.
6 Heil, John. Telephone interview. November 1999.
7 "Identifying Exceptional Talent." 1998. *Penn State Sports Medicine Newsletter* 7(4): 7.
8 Levine, Al. January 30, 2000. "When They Were Young." *Atlanta Journal-Constitution*, E-19.
9 Bollettieri, Nick. 1999. *Identifying Talent.* Audiotape. United States Professional Tennis Association. Convention Tapes International.
10 Côté, Jean. 1999. "The Influence of the Family in the Development of Talent in Sport." *The Sport Psychologist* 13: 395-417.
11 Rose, Russ. Telephone interview. December 1999.
12 Yukelson, David. Telephone interview. June 1999.
13 Ravizza, Kenneth. Telephone interview. December 1999.
14 Volleyball Competition Evaluation Form. 1997. *Penn State Sports Medicine Newsletter* 5(7): 2.

Chapter 4

1   Clark, Bill. Telephone interview. May 2000.
2   Verducci, Tom. 2000. "Change Is Good." *Sports Illustrated* 92(20): 50-54.
3   Quinn, Ron. Telephone interview. May 2000.
4   Hewitt, Paul. Telephone interview. April 2000.
5   Wootten, Morgan. Telephone interview. April 2000.
6   Pavlik, Mark. Telephone interview. March 2000.
7   Brown, Steve. Telephone interview. April 2000.
8   Simeone, Dave. Telephone interview. May 2000.

Chapter 5

1   Côté, Jean. 1999. "The Influence of the Family in the Development of Talent in Sport." *The Sport Psychologist* 13: 395-417.
2   Hill, Randy. Telephone interview. March 2000.
3   Hellstedt, J. C. 1987. "The Coach/Parent/Athlete Relationship." *The Sport Psychologist* 1: 151-160.
4   Hellstedt, J. C. 1995. "Invisible Players: A Family System Model." In *Sport Psychology Interventions*, edited by Shane M. Murphy. Champaign, IL: Human Kinetics. 117-146.
5   Bloom, B. S., ed. 1985. *Developing Talent in Young People*. New York: Ballentine.
6   Regnier, Guy, J. Salmela, and R. Storm. 1993. "Talent Development in Sport." In *Handbook of Research on Sport Psychology*. New York: McMillan.
7   Malina, Robert. 2000. "Talent Identification and Selection in Sport." East Lansing, MI: Michigan State University Institute for the Study of Youth Sports.
8   Wood, Carol. Telephone interview. July 2000.
9   Saviano, Nick. 1999. "Establishing a Developmental Plan." *High Performance Coaching* 1(1): 1, 8.
10 Sands, Bill. Telephone interview. May 2000.

Chapter 6

1   Grice, Tony. 1999. "The Development of Talent: A Talent Identification Inventory for Predicting Success in Sports for Children." Unpublished paper.
2   "Identifying Exceptional Talent." 1998. *Penn State Sports Medicine Newsletter* 7(3): 7.
3   Sampras, Stella. Telephone interview. February 2000.
4   Clark, Bill. Telephone interview. March 2000.
5   Pavlik, Mark. Telephone interview. February 2000.
6   Kater, April. Telephone interview. May 2000.
7   Brown, Jim. 1999. "Good Coach, Bad Coach." *The Washington Post*, Health: Family Special Issue: 34.
8   "Youth Strength Training." 1998. *Current Comments*. American College of Sports Medicine.
9   Bernarde, Scott. November 5, 1998. "Kids' Use of Controversial Creatine." *The Atlanta Journal-Constitution*.
10 "Creatine Supplementation." 1997. *Penn State Sports Medicine Newsletter* 6(4): 4.
11 Brown, Arlene P., and Jim Brown. 1999. "The Creatine Craze." *Raising Teens*: 18-21.
12 Coleman, Ellen. 1996. *The Ultimate Sports Nutrition Handbook*. Palo Alto: Bull.
13 Brown, Arlene P., and Jim Brown. 1999. "The Creatine Craze." *Raising Teens*: 22.

Chapter 7

1 Yukelson, David. Telephone interview. February 2000.

2 Côté, Jean. 1999. "The Influence of the Family in the Development of Talent in Sport." *The Sport Psychologist* 13: 395-417.

3 Heppler, Bruce. Telephone interview. December 1998.

4 Participation in Varsity Intercollegiate Sports at 4-Year Colleges. 1996. Washington, DC: The Center for Educational Statistics.

5 Ferguson, Andrew. July 12, 1999. "Inside the Crazy Culture of Kids Sports." *Time* 54(2): 52-60.

6 "Baseball." American Sports Medicine Institute. Available: **www.asmi.org/sportsmed/sport/baseball.html** [2000].

7 "Coaching Your Children." 1997. *Penn State Sports Medicine Newsletter* 6(2): 6.

Chapter 8

1 The President's Challenge. 1999-2000. Washington, DC: The President's Council on Physical Fitness and Sports.

2 Cook, Gray. Telephone interview. January 2000.

Chapter 9

1 NCAA Guide for the College-Bound Student-Athlete. National Collegiate Athletic Association. Available: **www.ncaa.org** [2000].

2 Zembower, Keith. Telephone interview. June 2000.

3 *1999-2000 NCAA Division I Manual*. Indianapolis, IN: National Collegiate Athletic Association.

4 Dempsey, Cedric. NCAA Guide for the College-Bound Student-Athlete. National Collegiate Athletic Association. Available: **www.ncaa.org** [2000].

5 Goetz, Al. Personal interview. January 2000.

6 Clark, Bill. Telephone interview. March 2000.

7 Weaver, Paul. Telephone interview. December 1999.

Chapter 10

1 Zembower, Keith. Telephone interview. May 2000.

2 Goetz, Al. Personal interview. January 2000.

3 Weaver, Paul. Telephone interview. December 1999.

4 "Baseball Running Speed." 1999. *Georgia Tech Sports Medicine & Performance Newsletter* 7(11): 7.

5 "Identifying Exceptional Talent." 1998. *Penn State Sports Medicine Newsletter* 7(3): 2.

6 Hall, Danny. Telephone interview. February 2000.

7 Guy, Jeff. Telephone interview. February 2000.

Chapter 11

1 Hewitt, Paul. Personal interview. April 2000.

2 Hendrickson, Bonnie. Telephone interview. January 2000.

3 Cremins, Bobby. Telephone interview. January 1999.

4 Wootten, Morgan. Telephone interview. April 2000.

5 Wooden, John. Faxed response. March 2000.

6 Ruedlinger, Rick. Telephone interview. April 2000.

7 Nierwinski, Al. Telephone interview. April 2000.

8 "On the Average." March 16, 2000. *USA Today.* 10C.

9 "Identifying Exceptional Talent." 1998. *Penn State Sports Medicine Newsletter* 7(3): 2.

Chapter 12

1 Martin, Joe. Telephone interview. January 2000.

2 Zembower, Keith. 2000. Texas high school football recruiting data. Unpublished data.

3 Tate, Tommy. Telephone interview. January 2000.

4 Kraemer, William J., and S. J. Fleck. 1993. *Strength Training for Young Athletes.* Champaign, IL: Human Kinetics.

5 Osborne, Tom. Telephone interview. November 1998.

6 Davis, Greg. Telephone interview. January 2000.

7 Gentry, Mike. Telephone interview. March 2000.

8 Conley, Bill. Telephone interview. February 2000.

9 New, Larry. Telephone interview. February 2000.

10 Collins, Mike. Telephone interview. February 2000.

11 "Predicting Performance at Nebraska." 2000. *Georgia Tech Sports Medicine & Performance Newsletter* 8(8): 1-2.

12 "NFL Scouting Combine Results." April 2000. *USA Today.* 16C.

Chapter 13

1 Martino, Rick. Telephone interview. February 2000.

2 Nelson, Derek. Telephone interview. February 2000.

3 Roer, Judy. Telephone interview. February 2000.

4 Arizona Classic, Golf Texas Junior Classic. Top five scores. American Junior Golf Association. Available: **www.ajga.org** [May 2000].

5 "Identifying Exceptional Talent." 1999. *Georgia Tech Sports Medicine & Performance Newsletter* 1(1): 4.

6 Brown, Robert. Telephone interview. January 2000.

7 Vollstedt, Linda. Telephone interview. May 2000.

Chapter 14

1 Eaton, Geoff. Telephone interview. April 2000.

2 Spini, John. Telephone interview. April 2000.

3 Karolyi, Bela. Telephone interview. May 2000.

4 Kaitschuck, Debbie. Telephone interview. June 2000.

5 Sands, William, and J.R. McNeal. 1999. "Body Size and Sprinting Characteristics of 1998 National TOPs Athletes." *Technique* 19(5): 34-35.

6 Smith, Kristin. Telephone interview. April 2000.

7 *Talent Opportunity Program.* USA Gymnastics. Available: **www.usa-gymnastics.org/women/tops/** [2000].

8 USA Gymnastics—Women. 1993. "Talent Opportunity Program." Indianapolis, IN: United States Gymnastics Federation.

9 *Future Stars Program.* USA Gymnastics. Available: **www.usa-gymnastics.org/men/future-stars** [2000].

Chapter 15

1 Mason, Ron. Telephone interview. June 2000.
2 Brennan, Dan. Telephone interview. June 2000.
3 Rennie, Tom. Telephone interview. June 2000.
4 O'Connor, Bob. Telephone interview. June 2000.
5 USA Hockey National Team Training Program Post Season-Pre Season 1999 Testing. 2000. Ann Arbor, MI: USA Hockey, Inc.
6 Gwozdecky, George. Telephone interview. June 2000.
7 Roster data. 2000. University of Denver, University of Massachusetts, University of Michigan, Michigan State University, University of Minnesota, University of Notre Dame Web sites.
8 Kay, Karen. Telephone interview. July 2000.

Chapter 16

1 Hart, Tom. Telephone interview. May 2000.
2 Simeone, Dave. Telephone interview. May 2000.
3 Kirkendall, Don. 2000. United States Soccer Federation Test Norms. Chapel Hill, NC: United States Soccer Federation.
4 Kater, April. Telephone interview May 2000.
5 Gorman, Barry. Telephone interview. May 2000.
6 Olympic Development Program. United States Youth Soccer. Available: **www.usysa.org** [2000].
7 "Identifying Exceptional Talent." 1999. *Georgia Tech Sports Medicine & Performance Newsletter* 1(1): 4-5.
8 Quinn, Ron. Telephone interview. May 2000.
9 Beswick, Bill. Email response. September 2000.

Chapter 17

1 Mays, Larry. Telephone interview. June 2000.
2 Kempf, Cheri. Telephone interview. June 2000.
3 Kempf, Cheri. 2000. Unpublished pitching velocity data. Nashville, TN.
4 Kempf, Cheri. 2000. Unpublished throw-down time data. Nashville, TN.
5 Kempf, Cheri. 2000. Unpublished home-to-first, home-to-home times. Nashville, TN.
6 Junior Olympic Program. Amateur Softball Association. Available: **www.softball.org** [2000].
7 Mendoza, Maria. Telephone interview. June 2000.
8 "Identifying Exceptional Talent." 1999. *Georgia Tech Sports Medicine & Performance Newsletter* 1(1): 5.
9 Lenti, Eugene. Telephone interview. June 2000.
10 Ivey, Sam. Telephone interview. June 2000.

Chapter 18

1 Herr, Larry. Telephone interview. June 2000.
2 Anthropometry on 1999 Girls/Boys Select Camp, 2000 Girls/Boys Select Camp, and 1998-1999 Men's/Women's National Teams. 2000. Colorado Springs, CO: USA Swimming.

3 Stopkotte, Ken. Telephone interview. June 2000.

4 Sheridan, Jim. Telephone interview. June 2000.

5 Young, Tony. Telephone interview. June 2000.

6 Burnham, Brad. Telephone interview. July 2000.

7 Sterkel, Jill. Telephone interview. July 2000.

8 "Identifying Exceptional Talent." 1998. *Penn State Sports Medicine Newsletter* 7(3): 1.

9 Urbanchek, John. Telephone interview. June 2000.

10 Roster Information. 2000. University of Texas, University of Washington, UCLA, University of Arizona, University of Tennessee, The Ohio State University, Iowa State University, and Stanford University Web sites.

11 Reese, Eddie. Telephone interview. July 2000.

Chapter 19

1 Sampras, Stella. Telephone interview. February 2000.

2 Case, Rick. Personal interview. January 2000.

3 MacCurdy, Doug. Telephone interview. January 2000.

4 McKee, Bobby. Telephone interview. February 2000.

5 "Identifying Exceptional Talent." 1998. *Penn State Sports Medicine Newsletter* 7(4): 7.

6 USTA Elite Player Protocol and Tests Results. 2000. Key Biscayne, FL: United States Tennis Association.

7 Saviano, Nick. Telephone interview. February 2000.

8 Gould, Dick. Telephone interview. February 2000.

9 Bollettieri, Nick. 1999. *Identifying Talent.* Audiotape. United States Professional Tennis Association. Convention Tapes International.

10 Talbert, Henry. Telephone interview. February 2000.

11 Wallace, Michael. Personal interview. February 2000.

Chapter 20

1 Groves, Harry. Telephone interview. July 2000.

2 Hinsdale, Grover. Telephone interview. July 2000.

3 Sellers, Cathy. Telephone interview. July 2000.

4 Barber, Mike. Telephone interview. July 2000.

5 Henry, Pat. Telephone interview. July 2000.

6 Dilley, Mike. Telephone interview. July 2000.

7 van Niekerk, Owen. 2000. *Coaching Athletics I, II.* Johannesburg, South Africa: Print Associates.

8 "Identifying Exceptional Talent." 1998. *Penn State Sports Medicine Newsletter* 7(3): 2.

Chapter 21

1 Pingel, Tom. Telephone interview. March 2000.

2 Pavlik, Mark. Telephone interview. March 2000.

3 Gambardella, Bob. Telephone interview. March 2000.

4 USC team roster. University of Southern California Athletics. Available: **www.usctrojans.fansonly.com** [2000].

5 Rose, Russ. Telephone interview. December 1999.

6 USA Volleyball Elite Player Test Results. 1999. Colorado Springs, CO: USA Volleyball.

7 "Identifying Exceptional Talent." 1999. *Georgia Tech Sports Medicine & Performance Newsletter* 1(1): 5.

8 Beal, Doug. 1999. "Scouting Report—What the Coaches Look For." *Performance Volleyball Conditioning* 6(7): 8.

Chapter 22

1 Gable, Dan. Telephone interview. January 2000.

2 Duroe, Mike. Telephone interview. January 2000.

3 Smith, John. Telephone interview. January 2000.

4 Women's Wrestling Growth Trends. 2000. Colorado Springs, CO: USA Wrestling.

Index

About the Author

Jim Brown, PhD, is the executive editor of the *Georgia Tech Sports Medicine & Performance Newsletter*, a columnist for CBS Sportsline, and a member of the Wilson Sporting Goods Advisory Staff. As a former teacher and coach, Brown has worked with athletes of all ages and has a good grasp of the complex issues involved in developing talented athletes. He understands how coaches, scouts, and sport scientists approach each situation, and he is also sensitive to the emotions and difficulties athletes and parents face in their quest to reach the top tiers of sport.

Dr. Brown has written, coauthored, or edited ten books, two national newsletters, one magazine, and hundreds of articles on sports, sports medicine, health, and education. His work has appeared in such notable publications as *Sports Illustrated for Women*, *Better Homes & Gardens*, *Washington Post*, *New York Post*, *Raising Teens*, *Ivanhoe Broadcast News*, and *Health Education*.

Jim and his wife, Arlene, live in Atlanta, Georgia.

You'll find
other outstanding
sport resources at

www.humankinetics.com

In the U.S. call

1-800-747-4457

Australia 08 8277 1555
Canada............................1-800-465-7301
Europe ....+44 (0) 113 278 1708
New Zealand 09-523-3462

HUMAN KINETICS
The Premier Publisher in Sports and Fitness
P.O. Box 5076 • Champaign, IL 61825-5076 USA